When the Light Is Fire

When the Light Is Fire

Maasai Schoolgirls in Contemporary Kenya

HEATHER D. SWITZER

Portions of this work have been previously published.

"Disruptive Discourses: Kenyan Maasai Schoolgirls Make Themselves," *Girlhood Studies* 3, no. 1 (Summer 2010): 137–55, with the permission of Berghahn Books, is part of chapter 4.

"Precarious Politics and Girl Effects: Exploring the Limits of the Girl Gone Global," with Emily Bent and Crystal Leigh Endsley (© 2016, The Johns Hopkins University Press). This article first appeared in *Feminist Formations* 28, no. 1 (Spring 2016): 33–59, and is part of chapter 5.

"Oppositional Girlhoods and the Challenge of Relational Politics," *Gender Issues* 33, no. 2 (June 2016): 122–47, with Emily Bent (© Springer Science and Business Media, New York), with the permission of Springer, is part of chapter 5.

"(Post)feminist Development Fables: The Girl Effect and the Production of Sexual Subjects," *Feminist Theory* 14 no. 3 (December 2013): 345–60, reprinted by permission of SAGE Publications, and is part of chapter 6.

© 2018 by the Board of Trustees
of the University of Illinois
All rights reserved
1 2 3 4 5 C P 5 4 3 2 1
∞ This book is printed on acid-free paper.

Library of Congress Cataloging-in-Publication Data
Names: Switzer, Heather D., 1970– author.
Title: When the light is fire: Maasai schoolgirls in
   contemporary Kenya / Heather D. Switzer.
Description: Champaign, IL: University of Illinois
   Urbana Champaign, [2018] | Includes bibliographical
   references and index.
Identifiers: LCCN 2018015070| ISBN 9780252042034 (cloth
   : alk. paper) | ISBN 9780252083723 (pbk. : alk. paper)
Subjects: LCSH: Girls, Maasai—Education—Kenya—
   Kajiado District. | Maasai (African people)—
   Education—Kenya—Kajiado District. | Women,
   Maasai—Kenya—Kajiado District—Social
   conditions. | Educational anthropology—Kenya—
   Kajiado District. | Kajiado District (Kenya)—Social
   conditions—21st century.
Classification: LCC DT433.545.M33 S95 2018 | DDC
   305.896/55226—dc23
LC record available at https://lccn.loc.gov/2018015070
Ebook ISBN 978-0-252-05077-0

for Maasai girls
past, present, and future

*I dedicate this book to my mom
Patricia Ann Kageals Switzer
1944–1995*

Contents

Acknowledgments ix

Introduction. "Girls are the most powerful force of change on the planet": Situating Schoolgirlhood 1

Chapter 1. "Now is not like before. The world has changed": Maasai Education in Cultural and Historical Context 29

Chapter 2. "I see that when I am in school, I will have a good life": Producing and Performing Schoolgirlhood 58

Chapter 3. "The medicine for fire is fire": Negotiating Schoolgirlhood 88

Chapter 4. "We are not enkanyakuai. . . . We are just girls": Embodying Schoolgirlhood 114

Conclusion. Becoming "People Who Use Both Hands" 145

Notes 169

Works Cited 195

Index 217

Acknowledgments

They say the road is made by walking. Mine is clearly not the first book ever written, but it is the first book written by me. The image of the road materializing with each step the walker takes reflects how the process of making this book has felt for me. It has taken much longer to write than it might have, as the road, like life, has unfolded in wild, unanticipated ways. Throughout the process, as much as anything, I've worried over my ability to render an account of contemporary Maasai girlhood that reflects a fraction of its complexity and wonder, challenges and possibilities. I would like to thank all the Maasai schoolgirls, teachers, mothers, elders, and community members who shared aspects of their lives with me. My debt—for their generosity, good humor, wisdom, patience, and time—is immeasurable. I hope that this book in some small way does justice to their insights and experience. Any mistakes are mine alone.

There are many people in Kenya I want to thank and to whom I am deeply grateful for their support, insight, and time in this road-making process. I thank Agnes Sereti Meja Kiluswa for welcoming me into her family and community, for being there to laugh (and laugh and laugh), and for introducing me to her brother, John Kintalel, a tireless advocate for his community. I thank John and his wife Esther for opening their home to me several times over the years and for making any research I do in Maasailand possible. I thank the communities of Loodariak and Eroret for making a place for me on the "goat truck," greeting me in the center, and welcoming me into their lives. I give thanks to all of the schools and surrounding communities I spent time in, to the teachers who gave my research assistant and me their beds and shared their food, to families who provided homestays, and to the local drivers who transported us to and from relatively remote locations with care. I also thank John for introducing me to the honorable Joseph ole Simel; without his wisdom, guidance, and generosity this book would not exist. I've worked with Eunice Sinore Nkopio for ten years. Her dedication to her community, and particularly to Maasai girls and young women, is an inspiration. I am truly grateful for her time, attention, wisdom, and care. I thank Rebecca Shempere Kitesho for her quick wit, sharp intellect, and savvy, and Mary Muyaki Kiok for her gentle wisdom, attention to detail, and keen insights; I am honored to know them both. I want to thank Eliakim (Oji) Okiddy and his family for opening their home to me in Nairobi and for their long friendship, patience, good humor, and care. Okiddy's TEKKO family made office space available, answered my questions with patience, and provided invaluable transport. I thank others in Kenya who have graciously supported my work in Kenya over the years: Professor Sarone ole Sena, Njoroge Maina, Sophie Matura, James Sakuda, Leah Meja Sonkoi, Dennis Sonkoi, Anne Samante, Patrick Mushanki, Benson Kitesho, Reverend Samuel Pulei and his late wife, Edith (Babu and Shosho), Leonard Pulei, Alex Kayiao, and Mercy Musomi.

In many ways the road-making for this book started about twenty years ago, during my service as a Peace Corps volunteer teaching in a secondary school in rural Ethiopia in the late 1990s (shout out to all of my dear RPCV friends!) and then in the early 2000s through several short-term volunteer engagements with community-based organizations in Kenya's Maasailand. I thank Lea Pellet, Camilla Buchanan, and Debra Hill for their work with Maasai community leaders to support Maasai women, girls, and the communities in which they live, for allowing me to be a small part of their work in the beginning, and for introducing me to a varied network of Kenyan friends and colleagues who have made this research possible.

My experiences in Ethiopia and Kenya led me to doctoral study in the School of Public and International Affairs (SPIA) at Virginia Tech. My initial focus on transnational feminist collaborations as a function of the "NGO-ification" of development afforded me the opportunity to learn from scholars whose influence remains with me today, particularly Max Stephenson and Wilma Dunaway. Carol Bailey not only taught me qualitative methodology, she modeled for me feminist pedagogy. I owe a debt of gratitude to Charles Good, Brett Shadle, Patricia Proudfoot Kelly, Bernice Hausman, and Timothy Luke for graciously and wisely guiding my intellectual development and for making the doctoral process positive and generative. I am especially grateful to Bernice for modeling how to mentor graduate students with humanity, care, and respect. I thank Tim for offering key insights and grounding my humanities-inflected interdisciplinary project and committee in SPIA and therefore making my project possible.

I want to give special thanks to Charles Good for generously pausing his retirement, at my request, to lead a course on African Political Economy and for encouraging me to immerse myself in the demographic, economic, and comparative education literatures on girls' education. In the process I learned that in-depth, qualitative accounts of girls' experiences in schooling as a transnational process were few. His guidance shaped the direction my doctoral research and writing would take and the road along which the seeds of this book would take root.

As a small-town girl from the magnificent Blue Ridge Mountains of Appalachia in southwestern Virginia, I never imagined that I would complete this book in a sprawling city in the beautiful Sonoran Desert. I have benefited tremendously from intellectual and social engagements with my colleagues in Women and Gender Studies and the School of Social Transformation at Arizona State University. I want to thank Georganne Scheiner Gillis, Yasmina Katsulis, Lisa Anderson, Rose Weitz, Alesha Durfee, Sujey Vega, Kim Scott, Marlon Bailey, Michelle McGibbney Vlahoulis, Karen Leong, Ann Koblitz, Sally Kitch, Vera Lopez, Aviva-Dove Viebahn, April Miller, and Elsie Moore for their gracious support, encouragement, and friendship over the years. Tami McKenzie's administrative genius and good-humored patience ensured all the right forms always got to the right people. Very special thanks go to Mary Margaret Fonow and Beth Blue Swadener for reading versions of the manuscript and for believing in me all along. Karen Leong and Ann Koblitz both read the manuscript at key moments; their insights and encouragement were invaluable for shaping the final draft. Outside of ASU, Dorothy Hodgson's astute insights have been instrumental to shaping this book; she read and responded to my earlier writing as well as drafts of the book as it developed over time. I cannot thank her enough for her intellectual guidance and inspiration. I want to express my appreciation for Jackie Kirk, in memoriam, whose insistence on girls in the Global South as experts on their own lives without romanticizing or overdetermining the notion of "voice" continues to inspire me. It's through Jackie's work that I stumbled upon the vibrant scholarly, activist, and advocacy community of girls' studies. I have benefited immensely from and am grateful for social and intellectual engagements with girls' studies colleagues and friends: Elaine O'Quinn, Jessica Ringrose, Emma Renold, Claudia Mitchell, Crystal Leigh Endsley, Marla Jaksch, Marnina Gonick, Wendy Hesford, and Shenila Khoja-Moolji. I am so very grateful to my writing collaborator and partner in crime, Emily Bent, for her tireless support, intellectual insights, and friendship; I hope to be as helpful to her as she writes her own book as she has been to me through this long process. Jerryll Moreno's editorial guidance and technical expertise were as essential for the book's development as they were for my peace of mind; I am certain I would still be writing in circles without her kind and generative interventions. Lindsey Allemang helped me prepare the manuscript for submission to the press as part of her undergraduate research assistantship with me; her keen attention to detail made that task less painful than it otherwise might have been, and I am grateful.

There are many people I want to thank for making this road with me—for answering the phone, cooking the food, pouring the drinks, turning up the music, and reminding me that no pursuit, no matter how lonely it feels, is completely solitary. I want to thank these friends, old and new, for being smart and funny and for keeping me grounded—intellectually and emotionally: Chantelle Eversole, Kate Saacke, The Aunties (Lissa Bloomer, Cathy Skinner, and Aileen Murphy) and the Mojitás (Marcy Schnitzer, Nicole Sanderlin, Veronica Arroyavé, and Angela Mendes), Aberash Berek Weji Ashenafi, Paul Heilker, Kim Foulds, Emily Bent, Ersula Ore, Karen Kuo, Chris Holman, Jenny Sandlin, Joe Forte, Rachel Christensen, Shauna Pomerantz, Emily Henderson, Ken Urakawa, Lisa Morley, Nick Markette, Juliann Couture, Kate Harper, Debjani Chakravarty, Paulette Stevenson, and Karishma Desai. Special thanks go to my (former) students, Rachel Reinke and Anastasia Todd. I became their doctoral advisor just after I joined ASU in 2010; in the time it has taken me to complete this book, they have each started and completed a PhD in Gender Studies! I am grateful for their patience and fortitude, and I look forward to supporting them as they embark on their next steps, including writing books of their own.

I thank Larin McLaughlin and members of the National Women's Studies Association and the University of Illinois First Book Contract Committee for seeing this book's early draft as a diamond in the rough and selecting me as a finalist. Although I am sure she does not remember, a fortifying comment at NWSA in 2011 from a member of that committee, Amanda Locke Swarr, encouraged me to see that I have something worth saying. Dawn Durante has been a pleasure to work with. I am grateful for her patient dedication to this book and her faith in me to give it life. I would also like to thank an anonymous reviewer whose compelling and careful feedback helped me strengthen my arguments.

My research and writing have been generously supported by the Association of University Women Dissertation Completion Fellowship, faculty research funds, and a travel grant from Women and Gender Studies, the

School of Social Transformation, and the College of Liberal Arts and Sciences at Arizona State University, and a seed grant from the Institute for Humanities Research at Arizona State University. I am grateful to the Kenyan Ministry of Education, Science, and Technology for permission to carry out this research and to Kenyatta University for affiliation and support.

This book is dedicated to my mom, Pat Switzer, who was taken from us too suddenly and too soon. My own girlhood was shaped by her steady love, easy laugh, hard work, and dedication to our family. She died just as I was negotiating my own in-betweenness, just as we were starting to know each other as women in this world together. I think she would've been delighted and amazed, but not the least bit surprised, to hold this book in her hands. My dad, Charles Switzer, and my stepmom, Rita Montrosse, have been a constant source of unconditional love, encouragement, and wise counsel. I am so grateful for their presence in my life and happy beyond measure that they've traveled to Kenya, met my friends who have become theirs too, and cultivated their own love for the place and its people. To my brother Scott and his wife, Ashley, two talented people immersed in their own labors of love, I hope this book helps you understand what has monopolized my time and attention all these years. I thank my in-laws, Bill and Carmen Deshler, for their kindness and confidence as well as their patience with this long process. Special thanks go to my dear cousin Leslie Forstadt-Villeneuve, who paved the way as the first person in our extended family to earn a PhD (we are only two so far); her support over the years in this and other journeys of the heart have steadied me. And last, after all these thousands of words, I struggle to find the right ones to express my gratitude to David Deshler, my husband, partner in life, and by far my favorite human being. He has been my cheerleader, confidant, and gentle critic. He and our sweet dog Kidogo (and our half-feral cat, Wazimu) bring light, love, and laughter to my life every day. I thank him for the past twenty years that have brought us to this moment and look forward to rest of our lives together.

When the Light Is Fire

INTRODUCTION

"Girls are the most powerful force of change on the planet."
Situating Schoolgirlhood

The danger of a single story . . . is not that [it] is not true, but that [it is] incomplete.
—Chimamanda Ngozi Adichie

"Do you circumcise girls in America? What do you put on your skin to make it white? Do you have poor people in your country? Do you have black people in your country? Do you have cows in America? Do you have schoolgirl pregnancy in your country? Do schoolgirls drop out of school? Are girls married off to old men in America? What foods are there in your country? Is there corruption in your country? Do you walk long distances in your country? Do parents beat children in your country? Did your dad beat you? Do you have a husband? Where is he? Do you have your own children? Do you believe in God? Are you a Christian? How far have you gone in your education? Who supports you in your education? What will you do with your education? Have you come to Kenya just to ask these questions of Maasai girls?"

Slender arms shot in the air with each question. Often the group didn't wait for our answers before someone insisted "Teacher! Teacher!" and the next question was hurled through the dry, dusty space between them and us. Alice, one of my research assistants, and I stood in front of thirteen Maasai primary schoolgirls, ages twelve to seventeen, who had been gathered by the head teacher in an empty classroom close to the end of the school day.[1]

Innyonyorri Primary School is a small, coeducational, government-run day school located in southern Kenya, about fifteen kilometers west off the paved Magadi Road along the loose rock and hardpack dirt road local elder and my host David ole Kilusu jokingly calls "the Loodariak highway." Innyonyorri Primary School and the surrounding community with the same name would not show up on most maps of Kenya. This sublocation was one of nine similarly small, rural, and relatively remote communities I visited over the course of three research trips to Kenya.[2]

My home base was in Loodariak, about twenty-five kilometers off Magadi Road, where I rented a single, stand-alone room in Ruth and David ole Kilusu's homestead. Over the course of fieldwork, I worked with two different research assistants, first Maria and then Alice,[3] who also lived in the Loodariak area with their families (Maria with her paternal uncle's family; Alice with her mom and younger siblings). From there we traveled by local pickup *matatu*[4] or arranged a ride to the schools that made up the study with the local Maasai nongovernmental organization (NGO) that facilitated my research. At each school we conducted interviews and observations for three to four days while living in teachers' housing on school compounds or with local families in nearby homesteads.

Even though Innyonyorri Primary School was the closest school to Loodariak, it was the second-to-last school we visited. By this time, at the end of February 2008, Maria was still in a holding pattern as the postelection violence in the wake of the December 2007 contested presidential election had started to simmer down in Nairobi's city center, and University of Nairobi officials planned to reopen the gates for her new life as a university student to begin. After many weeks together, Alice and I had finally found our own rhythms with the research despite the fact that everyone was still on edge. The Maasai communities in Keekonyokie Central Location (KCL), Ngong Division, Kajiado District, where the research was conducted, had remained largely untouched by direct violence.[5] Nonetheless, everyone was shaken by the election, its conflicting results, and the stories of rage, pain, and deadly destruction that erupted in many parts of the country. To add to national anxieties, regional worries connected to recurring drought deepened. In the arid and semi-arid drylands (ASALs) of the southern Rift Valley, the short rains had barely fallen; the staggering heat of the lingering dry season seemed to swallow everything whole.[6] Livestock suffered and died while Maasai men and their sons migrated out of the valley to higher ground to find grass for grazing their animals, and women consolidated households and did what they could to keep school-going children in school.

And still, every visit to a new school started this way, with a vibrant and fascinating onslaught of questions. After an introduction by cellular phone or in person by a staff person from the local Maasai NGO, I explained my intentions and needs to each head teacher, and he, or his deputy head teacher, gathered a group of girls to be interviewed over the course of three to four days.[7] As requested, before we met with each girl privately for her individual interview, we met with the group all at once to introduce ourselves, explain the research in basic terms, explain the interview process, and request their participation. These group meetings also gave the girls a chance to freely ask us questions. As local young women who had completed secondary school and gained employment (if informal) as research assistants based on their credentials as graduates, Maria and Alice embodied success for Maasai schoolgirls. I hoped the primary schoolgirls would see Maria and Alice as knowledgeable resources who could answer questions about their own experiences in secondary school, the search for colleges, and working outside of the pastoral economy.

I also wanted to present myself to them in a very open manner and to underline what I hoped would be a casual, nonthreatening, but also serious exchange of ideas and inquiries. In this sense I hoped to destabilize the standard didacticism that characterizes most Kenyan teacher-pupil relations within the classroom, lessen the distance between the girls and me as an adult and a white foreigner, and ultimately foster a less rigid but nonetheless engaged dynamic. We talked in this unstructured way for an hour or so with each group in each school. These discussions, like the individual interviews, were conducted in a mixture of three languages, English, Kiswahili, and Maa, depending on the language(s) each schoolgirl felt most comfortable using, and Maria and Alice translated for the schoolgirls and me as necessary. More than one hundred individual, semi-structured interviews across the nine schools lasted anywhere from thirty to seventy-five minutes, depending on how much time each schoolgirl was allowed to take out of her school day.[8] In some sublocations more than others, I also had opportunities to interact informally with schoolgirls within the daily ebbs and flows of community life, but most specifically in the context of, and physical spaces of, school.

When the Light Is Fire is my attempt to weave together engagements like these and others into an account of Maasai girls and shifting notions of Maasai girlhood that mark a departure from much of what we in the Global North often see or hear about poor girls in the Global South, particularly in Africa.[9] Like poor racialized girls elsewhere, Maasai schoolgirls have been conventionally regarded as the objects of expert knowledge rather than the subjects of their own stories. In recent years, as the result of feminist critique of these silences and erasures, girls' voices from "the developing world" are now more likely to be sought after, amplified, and circulated in development discourse. As I go on to discuss, however, often only certain representations of girls are deployed in ways that reassert already-agreed-upon normative ideas about girls' lives that flatten their experience into a single story of girls' "empowerment." I focus on Maasai schoolgirls' subjective perceptions of education in their daily lives because schoolgirls are knowledgeable subjects with singular, incisive insight into their own lived experience of development that reflects hegemonic ideas, as well defies and exceeds the neat boundaries of normative claims.

Questions like those posed during our group meetings and at the end of each interview when we turned our inquiry over to the interviewee reveal some of the girls' curiosities but also the multiplicity of their commitments, aspirations, and desires. In moments like the opening scene in Innyonyorri, I was routinely struck by how astute their questions and how resounding their curiosity could be. It was as if in those dusty, hot rooms all the clarity and sheer energy needed to surmount the impossible congealed into slender arms and coalesced into rapid-fire questions. At this school, like all the schools we visited, during the group meetings some girls giggled and looked shyly away, some sat in disciplined silence, and some responded quite vigorously (almost always in English) to our invitation to ask us anything at all. They often posed questions I did not anticipate, from the scientifically curious ("Which geological processes have shaped the mountains in your country?") to the poignantly mundane ("What can you do to help Maasai girls?"). Sometimes I learned more from what they asked, and my attempts to answer, than from the answers they sometimes struggled to give me. Girls' experience of schooling, their perceptions of development in their daily lives, and the ways they rework the idea of "the schoolgirl" as she comes to them from messages at home, in school, in NGO workshops, at church, on the radio, from other outsiders like me, and elsewhere in everyday discourse, are the issues that continue to animate my own desire to learn about and from them. The recent focus on girls' education as the silver-bullet solution to eradicating poverty and ensuring global economic growth found at the center of an assemblage of discourses I refer to in this book as *girl-effects logic* has helped to create the conditions in which a new category of gendered childhood can emerge for Maasai girls who go to school. For Maasai schoolgirls and their communities, "the schoolgirl" as a social category and form of personhood far exceeds the static demographic indicator of a girl enrolled in school.

Situating Schoolgirls

Conceptually central to my analysis is what I came to see as Maasai schoolgirls' embodied and inhabited agency.

> If the ability to effect change in the world and oneself is historically and culturally specific (both in terms of what constitutes "change" and the means by which it is effected), then the meaning and sense of agency cannot be fixed in advance, but must emerge through an analysis of the particular concepts that enable specific modes of being.... In this sense, agentival capacity is entailed not only in those acts that resist norms but also in the multiple ways in which one *inhabits* norms. (Mahmood 2005, 14–15, original emphasis)

Thinking of agency as de-linked from a fixed idea or specific result and reconceptualizing it as an embodied and discursively produced array of capacities helps to break down vague notions of "empowerment" dubbed over schoolgirls' experiences. If agency is the capacity to inhabit existing and constraining norms in ways that slowly shift cultural meanings and enable new possibilities, then schoolgirls' "empowerment" can be seen as locally mediated and embedded in Maasai life. The schoolgirls in this study do not perform or enact agency in the classical liberal or even liberatory sense. They are not fully autonomous; they do not necessarily act with free will; they do not necessarily or knowingly resist or reject dominant modes of power, and certainly not in overt ways (Ahearn 2001; Madhok, Phillips, and Wilson 2013). They are limited by a variety of structural material and constructed ideological barriers to freedom. Yet, the ways in which they inhabit and embody a repertoire of negotiative strategies for making sense of their realities as schoolgirls belies the conventional figuring of their complete victimization as female children.

Despite the very recent tendency to depict poor girls in the Global South as "full of potential," the African "girl-child" from pastoralist communities is still often represented as the helpless and often hapless victim of local cultural pathologies and immutable conservatism. Particular social arrangements and practices, including arranged marriage, early and forced marriage, female genital cutting, and resistance to female education, are often presented as emblematic of oppressive gender relations and lack of development in pastoralist communities generally and Maasai communities specifically. Yet, these elements of social reproduction often come to global public consciousness within a narrow, oversimplified, and static rendering of Maasai life. As Thomas Spear (1993, 1) asserts in his introduction to *Being Maasai: Ethnicity and Identity in East Africa*, "Everyone 'knows' the Maasai":

> Men wearing red capes while balancing on one leg and a long spear, gazing out over the semi-arid plains stretching endlessly to the horizon, or women heavily bedecked in beads, stare out at us from countless coffee-table books and tourists' snapshots. Uncowed by their neighbours, colonial conquest, or modernization, they stand in proud mute testimony to a vanishing African world.... Or so we think. Reality is, of course, different.

The enduring masculinized image of the pastoralist elder honed throughout Kenyan history is alive and well today in travel brochures, Kenyan textbooks, and in the broader popular imaginary inside and outside of Kenya, and, to some degree, in the daily life experiences of Maasai individuals—the recalcitrant patriarch, *rungu* on his belt, staff in hand, lording over his wives, children, and livestock (Hodgson 2001a).[10] Spear suggests that the coffee-table-book image of Maasai social forms is reductive and romanticized. Nonetheless, his portrait also makes clear that the Maasai "everyone knows" are adults. Images of men and women are evoked here, but somehow the patriarch gazing over the endless plain becomes the specter of reference for the "girl-child," not the bead-bedecked woman she is to become. The girl-child, imagined as inherently vulnerable to patriarchal power, submissive to authority, and reticent to speak (having never been asked), is absent from this portrayal. She is implicated only in relation to the "uncowed" patriarch and his plans for her future symbolized by the distance across the open plain.

Given my reading and study across a variety of literatures and conversations with Kenyan friends and colleagues, including Maasai, I also expected to hear stories of oppression, abjection, and even violence as central features of Maasai girls' lives. I had "fixed in advance" ideas about the oppressions Maasai schoolgirls must face and therefore likewise fixed in advance the resistance, overdetermined as a narrow definition of "agency," that I hoped to see. My assumptions about schoolgirls' oppression not only delimited the possibilities of their agency, they also fixed in advance Maasai "culture" as monolithic and static. Actual fathers and the generalized reference to "fathers" as indexical to kin-based patriarchal power, particularly regarding decisions about girls' lives, loom large in this book. The trope of the authoritarian father recurred in every interview, even in stories in which it was also clear that individual fathers supported girls' education and individual mothers evoked and benefited from "patriarchal" authority. Despite the discursive salience of "fathers" as a powerful structural force in girls' lives, I interviewed very few individual fathers unless they also happened to be teachers or NGO staff with whom I often interacted. Very early in the research I was told repeatedly that if I wanted to learn more about girls, I needed to talk to mothers.

Fathers, everyone agreed, would not know their daughters in the ways that mothers would and therefore would have nothing to offer in terms of insights about their lives, in part because of cultural taboos around affective relations (emotional, physical, and sociopolitical) between fathers and daughters (that are powerful cultural habits; see chapter 3). After only a few interviews, however, it became very clear to me that despite the fact that fathers cannot "know" their daughters as their mothers might, fathers are indeed central to decisions concerning girls' education. Unfortunately, men of all ages living exclusively according to the pastoralist economy were overwhelmingly absent from the case-study communities as they migrated with livestock away from the drought. The actual absence of men compounded the cultural consensus that even if they were readily available, they would have no useful insights to offer anyway.

Yet, on the whole, fathers are not always or even the only adults involved in decisions concerning daughters. Fathers, mothers, and other adults (women and men) tend to have a say, if not a stake, in girls' futures. Maasai parents' decisions regarding girls' schooling and marriage arrangements are less about absolute patriarchal power and more about attempting to account for daughters' needs, household needs, and the challenges of pastoral livelihoods in the face of shrinking resources and increased poverty (Archambault 2011). Everyday livelihood insecurity and ongoing pastoral crisis is as operative in Maasai girls' lives as cultural beliefs and practices that limit their options and opportunities. As I hope the arguments in this book make clear, education is a central process, and school a key site, through which Maasai communities struggle to imagine and craft their futures. I listened as Maasai schoolgirls shared stories describing the obstacles they faced in their pursuit of schooling and their worries about the future, and many expressed frustration, fear, and even pain. But they also expressed something else: pointed, provocative hope and a particular knowledge about who they are and who they want to be.

Schoolgirls' aggressive faith in the promise of schooling troubles reductive notions of the abject Maasai girl struggling within an inherently oppressive culture. Their collective insistence on the possibilities of schooling for changing key aspects of their lives likewise reveals the possibilities and, as I will go on to discuss, the paradoxes of gendered social change in Maasai communities as elsewhere. The emergence of the schoolgirl as a normative social category and schoolgirlhood as an increasingly common cultural space are effects of, as well as producers of, a new commonsense about the crucial role school(ing) girls plays in development as economic growth. These chapters begin to map the contours of these experiences for a group of Maasai schoolgirls in rural communities navigating the gendered cultural effects of increased institutional access to school based on sex in the context of a globalizing exuberant embrace of girls' education as the "key" to development.

• • •

How has "the girl," who has historically been represented as the most vulnerable and disempowered member of nearly every society, been recast as the exceptional subject of education and economic success? How are "the girl" and her new "power" constituted? From within what meaning systems has she come into effect? My conversations with Maasai schoolgirls during various trips to Kenya between 2007 and 2012 occurred as ideas about the interdynamics of girls' education, gendered social change, and economic growth were becoming widely available outside of conventional development channels through social marketing campaigns circulated via Web 2.0 social media platforms, particularly YouTube, Facebook, and Twitter. Over the past ten years, discourse extoling the wisdom of investing in poor, racialized, adolescent girls in the Global South seems to be everywhere, from corporate marketing conference rooms in the Global North to the halls of the UN, the World Bank, national governments, and the dusty primary-school compounds of Kajiado County, Kenya. *The logic of girl effects*—the purported outward ripple of positive social and economic benefits resulting from an investment in adolescent girls—has since come to dominate the market in girls' empowerment as the singular authoritative narrative about poor girls in the Global South (Switzer, Bent, and Endsley 2016; Bent and Switzer 2016). The ideas of empowerment that animate girl-effects logic are not created in a vacuum but gather meaning and affective value within systems of interrelated and interwoven discourses and historical legacies. The cultural and political-economic conditions that make increasingly hegemonic ideas about "the schoolgirl" in the Global South the "key to every solution" provide the context in which Maasai schoolgirls', mothers', and teachers' narratives in this book play out (The Girl Declaration, n.p.).

"Girling the [Neoliberal] Subject"[11]

A diverse array of scholars has documented the various ways over the course of the twentieth and into the twenty-first century the category of girlhood has been "a container for cultural anxieties about social change" (Harris 2004, 128; Gonick 2006; Aapola, Gonick, and Harris 2005).[12] The historical emergence of "the girl" as a subject-position and girlhood as a transnational cultural form has indexed wide-ranging efforts to define proper gender and generational, as well as racial and classed, relations of power and authority through the expansion of capitalist modernity, particularly imperialism, colonialism, industrialization, globalization, and development.[13] In the past twenty-five years, a cultural consensus in Western societies has formed around the figure of "the girl" as the subject best suited to excel in current sociocultural and political-economic conditions. Within neoliberalism as the organizing feature of contemporary capitalism, including economic policy prescriptions as well as the cultural ideology of our time, social legitimacy and belonging are intimately tied to one's capacity to participate in the market.[14] Girls in the Global North are thus ascribed a new kind of gendered "power" commensurate with the performance of specific modes of normative white femininity and youthfulness encapsulated by the ambiguous term "girlpower."

For girls in the Global North, girlpowered girlhood is characterized by educational achievement, delayed childbearing, career advancement, and market participation. Successful girls (and young women, in which female people older than eighteen self-identify, and are positioned as, "girls") are the creators, curators, and consumers of culture at the center of service and lifestyle economies (Harris 2004). Heterosexual marriage and motherhood may be part of the equation, but these conventional feminine aspirations are carefully considered as part of strategic process of rational self-styling and life-making (Aapola, Gonick, and Harris 2005). In this ideological context, girls are represented as the beneficiaries of feminism. Girlpower ideology relies on the (erroneous) popular sensibility that in Western democracies, gender discrimination is over, gender equality has been reached, and feminist political struggles for gender justice are no longer needed. Moreover, collective feminist politics and activism aimed at structural transformation are disavowed (McRobbie 2009). Ideas about girls in the Global North as the winners in a new feminized economy are thus tethered to this notion of "postfeminism" as a very narrow version of feminism focused on individual achievement, entrepreneurial investment, and self-making (Rottenberg 2014; Gill and Scharff 2011). These days, girls and young women are "not only recognized as subjects within discourses of neo-liberalism, they are its subject par excellence" (Gonick 2007, 438; Walkerdine 2003). As this prevailing sentiment goes, every individual girl can succeed if she works hard enough.

It is important to note that girlpower is neoliberal postfeminist empowerment embodied; as such, it is not readily available to all girls in the Global North. Those girls better positioned to participate by race, ethnicity, class, citizenship status, sexuality, gender identity, ability, and geopolitical location are hailed as successful subjects, whereas their less "ideal" counterparts are further marginalized and disproportionately criminalized and institutionalized for failing to leverage the purportedly universal access to empowerment.[15] In this globalizing cultural schema, any girl and any woman are expected to succeed according to a narrow rubric of girlpowered consumer citizenship, although not all girls and all women are equally positioned to do so. Neoliberal postfeminist girlpower ideologies require and create new social categories and political subjectivities in contradictory ways. These contradictions produce (and reproduce) difference structured as inequality and exclusion at multiple scales rather than radically intervening in the logic of white supremacist, heterosexist capitalism. In the contemporary context, intersectional gender oppression and multiple marginalization in the Global North have by no means disappeared; they have instead taken on new forms (hooks 1994; Griffin 2004; Mohanty 2013; Wilson 2011 and 2013).

Girlpower Travels South

As transnational feminist theorist Chandra Talpade Mohanty (2003b, 514) reminds us, "It is especially on the bodies and lives of women and girls from the Third World/South—Two-Thirds World—that global capitalism writes its script." Current manifestations of development have ideological roots in centuries of Western imperialism. Colonial political-economies were designed to maximize capital accumulation for the imperial power through exploitation and extraction of natural and human resources and to enculturate the colonized through European civilizational norms and forms. Colonial states were thus often violently productive of identities and lifeways as categories of social and political control. Development continues to be a central mechanism for expanding capitalism and producing identities and subjectivities that fall in line with a capitalist ethos.

In the twenty-first-century version of the nineteenth- and twentieth-century imperialist narrative, "economic growth" is necessary and good for everyone, not just the arbiters of empire who hold global power. The neoliberal variant of capitalist epistemologies and ways of being extend market-based principles and practices (competition, entrepreneurialism, commodification, exchange, value, capital, regulation, investment, returns, risk, and so on) into every realm of social life, including our internalized self-understandings (Ong 2006; Sparke 2015). Economic logic has come to shape our ethical frameworks so that thinking through individually centered, cost-benefit analyses is taken for granted as commonsense. Neoliberal ethics require *all* subjects to make rational strategic sense of their "individual biographies in terms of discourses of freedom, autonomy and choice—no matter how constrained their lives might actually be" (Gill and Scharff 2011, 6). In this frame, "elements of feminism have been taken into account, and have been absolutely incorporated into political and institutional life ... converted into a much more individualistic discourse ... [and] deployed ... by Western governments as a signal to the rest of the world that this is a key part of what freedom now means" (McRobbie 2008, 1). Consequently, the form of empowerment that frames expectations for girls and their girlhoods in both the Global North and South is a function of this depoliticized ethical-economic thinking. Although their lives and needs are not identical, girls' lives in both geopolitical spaces unfold within the globalizing of girlpower; thus, representations of their instrumental value to capitalist expansion are linked, forming a new kind of ethio-commonsense about all girls in the global system (Bent and Switzer 2016).[16]

At first blush, nonetheless, postfeminist girlpower may seem like a misplaced concept for thinking about contemporary rural Maasai schoolgirls' lives. Yet, postfeminist sensibilities thoroughly infuse neoliberal development discourse and practice. It is precisely girlpower's appropriation of racialized gender oppression *and* gender equality that makes a consideration of its circulation pertinent to my framing. A growing archive of policies, programming, and funding mechanisms extends and transforms neoliberal assumptions about girls' "new" "power" in the Global North to poor girls in the Global South who are explicitly represented as "the world's greatest untapped resources" in which "investments in girls have significant economic returns. Their returns have the potential to uplift entire economies" (Girl Effect n.d.). According to this new commonsense in which adolescent girls themselves are a form of capital, assumptions about the central role they should play in development further reifies neoliberal principles of economic efficiency and ethical self-responsibility.[17] Historically invisible on development agendas, adolescent girls living in poverty in the Global South are now spotlighted for their newly determined capacity to embody development imperatives. My phrasing—*girl-effects logic*—alludes to a body of public discourse created and circulated online and offline between 2004 and 2015 by the Nike Foundation's Girl Effect.[18] As a result of a decade of coordinated effort, the Girl Effect as an institution and an idea has been instrumental in crafting and disseminating this framework for girls' empowerment and global economic growth. Important as a central organizing feature of development discourse, girl-effects logic today extends well beyond any single organization. The Girl Effect, therefore, asserts the schoolgirl is "the most powerful force of change on the planet,"[19] while other widely circulated commanding and compelling declarations from public-private partnership campaigns marketing girls' education announce "One girl with courage is a revolution";[20] "Girl Up!";

"Educate Girls, Change the World";[21] "#BasicMath: 'Education + Girls = A World of Possibilities!'";[22] and most recently, "Let Girls Learn!"

These examples evince the standard "grammar" (Abu-Lughod 2013, 203) for representing girls' education as the sine qua non of economic development and girls themselves as the ideal subjects of investment and intervention. Here, girls themselves are the subjects who act: they are collectively the courageous force of change the world (and its societies) and the planet (and its ecosystems) need if allowed to stand up and take advantage of possibilities denied to them. Within this discursive system, girls' education signifies justice for girls otherwise marginalized and oppressed, suturing this justice to global benefits for all. Yet as Lila Abu-Lughod (2013, 203) reminds us, "We have to take this language of justice seriously." What does this grammar permit and what does it refuse? Packaged neatly as "shareable" ideology for instantaneous circulation, repeated representations of girls' empowerment through education conflated with economic productivity work to systematically produce and perpetuate hegemonic ideas about who empowered girls must be and for whom. Moreover, part of the persuasive and productive power of the invest-in-girls discourse is that girls derive their new "power," capacity, and aspiration from exceptionalizing processes like going to school. Within these entangled discourses, the exceptional adolescent girl is most often constructed specifically as a schoolgirl. Education through formal schooling is presented as the singular solution to eroding local pathological patriarchal norms that oppress girls. By going to school, so the discourse goes, "the girl" is rightly removed from, and essentially becomes Other to, local practices deemed barriers to their participation as proper citizens of developed societies, growing economies, and legitimate states.

Troubling Schooling as the Silver-Bullet Solution

Girls' schooling in Africa as elsewhere has historically positioned girls' bodies in the crosshairs of modernity and tradition. "Formal education constituted an alternative organizing category that sought to restructure the totality of an individual's life" (Kanogo 2005, 206).[23] Schooling therefore often "mark[s] the definition, impact, and reshaping of new forms of gendered and generational differences" (Stambach 2000, 4; Archambault 2009, 2016) that in turn are productive of new forms of gendered and generational identity. Yet as Stambach (2000, 10) argues, deterministic perspectives, which assume "schools themselves are the main engines of social change," fail to consider the ways in which "people collectively invest schools with the cultural capacity to change social relations." Kenyan Maasai encounters with Western education as formal schooling have historically been fraught and ambivalent engagements. The communities with whom I spent time are nevertheless nearly unanimously interested in education for all children, including girls; schoolgirls themselves are deeply invested in what they, along with their mothers, teachers, and many local elders, believe is the cultural capacity of schooling to change social relations in positive ways along gendered and generational lines. Schools, however, are complex sites of cultural politics, production, and reproduction; changing gendered and generational social relations by school(ing) girls is by no means a straightforward affair (Vavrus 2003). Education is a transnational process and is therefore an important institution for understanding the production of identities. Global discourses (as ideologies and affects in circulation, and material processes like funding mechanisms and policy interventions) targeting populations for development have powerful influence on social relations and formations. While globally derived ideas about education and development can never fully determine local notions of educational inclusion and exclusion, in rural Maasai communities, everyday identities are formed, among other things, via one's relative relationship to schooling.

Faith in education to lift all boats in a rising tide of economic success is not new in Kenya. Although a focus on girls' education has been on the margins of everyday discourse for some time as Kenya has attempted to keep in step with global agendas concerning universal primary education, an emphasis on education as a human right for girls has taken on new urgency in the past fifteen years (Archambault 2011). In the process, girls' education in Kenya, as elsewhere, has come to signify gender equality in all aspects of life. For the Maasai schoolgirls we talked with, the global development imperative of "education for all," with particular reference to educating girls, has enabled spaces of rupture in the institutional fabric of Maasai life. "The schoolgirl" is now a new form of personhood, the contours of which continue to emerge but that I attempt to begin outlining in these chapters. I argue *as schoolgirls* Maasai girls and young women who have historically been constrained by virtue of the gender and generational structures in their lives can act and be in ways heretofore largely denied them, in part because they are seen (and they see themselves) differently. As schoolgirls, they have access to a limited empowerment with which to negotiate their own needs and desires in ways that their age-mates who are not in school do not have. As such, in Kenya, the "Maasai schoolgirl" is now a normative social category; poverty and livelihood vulnerability notwithstanding, families in the case-study area aspire to be families who educate their girls. Although Maasai are assumed to "hate education," a shorthand for the belief that Maasai patriarchal conservatism is inimical to modernity, particularly modern conceptions of gendered social life girls are supposed to learn in school, my conversations indicate the opposite: that Maasai are people who "love education" for all children, including girl children. Contrary to girl-effects logic, Maasai schoolgirls want education not because they want to leave Maasailand or be other-than Maasai, but because they want to be *better Maasai*. They see being better Maasai as integral to participation in a national narrative of development.

The problem is that overly affirmative rhetoric and education policy promotion consistently fail to address "gendered relations of power in cultural, economic, and political domains that are not easily rectified through schooling" (DeJaehere and Vavrus 2011, viii). The openings created by relatively new forms of girlhood are constantly under threat of closure, as schoolgirls are implicated in development as a regulatory regime that requires and valorizes certain ways of being over others (including biosocial bodily attributes like sexuality and fertility), and they live in economic circumstances that reinforce limited opportunities rather than expanding them. Further, persistent Maasai gender and generational ideologies that can reinforce *dis*empowerment play out in these same political and economic contexts and can work against gendered social change despite widespread desire for girls' education. Maasai schoolgirls, like schoolgirls elsewhere, live in local and transnational "contexts that are hostile to the transformations that education can bring about" (Weinstone 2004, 6). Moreover, "economic imperatives which construct schooling as an unequivocal social good have provided little space for the consideration of the possible adverse effects of schooling on the reinscription of gender inequalities rather than their amelioration" (Dunne, Humphreys, and Leach 2006, 77). Axiomatic claims regarding the new commonsense about girls and development—that there are direct, causal, and unequivocal linkages among girls' education, girls' empowerment, and economic growth (and concomitant poverty alleviation)—do not clearly account for the gendered and generational implications of school(ing) girls.

The Logic of Gendered Labor and Girl-ed Effects

There is more at stake in the increasingly hegemonic rallying cry for girls' education as a panacea (Vavrus 2003). Enthusiastic declarations of girls' empowerment through education as the most efficient and effective way to ensure economic security and gender equality relies on age-old assumptions about "Third World difference" (Mohanty 2003a, 19) transfigured by girl-effects logic into what Kathryn Moeller (2013, 614) calls "Third World potential." I argue that calling on girlpower as a specific social modality concerned with girls' intimate interactions with market forces (primarily as consumers but also as "new" kinds of workers for "new" kinds of work) has become a pervasive (and persuasive) authorizing discourse because it sutures consumer power ascribed to girls in the Global North to labor power ascribed to girls in the Global South. As an effect of this merging of girl-subjectivities, the figure of the homogenized and racialized Third World Girl is constructed, circulated, and celebrated. "The adolescent girl" living in poverty in the Global South has thus become the quintessential object of efficient and ethical human capital investments. This figure of the Third World Girl animates the ubiquitous and troubling claim that girls and their bodies *require* development investment in order to realize their "full human potential."[24] According to this purported ethical-economic reasoning, girls' lives become sites for extraction because girls' gendered labor produces "dividends" that everyone, from their immediate families to the global economy, can—and should—count on (Girl Effect, n.d).

In this ideological context, the social benefits of educating girls, such as the potential for increased individual decision-making power and access to and power over resources, are wrapped up into a means equation for economic growth as the end goal. In other words, positive social, intellectual, spiritual, and psychological benefits for girls, while sometimes acknowledged as an end to themselves, are never the only—or even the primary—reason to consider girls' experiences in (or out of) development. Rationalizing girls' education as "smart economics" makes it easy for development institutions and the global public to think about girls' bodies in simple economic terms as labor lost to the "opportunity costs" of school dropout, precocious pregnancy, and joblessness—or gained through school completion, delayed fertility, and formal employment.[25] This logic links access to education directly to measurable, formal productivity as a girl's gained labor is appropriated and distributed from her to others. If we position "the girl" as the consummate future worker and therefore future consumer, her only viable life course becomes formal economic participation.[26]

As I discuss more extensively in the concluding chapter, neoliberal postfeminist girlpower ideologies therefore accommodate (and rely on) rather than challenge the globalizing policies that extend "the feminisation of responsibility and obligation" (Chant 2008) regarding gendered labor, conventionally ascribed to women, *to girls*. The incorporation of poor, non-Western girls of color within this often oppressive logic is a consequence of, and rationale for, girlpowered development, and it actively shapes normative expectations of girls as instrumental to development based on their "natural" capacity as gendered subjects to shoulder the burden of local and global social reproduction by "succeeding" in the marketplace. Girl-effects discourses emphatically focus on catalyzing girls' purportedly natural economic capacity, yet cover over the fact that women, young women, and girls already disproportionately do the majority of global work (Chant and Sweetman 2012). They are the world's subsistence farmers, informal marketers, and invisible pastoralists; they collect fuel as wood or dung; they collect water for human consumption, livestock consumption, and household use; they raise other peoples' children and clean their homes, workplaces, churches, and public facilities; they accomplish all of the unpaid labor of reproducing their own households, including carrying and raising children, caring for the ill and elderly, as well as ensuring food, shelter, schooling, and healthcare for their families, including their male partners, siblings, and children (Marphatia and Moussieé 2013). As Grosser and van der Gaag (2013) point out, drawing from Diane Elson's work on the invisible care economy, "If the value of this work was counted in global financial terms, global output would be 50% higher" (ILO 2009, quoted in Grosser and van der Gaag 2013, 80).

This linkage between "geopolitics and biopolitics" (Grewal 2005, 17) continues to rely on oppositional categories of gendered and racialized subjects. According to this commonsense, some girls are the beneficiaries of late modern consumer culture and "Other" girls are the eternal victims of poverty and patriarchy. This framing sustains and justifies interventions in the name of "development" as the unfolding of progress according to Western norms (Abu-Lughod 2013; Mohanty 2003a; Narayan 1997). As I argue in the concluding chapter, these discursive and affective moves mark a shift toward centering girls and their girlhoods in the genealogy of approaches to women, gender, and development that is full of paradox as well as possibility.

Reimaging Maasai Girls, Rescripting Their Girlhood(s)

Within and against global girl-effects logic as a straightforward account of human capital investment entangled with prevailing Kenyan popular commonsense that Maasai "hate education" and always have, and that Maasai girls are always and already victims of "culture," Maasai schoolgirls (as well as mothers and teachers) unanimously believe that education is the only achievement that will qualify them to succeed in their world. One goal for this book, then, is to contextualize commonsensical claims about Maasai girls who go to school within transnationally scripted and locally embodied gendered ethnic formations.

Hannah, a mother in Loodariak, made comments during her interview that provide insight into the powerful affective attachments that coalesce around education in KCL that illuminate these ideological narratives. Hannah "was never taken to school" as a girl. Widowed, she ran a small, single-room café called "the Hilton," made of a corrugated metal roof on a wooden frame with a dirt floor, where she sold bowlfuls of beans with *chapati* and cupsful of chai that she prepared over an open fire. She worked hard to put all of her children in school because she recognized that graduating from secondary school is the bare minimum requirement for jobs in Kenya's formal economy.[27]

As we talked about the importance of education for Maasai children, and particularly girls, she made reference to a version of what Archambault (2007, 40) claims is a common "joke." A matatu driver recounted the "joke" for Archambault in this way: "The driver received a phone call from his tout asking how full the matatu was. The driver responded, 'Well, I have twelve people and one Maasai.'" It is hard to discern the humor in Hannah's account:

> Education is the head of everything because educated people know many things which illiterate people do not know. Those who are educated take the illiterate as if they are not people. For example, a car gets an accident; they say there were ten people and one Maasai as if the Maasai are not people—as if the illiterate is not somebody. So education gives you value.

For Hannah, "being educated" is an existential matter. "The illiterate" are "not people." "The illiterate" is "not somebody." Arguably, the Maasai subject as other-than human is interpellated by mainstream Kenyan beliefs about inherent Maasai otherness encapsulated by the "joke." In another encounter, when I submitted my request for research clearance, the ministry of education official who received it (a non-Maasai man) commented with a heavy sigh, "I am happy to see this research. *Something needs to be done for those Maasai girls!*" (his own emphasis). In the frame of reference created by the joke, Maasai are immutably outside of "the educated" and "the developed." Maasai are literally not counted among persons and therefore exist naturally outside of the aspirational life of the nation. The ministry official's comment, like so many casual comments I heard from Kenyans, specifies the gendered and generational profile of ethnic otherness and, paradoxically, spotlights Maasai girls for specific kinds of recognition. Hannah's assertion that "education gives you value" illustrates how, for Hannah, personhood—having "value" to others as belonging among the community of persons—is deeply sutured to being educated. Like all the mothers we talked to, Hannah wanted her Maasai children, and particularly her girls (see chapter 2), to be seen, counted, and therefore endowed with personhood and belonging to the nation.

Representations that circulate in discourse targeting ideological and material investment in girls' education and local Kenyan parlance that marks Maasai girls out as exceptional subjects of such investment authorize interventions on their behalf that have material consequences. Hannah's aspirations for her daughters' futures as educated citizens reflect this confluence of discourses that produce the schoolgirl as a social category and desired subject-position in rural Maasailand today. Qualitative accounts of schoolgirls' insights about who they are and want to be and how schooling figures into the lives they imagine for themselves, as well as the ways in which they inhabit certain norms and the actions they take concerning school, help me document and understand how a group of Maasai schoolgirls see their current lives and future prospects; their narratives give insight into their quotidian experience as "targets" of development intervention.

The use of the "the modern girl" as a "heuristic device" in the Weinbaum et al. (2008) comparative study of the modern girl ideology is a worthwhile reference for the relations I examine. The authors emphasize how the notion of the modern girl in the early twentieth century, conventionally understood as a "local" incarnation, was actually a dispersed global phenomena that evinces how "the local comes into being through complex global dynamics" (4). As I talked to schoolgirls, I came to understand the figure of "the schoolgirl" as indexical to a range of social, cultural, and economic processes in Maasailand today. In each chapter, I draw on examples of the newly visible "schoolgirl" in development policy promotion along with actual schoolgirls' everyday embodied experiences to show how the nexus of global and local discourse authorizes hegemonic "truths" that create social realities with often uneven effects. Examining transnational discourses of girls' education as a multiplier of economic development helps illuminate the ideological conditions that have helped to make "the schoolgirl" as a social category possible and enabled a new, if narrow, set of social capacities for Maasai girls who go to school, as well as produced new constraints.

Relative to "the schoolgirl" as a social construct, Maasai girls who go to school are living, breathing young people who daily inhabit and negotiate norms; they are at once shaped by, and contribute to shaping, the powerful discourses that circulate about and around them. A consideration of the variable girlhoods "the schoolgirl" construct makes possible also helps me "shift the focus away from simpler oppositions of agent or victim . . . towards the complex ways in which agency and coercion are intertwined" in the interest of foregrounding embedded transnational, historical, and affective relations (Madhok, Phillips, and Wilson 2013, 3). The insights of actual school-going Maasai girls and some of the key adults in their lives have a great deal to teach us about shifting meanings around gender and generational norms that shape (and are shaped by) girlhood as a contingent and dynamic cultural formation.

Tracing the Outlines of Schoolgirlhood

The schoolgirls we talked with around KCL understand their positioning as exceptions to many conventional gender and generational assumptions about Maasai girlhood as a space of passivity, submission, and subservience, as well as playfulness and relative freedom from the responsibilities associated with womanhood. Unlike a "girl at home" who, according to schoolgirls, is doing "nothing" but "waiting for a husband," schoolgirls see themselves as actively working toward a future that is a bright unfolding of possibilities that include, but are not limited to, marriage and motherhood. At the same time, schoolgirls understand that their exceptionality comes with its own "hard work" and intensification of responsibilities associated with maintaining what I have come to think of as *schoolgirlhood*: a relatively new and different kind of gendered cultural space formed through the process of going to and staying in school that extends childhood and codifies adolescence for girls.

A clear parameter of schoolgirlhood that emerged in the interviews is an ardent desire on the part of the girls to stay in school. Schoolgirls *want* to be exceptional; they are invested in the boundary maintenance work, as well as the actual labor, required for the proper performance of schoolgirlhood. A successful performance requires the near-constant negotiation of conventional Maasai gendered obligations to family and relational affective investments in community potently and dynamically entangled with "modern" gendered and generational expectations for independence, autonomy, and continuous self-making conveyed by the discourse of girls' economic empowerment through education. In other words, schoolgirls have internalized the fundamental message of girl-effects discourse because it is in many ways consonant with local ideas regarding normative behavior for girls and young women who go to school. Despite their positioning as the most vulnerable members of society, successful schoolgirls are valorized for their almost superhuman capacity to mitigate their own precarity. For example, all the schoolgirls we talked with deeply understand that avoiding further marginality through "schoolgirl pregnancy," school "dropout," and "early marriage" is their responsibility alone, rooted in individual self-will, self-discipline, and hard work against all odds. Inhabiting this often ambivalent mixture of "old" and "new" norms means that schoolgirls frequently came across as subjects caught in the interstices of changing social forms and shifting commonsense. This milieu, often described by schoolgirls as "the world of today," hailed a range of capacities to enact and inhabit conventional norms in novel ways in order to negotiate who they wanted to be or what they wanted to do against or around what was expected of them.

Take, for instance, a moment with Sereti. When I met Sereti, she was a precocious fifteen-year-old schoolgirl in Class 7 (seventh grade) at Loodariak Primary School. In her interview she was animated, forthcoming, and generous with her insights; despite a difficult story to tell about her family's struggle, she stood out among her peers for her talkative, inquisitive demeanor. Because I lived in the Loodariak area, I often ran into Sereti outside of school. One day as we walked together, she suddenly grabbed my arm and pulled me off the main rocky dirt road leading to the Loodariak "center" and down a winding footpath through the thorny brush that characterizes the southern Rift Valley. She surprised me, but I complied because she was smiling. Once we were a few feet down the footpath, I asked her what we were doing.

She gestured toward a group of adult men, elders (in Kiswahili, s. *mzee*, pl. *wazee*), who were gathered along the road chatting in the sliver of shade cast by a stand of acacia. Sereti laughed mischievously: "Did you not see the group of wazee there ahead? If we go there, we can only walk with our heads bowed! It is better to pass here." I had seen the men but didn't think much of this familiar scene. She explained that if we continued down the main road we would soon meet the men, and we would have to "show them respect" which, she added, would "take our time."

I was delighted at her quick thinking and a little relieved to avoid the men on the road. By "showing them respect," "with our heads bowed," she meant that because she was a girl, circumcised or not, and because I was a classificatory "daughter" and even "granddaughter" to most of the men gathered, we would be expected to show our respect by way of proper greeting. We would slowly and deliberately walk silently up to each mzee, bend our heads slightly toward the ground, and receive his greeting—the palm of his hand laid gently and quickly on the top of our heads in turn. We would say nothing; each man would say "my child" (s. *enkerai*, pl. *inkeran*) as a greeting, an acknowledgment of our respect (*enkanyit*), a phrase of endearment, and a recognition of a communal responsibility and paternalism toward all children (women are categorized as inkeran, children/dependents: see Hodgson 1999) and social juniors (like me—although I was an adult, I am a woman and younger than the men gathered, who were senior and retired elders). Not only would we need to properly greet everyone, but I surmised also that we would be waylaid by questions, as Sereti would be asked to explain my presence with her: why we were together, what we were doing, where we had been, where we were going, and so on. I had come to enjoy showing my respect to elders (men and women), even though sometimes as an outsider I was a bit confused as to my status relationships because I was often also a classificatory "wife" of men around my age and could therefore shake hands in greeting. But sometimes it was hard for me, and for Maasai I encountered, to tell on sight our relative positions.

Sereti, however, quite clearly understood the social expectations of passing a group of wazee on the road. In fact, this way of greeting was mentioned in almost every interview, as schoolgirls referred to this ritual as one example of why "nowadays" female circumcision (*emurata,* for both boys and girls) is "meaningless." In their minds this customary rite affords them no social status upgrade, as they are "still just girls" because they are in school and therefore have to "give their head" in greeting. In this instance, Sereti actively and decisively avoided engaging in the performance of proper Maasai girlhood by skirting the group altogether and following the footpath through the dense thicket and behind a row of one-room shops. We were in a hurry; dodging the wazee got us to where were going without delay. There would be absolutely no way for a Maasai girl and foreign woman to "hurry" the process of properly greeting and answering the insistent questions of ten to twelve wazee standing in the shade. Better, she calculated, to avoid the situation altogether.

By singling out and presenting this interlude with Sereti, I don't mean to suggest that she is the only Maasai girl to ever dodge a group of wazee. Indeed, her swift maneuver indicated to me that avoiding her elders like this, and the structural requirements of encountering them, was not uncommon for her, and likely for many Maasai children (boys and girls) through the course of any given day (Pratt 2003).[28] I do, however, think her lesson teaches us something fundamental about the negotiations Maasai schoolgirls make daily among conventional expectations and practices (particularly as the map to gender and generation), social expectations attached to being in school, and shifting conceptions about who girls are and can be. These seemingly contradictory actions—dodging expectations in order to conform to them—can help us to see how power relations are historically shifting, if in very small and seemingly trivial ways and in light of "new" ways of being in Maasai life (Abu-Lughod 1990). These negotiations, as I argue throughout *this book*, are manifest in the ways the schoolgirls talked about education and development, the ways they inhabited certain norms, and the actions they took in the context of schooling that mark them as exceptional to some normative expectations and beholden to others.

In this brief moment on the dusty road we can see the outlines of the schoolgirl social category and schoolgirlhood as a cultural space in formation.

The schoolgirl is a construct that is constituted by social, cultural, political, spatial, institutional, and historical relations and processes that intersect to produce and perpetuate the idea of the schoolgirl. In this sense the schoolgirl and her schoolgirlhood are contingent creations, enactments, and embodiments. That is, the Maasai schoolgirl as a social category, form of personhood, and lived experience has emerged over time from within dynamic systems of meaning. At the same time, Maasai schoolgirls (as well as the discourses, structures, and people around them) continually produce (disrupt, reify, modify, and negotiate) meanings about themselves and thus participate in the construction of the social worlds they inhabit.

Sereti's decisive detour effectively disrupted her performance of Maasai young femininity as this subjectivity has been articulated and rearticulated through the institutions, like displays of respect in the greeting of elders, that characterize Maasai social relations. Her disruption was not extraordinary. In fact, her disruption was brief; it amounted to the time it took us to duck into the thicket and avoid the group of men. The wazee were not, at that moment, aware of Sereti's disruption. Nonetheless, she maneuvered in such a way that she could preserve social respect for her elders (and thus her legitimacy as a proper Maasai girl) and do what she felt she needed to do according to her desires at the moment. Her disruption was minor, maybe even meager. Yet the precocity with which she executed her dodge suggested to me in that moment that it *felt* bigger and more profound to her at that time than it seems now looking back or even relating the story here. That is, simply, Sereti knew what she was doing. Moreover, what she was doing enabled her to know herself differently. In that moment she enjoyed her own ingenuity as a set of honed navigational skills, not just knowing where and how to step out of sight into the bush to avoid her elders, but how to strategically manage expectations and norms, all the while inhabiting them, to her own benefit. She certainly enjoyed sharing this particular strategy with me.

For Sereti and her peers, the institutions that govern social relationships, such as the progression of males through the age-grade system, are in significant flux in her community. As a girl in school in a community largely in agreement with school(ing) girls, both Sereti and the wazee along the road inhabit unstable normative positions. In that moment, Sereti embodied the norms that have come to define schoolgirl subjects which are themselves contradictory—on the one hand, cleverness and, on the other, disrespectfulness. Yet her status as a girl-child positioned her to have to walk the purported line between the schoolgirl and the girl-child, never fully one, to the exclusion of the other. Understanding the subject as always in-process and constituted by sociocultural and political-economic processes (macro as well as micro) allows us to see Sereti's dodge as less an absolute rejection of or rebellion against elder male authority—even though her father was not among the gathered men, all the men gathered were her "fathers"—and more a negotiation among the multiple structural expectations and modes of being that were in play at the moment, including Sereti's own desires.

This brief scene illustrates a small example of how relationships of authority among categories of persons continue to shift, particularly as categories of persons themselves—of which the schoolgirl is an excellent example—are not settled. Moreover, as Pratt (2003) has argued and as will be discussed throughout each chapter, the struggles over these shifts have often involved "who has access to girls' bodies, who has control over where girls should be and at what time, and for whom girls should work" (Pratt 2003, 268). In a structural sense, Sereti, as a girl ducking into the thicket to avoid showing her respect to the wazee, was a "person out of place" (Pratt 2003) in the Maasai worldview. Yet that she orchestrated her dis-placement suggests the struggles and opportunities schoolgirls face in a gradually changing landscape of female personhood in Maasai communities for which historical and "traditional" structural relationships have eroded, continue to shift, and in some cases have disappeared (Hodgson 1996a). "Girls become girls by participating within the available sets of social meanings and practices" rooted to a particular place, cultural landscape, and historical moment (Gonick 2003, 5). As I hope to show, Maasai schoolgirlhood marks off a specific kind of gendered and generational social space and cultural place for girls who go to school that affords them new, if narrow, social meanings with which to craft new, if narrow, social identities, even as it also creates new kinds of constraints.

Reading This Book

In order to begin to account for the entangled processes of education, development, and gendered identity that configure schoolgirlhood as a relatively "new" cultural space in which some Maasai girls grow up, I have become a "scavenger methodologist" as a strategy for creating a place for schoolgirls.[29] In this vein, I have assembled an interdisciplinary archive of insights from critical feminist theoretical literatures concerned with the construction of gendered subjects in late capitalism and critical development literatures concerned with the contradictory processes of development and their gendered, and gendering, effects. I draw specifically from girls' studies as a subfield of feminist cultural studies; feminist media studies; feminist cultural theory; transnational and postcolonial feminist theory; political geography; feminist anthropology; Maasai ethnography and ethnohistoriography; studies in critical and comparative education; and the range of literatures that constitute women, gender, and development studies. As a scavenger, I have been less invested in cohesive disciplinary frameworks and more attuned to collecting and collaging together insights from here and there that help me attempt to capture the intricate, intimate, multifaceted, and still unfolding parameters of schoolgirlhood.

As a result of this scavenging, my analysis sits at the nexus of several bodies of knowledge that might not typically intersect. For example, girls' studies has emerged to counter the historical tendency for feminist scholarship to center adult women and marginalize girls (Kearney 2009). Nevertheless, girls' studies has historically focused primarily on white girls' lives in the Global North.[30] When girls' studies scholars sometimes look south, they do not often engage gender and development literatures. Similarly, the literature focused on ascertaining demographic trends and examining constraints to, and benefits of, girls' education in the Global South has devoted significant attention to gender inequalities in schooling, such as sex-based disparities in education policy, provision, access, persistence, and success without the benefit of engaging critical girls' studies scholarship or transnational feminist theory.[31] While I believe feminist scholarship is fundamentally enriched by interdisciplinary, intersectional, and transnational approaches, regardless of the subject matter, my aim has not necessarily been to insert Maasai schoolgirls and their schoolgirlhood into the study of girlhood in comparative perspective, add feminist development knowledge to the study of girlhood, or infuse development studies with insights from critical girls' studies (though some of this might have happened). I am more concerned with tracing the emergence of schoolgirlhood as a social category and embodied experience as an analytical threshold for understanding the production of gendered subjects in the development process broadly and for girls specifically.

My analysis is also situated in tension with the education and demographic literatures that form the bedrock of girls' education discourse and girl-effects logic. On the whole, in their focus on the timing of demographic events, changes in per capita income, and changes in health and wellbeing, these literatures conclude that education has a positive impact on delayed marriage and sexual debut (Ikamari 2005), fertility (Ikamari 2005; Nekatibeb 2002), infant mortality, maternal mortality, the provision of education for the children of educated women, the ability of women to negotiate sex (Jewkes, Levine, and Penn-Kekana 2003; Wolff, Blanc, and Gage 2000), and reduced vulnerability to HIV infection (Fylkesnes et al. 2001; Hargreaves and Boler 2006). Moreover, studies indicate the benefits of girls' education are distributable for the human development of everyone in their households and correlate with economic growth (increased Gross Domestic Product [GDP]) and poverty alleviation (Al-Samarrai and Bennell 2003; Appleton, Bigsten, and Manda 1999; Chaaban and Cunningham 2011; Ikamari 2005; Levine et al. 2008; Malhotra, Pande, and Grown 2003; Manda, Mwabu, and Kimenyi 2002; Psacharopoulos and Patrinos 2002).

Qualitative and ethnographic studies of education in developing contexts complicate this seamless picture (Kiluva-Ndunda 2001; Mojola 2014; Stambach 2000; Vavrus 2003, 2007). Moreover, feminist scholars have troubled faith in "education as panacea" (Vavrus 2003, 2007) by documenting education as necessary but insufficient to positively transform gender relations. This work highlights aspects of formal schooling for girls in development contexts that work against empowerment and positive impact, including the high rates of sexual harassment and assault (including rape) in schools and in the context of schooling, the global persistence of HIV/AIDS among females of schooling age (from fifteen to twenty-four) (UNAIDS 2012), gender bias in student, teacher, and parental attitudes against girls' academic abilities (Davison and Kanyuka 1992; Mensch and Lloyd 1998; Mensch et al. 2001), and the ambivalence many communities still have around the "social death" young women face when they pursue schooling (Kanogo 2005).[32]

When the Light Is Fire sits most clearly in these critical feminist qualitative literatures. I do not dispute the efficacious and life-expanding benefits of education for girls anywhere and for poor girls everywhere. As I discuss throughout these chapters, Maasai schoolgirls and many of the adults in their lives are deeply invested in the positive benefits scholars document and promote. With this said, I am interested in troubling the overly affirmative rhetoric of girl-effects logic that too easily individuates responsibility, depoliticizes discourse, and deflects attention from structural analysis. Rather than viewing education a neutral public good inequitably provisioned and accessed, I understand education to be a transnational process, particularly in the regions of the world targeted for development investment, and it is thus a primary means by which individuals and collectivities are configured in a globalizing world.

My agenda as a U.S.-based academic researcher and my white, adult, female body are implicated in these transnational processes. While I might be a scavenger, I was not and cannot ever be simply a fly on the wall. Rather, my positionality as a white woman who is not "young" and an academic (who is also married to a man and is not a mother) is deeply implicated in all elements of the research process, from conducting a "formal" interview in a head teacher's borrowed office (the schoolgirl's classmates no doubt wondering why she was chosen and not them) to smiling with Sereti as she gently pulled me off the road to avoid the group of men, to figuring out how to arrange these sentences on this page and thereby (re)present the lives I encountered. How might have schoolgirls' self-representations, for example, been different if we had interviewed them at home and not on the school compound or in small groups under the shade tree outside of one of the local churches? How might schoolgirls' and mothers' insights have been complicated by fathers' narratives, had I been able to talk to fathers in the same way I talked to their daughters and wives? How might have my conversations with mothers unfolded if I had spoken with them directly rather than through a Maa and Kiswahili interpreter or been in the position to reference my own children's schooling as a point of connection? It is certainly possible that the community's willingness to invite me so generously into their schools and homes had something to do with the promise of development attached so securely to my white, educated, U.S.-based body as emblematic of the promises embodied by educated women, suppositions complicated by the fact that some Maasai children go to school as a result of sponsorships from individuals in the United States. I cannot account for all the possible answers to these speculations, of course. My task has been to consider the local, national, and global influences and interests that circulate transnationally to produce, reproduce, maintain, and normalize the gendered ideologies, discourses, policies, and practices that structure inequality and distort the just distribution of life chances for marginalized girls living in poverty in the Global South generally and rural Kenyan, Maasai schoolgirls specifically. I want to acknowledge, nonetheless, that the arguments I offer here are refracted through the very power asymmetries I work hard to illuminate and, hopefully, erode.

Overview

Maasai social norms and cultural structures involving the mutually reinforcing intersections of gender, generation, and ethnicity are co-productive of attitudes and behaviors concerning school that have bearing on how schoolgirls come to understand themselves in relation to their present and their futures. Chapter 1 focuses on how ideas about "being Maasai" and "being educated," beginning in the colonial period and extending into the formation of the postcolonial state, have changed and continue to be dynamic. Schoolgirls, mothers, and teachers today see education as a powerful antidote to historically produced ethnic otherness, political marginalization, and endemic economic insecurity. Across the interviews, everyone explained that "the world has changed" and so have Maasai attitudes about education. In chapter 1 I historicize and therefore politicize contemporary Maasai attitudes about education in the case-study communities, within and against still-salient ideas in the Kenyan social imaginary about Maasai as people who "hate" education. Drawing on history unfolding in the present, I explain how Maasai have in large measure come to see themselves as people who "love" education for all children, including girls.

In chapter 2 I explore the affirmative embrace of girls' education in the case-study communities. I show how girl-effects logic is localized through Kenyan gender and education policy and then produced and performed in local communities. Although the schoolgirls, mothers, and teachers I talked with had never heard of "the girl-effects dividend" per se, a very strong faith in girls' education to create positive social and economic "ripple effects" for individual girls, families, their communities, and Kenya as a nation saturated their perceptions of education as a pathway to development. I discuss the ways in which Maasai mothers' and teachers' expectations for development as increased household security and community advancement worked to shape schoolgirlhood as a normative category. I then show how schoolgirls worked hard to perform the attitudes, attributes, and actions expected for schoolgirls.

In chapter 3 I show the instability of the ubiquitous dichotomy that has come to represent young female subjectivity in the poverty contexts of the Global South: the girl-child and the schoolgirl. I focus in on Nashipae's and Felista's stories to illustrate how the experience of Maasai schoolgirlhood exceeds oversimplified accounts of gendered vulnerability or gendered agency. Nashipae's struggle for school calls into question the inherent vulnerability of the girl-child. Felista's situation, conversely, alerts us to the contradictions of the schoolgirl as unequivocally empowered. These girls' stories, along with my research's assistant's advice (and her own schoolgirl story), show the challenges Maasai girls face as they work individually to circumvent, reinvent, and ultimately surmount structural relations of power in order to embody and perform schoolgirlhood. Chapter 3 foregrounds what girl-effects logic often elides: Maasai schoolgirls are relational subjects enmeshed in social formations and power relations as Maasai daughters.

Chapter 4 considers how schoolgirls' "developing" bodies complicate their performance and negotiation of schoolgirlhood in a context in which "old" cultural norms are in tension with new social forms. Here I consider conflicting and conflicted accounts of *emuratare oo ntoyie*, girls' circumcision, and *enkanyakuai*, a female social category. My analysis highlights how schoolgirl subjectivity and schoolgirlhood as an index for the biosocial process of adolescence challenges conventional cultural structures, such as language, bodily practices, and the gendered and generational distribution of power and status. In this sense, schoolgirlhood proceeds as girl-effects logic would predict by destabilizing current meaning systems and rescripting girlhood as a place of possibility for girls who go to school rather than a relatively short life stage that ends abruptly at circumcision. At the same time, this chapter, as well as the book as a whole, also reveals how girl-effects logic cannot account for how important community identity and belonging are to Maasai girls who go to school. Girl-effects logic constructs girls who go to school as autonomous social actors who, by virtue of their participation in education, are divorced from cultural expectations and social norms that limit their capacity. Local discourse likewise positions schoolgirls as "tough" enough to resist and refuse still salient cultural claims on their bodies, time, and attention. Yet at both scales, assumptions about schoolgirls' abilities to "call the shots" collide with schoolgirls actual capacity to do so, not to mention their conflicted desires to be independent *and* to deeply belong as "Maasai" among Maasai. Thus community identity as relational recognition is constantly under threat by the schoolgirl identity, and any schoolgirl's tenuous hold on her place in school is constantly under threat by her relational affective attachments to family, friends, and "Maasai-ness."

In the book's conclusion, I consider the implications for the two strands of my analysis throughout the chapters. First, I elaborate what I see as the emergence of GID (Girls in Development) as a distinct paradigm for framing girls in development discourse and practice that is informed by and also distinct from WID (Women in Development) and GAD (Gender and Development). From there, I consider what Maasai schoolgirls' narratives tell us about what it is like to live as a "target" of development and how thinking about schoolgirlhood as a new form of personhood illuminates why identities matter in the discourse of development.

CHAPTER 1

"Now is not like before. The world has changed."

Maasai Education in Cultural and Historical Context

> We need to be suspicious when neat cultural icons are plastered over messier historical and political narratives.
> —Lila Abu-Lughod

Alice and I sat with Cherity on wooden chairs painted forest green to match the student uniforms required for children attending Enkoerroi Primary School.[1] As we talked, we were both struck by Cherity's gregarious personality; the majority of the schoolgirls we interviewed were incredibly shy and deferential; their voices barely above a whisper. Cherity, however, came across to us in her interview as what Maasai might call *entito naisosion*, a bright, clever, well-prepared girl, and in fact, she was the prefect of her class. Her outgoing nature might also have been explained in part by her age: at fifteen in Class 6, she was four years older than members of her Class 6 cohort who had started "on time" at age six and who had not repeated any classes. Her relatively mature character might also be explained by the challenging circumstances of her home life. She described her father as a "drunkard." Her mother contributed to her education to the extent that she could by selling firewood in hopes that, as a result, her children would be able to help her in the future. Cherity explained: "[My mother] just knows it is usually very difficult to get even shoes or food. She has to carry firewood to sell them to get money, so we also know [the struggles] we have passed through and the poverty that we are in so she knows that we will help her." At that point in her life, Cherity and her younger siblings had managed to stay in school through the combination of sponsorship from a faith-based international nongovernmental organization (INGO) active in the area and the concerted efforts of her mother, her educated uncle, and her uneducated older brothers.

Cherity was clear that education, including the successful completion of secondary school and university, is absolutely necessary for her to realize her aspirations. When we asked her why "education is important for her life," she asserted that it enabled her, among other things, "to see ahead" beyond the immediacies of the moment. Cherity wasn't the only schoolgirl (or teacher or mother) to use the imagery of "seeing ahead" to evoke the capacity—which one learns, everyone argued, through formal schooling—not only to plan for the future, but also to adopt new (and adapt old) strategies for living. Yet Cherity, like nearly everyone when asked about the importance of education for Maasai life in the present, invoked the future promise of the "fruits" of education by referencing the past, or more specifically, the differences between the present and the past. As one of Cherity's classmates, Damaris, explained: "Now is not like before." A persistent theme across the interviews suggests how the production of "the Maasai" subject as antithetical to participation in formal schooling in the past informs aspirational identities projected in the future that have implications for the present, and Cherity's insights offer a case in point. As we talked, she offered a detailed list of the ways educational participation enables new ideas about the present and the future that were for her unthinkable and impossible in the past because "there before" Maasai did not have access to schools or rejected the schooling on offer.

For Cherity, "seeing ahead" encapsulates a range of strategies and possibilities that she believes come from one's relative access to school. For example, "seeing ahead" means being able to communicate with non-Maasai and even non-Kenyans in Kiswahili or English because "there before [education], no one was there to talk [to outsiders] because of English, so now it's better because we [Maasai] are there with English." She equated planning for the future with being able to acquire vehicles for transporting goods and people to Kiserian, the closest market town, instead of walking and using pack donkeys because "at least now we have education [so] we have people having their own cars so they make the transport easier." Without the forethought she associated with educated behavior, her community would not have access through transnational networks to external donor support for borehole and spring-tapping projects for predictable and safe water instead of relying on intermittent streams, as "long ago there was no water in Maasailand; for example, they used only rivers [so] now educated people can get support from outsiders to [provide] water [via boreholes and piping from tapped springs] to avoid such diseases as typhoid."

Cherity noted that while education fosters access to material resources that lessen labor burdens, educated people are also able to directly engage the political process by demanding recourse from the state for protection from violence and exploitation—in evidence, for example, when "people the other day [in the past] were fighting and they [brought] the dead people and just [threw] them in Maasailand, dirtifying the place [but because] we never had any education, we never reported such cases, but now because we have some people who are educated they can report such cases to the police." What's more, she insisted, being able to see ahead engenders the local capacity to access formal employment, which has, for her, broad-reaching implications for everyday life. She explained that when communities can see ahead through education, "nobody will lack a job." Instead of "cutting down trees for firewood and charcoal to get money," behavior that, according to her, "finishes the land," people will "get money" through "their job." Even though her mother's petty trade in homemade charcoal had in part enabled her education, she also believed that deforestation would make Maasai life unlivable in the future "because later they will have no place to live because they have removed all the trees."

Finally, of all the reasons Cherity believes Maasai have suffered from the lack of education "there before" that can now be mitigated by the capacity to "see ahead" through education, one of her explanations was unique across all of the interviews with schoolgirls and adults: "There before [in the past] Maasai people did not get education [so] we were made to leave our place and [were] forced here to these deserts."

On the surface, Cherity outlined a typical and laudatory list of the benefits Maasai schoolgirls associate with education and development. She, like the other schoolgirls we spoke with, was unequivocal: education makes life healthier, safer, more secure, and easier for everyone. Nevertheless, I argue that Cherity's insights do more than articulate the promises of education for development as if she is reading from a girl-effects script. As Maasai schoolgirls, mothers, and teachers made repeatedly clear, "now is not like before" because "the world has changed." What about the world has changed for Maasai communities? Why haven't Maasai been able to rely on education before "now" to negotiate non-Maasai environments outside of their immediate communities, improve infrastructure, call on the state for protection from violence and injustice, or work in the formal economy instead of the informal economy? And what does she mean by being "forced to move to these deserts"?

Cherity's recognition that Maasai history is alive in the present prompts a consideration of the intertwining of historical and sociocultural forces that have produced, and in many ways sustained, mainstream Maasai marginality and lack of belonging that are both collectively felt and decidedly complicated by gender and generational positioning. As Lynn Thomas (2003) has argued regarding the politics and processes of sexuality and reproduction in colonial and postcolonial Kenya, the repeated reference across the interviews to the lack of educational access and interest in the past and the changes in both access and attitudes in the present require us to consider the politics and processes of education—both "there before" and "now"—as "historical entanglement[s]" (19). Entangled are indigenous and imperial, local, and global concepts of knowledge, agency, and development that are unevenly formed, negotiated, and reformed within a "wide range of power relations" (175). Moreover—and important for what an empirical understanding of girls' experiences as the targets of development discourse can achieve—by directing us to the past entangled with the present, these comments disrupt seamless affirmations of education's future promise articulated by girl-effects logic and instead do what girl-effects discourse never does: force a reckoning with the local politics of education in Maasai life. Western education as formal schooling in Kenya is not now and has never been a neutral public good equitably distributed, accessed, and experienced. Cherity's and other schoolgirls' insights call into question the myopia of the future-oriented, narrowly economic, apolitical discourse of girls' education as the key to development that orients girl-effects frameworks away from explicitly recognizing girls as subjects in and of history, even as schoolgirls and many of the adults in their lives also value seeing ahead through education as a key strategy for individual and community survival in a changed and changing world.

Following Cherity's lead, I attempt in this chapter to historicize Maasai schoolgirls' perceptions of education and development in their daily lives as a counter to the ahistorical articulation of girl-effects logic. Here I consider the continued unfolding of historical processes that have produced and continue to sustain persistent popular ideas inside and outside of Maasai communities regarding Maasai interests in and need for formal schooling. It is through her lens that I move from the present to the past and then back again, weaving together evidence of changing attitudes and aspirations expressed in our interviews with a cultural and political story of the "history of the present" as a way of tracing systems of meaning that have come to enable the notion that a girl who is "Maasai" can also be a "schoolgirl" as an aspirational subject position and identity category.

• • •

I looked for conversations about education everyday while in Kenya. On this particular day in Kiserian, the closest market town to the case-study communities, the conversations found me. I waited at the staging area with passengers headed to Loodariak and the surrounding areas in pickup matatu #43, owned and operated by David ole Kilusu's nearest neighbor, Ole Parsoi. Ole Parsoi and his assistant made space for a group of four men and their provisions along with burlap sacks of cabbage, kilos of flour, one kid-goat, and more than twenty people already wedged into the narrow Nissan truck bed.

As #43 lumbered and sagged its way down the dramatic escarpment into the southern Rift Valley, the foreman struck up a conversation with me. I learned that he owned the construction firm contracted to build an addition onto the African Inland Mission (AIM) church social hall, one of the two small churches in an area known as Loodariak's "center" where several *dukas*[2] supplied the sublocation with the basics: sugar, salt, matches, pencils, pens, various other sundries, and occasionally some vegetables.

By the time we reached the AIM church, most of the passengers and goods had been dropped off along the way. As we backed up to unload the crew's supplies, the foreman, stepping off the back of the truck bed, asked me, "So what is the subject of your research?" I told him I was studying Maasai girls' education and that I had been in the community for a few months and would remain a few more.

"Ah," he said, with a kind of recognition in his voice that indicated he'd heard the joke before and already knew the punchline. He continued: "Of course we know that Maasai hate education. They always have; they have never wanted it, and that's why they are so behind the rest of Kenya today."

This "hate" discourse and the confidence with which urban Kenyans delivered it were not new to me. But this time, I heard these familiar words standing in the center of a rural Maasai community, surrounded by Maasai people.

Even though I disagreed, I asked, "Really? What leads you to believe that?"

"Look around," he said with a mild laugh, "just look around; there is no development here" and with a shrug, he walked off to join his waiting crew, wishing me a "nice time."

Ole Parsoi, impatient to get home, quickly herded the few remaining passengers back into the truck. I found a place to stand facing forward, thighsto-waist against the back of the cab. A tall, slender young Maasai man dressed in "Western" clothes took his place beside me. As we lurched along, our faces in the wind, he asked me in English: "So, after your time here in this community, do you believe what he has said, that Maasai hate education?"

I felt the color rise to my face and knew that he had heard my conversation with the contractor. "No, I do not agree with him at all," I said. "What is clear to me from my time here is actually exactly the opposite, that many Maasai are hungry for education for their children and even for themselves."[3] "But you know," I continued, "that I also hear this other thing all the time, this thing that Maasai hate education."

"Yes," he said, "*Keh soba oleng* (it is very true). This is what they say about us."

He introduced himself as Gregory, a new teacher at the nearby Eroret Preparatory School, the only private primary school in KCL at the time. Indeed, the presence of a private school suggested the opposite of the contractor's view of educational demand, and Gregory pointed this out. He also noted that the presence of the contractor and his crew were clear indications of development, as the Loodariak community had come together to raise funds to expand the church. Moreover, that Ole Parsoi, a "traditional" (read: "uneducated") Maasai man, also owned and operated a matatu as a way to provide a fundamental service to his community and supplement his livelihood from herding cattle with cash suggested behaviors consonant with ideas regarding maendeleo.[4] In other words, he explained, the community was not only "seeing ahead" but also acting on plans for change and improvement for the present and into the future.

I agreed with him. The contractor's narrow understanding of "the Maasai" as coterminous with "uneducated" and "behind" led him to forgone conclusions, some of which could be rebutted by actually "look[ing] around" and getting to know the community. Nonetheless, I had also been a part of many conversations with Maasai community members, both educated and uneducated, regarding a still-prevalent reluctance (or incapacity) among some families to educate girls. So I asked, "If there is such a hunger for education and development, why are some families still resistant to educating girls?"

For the rest of our remaining short ride home he told me of his own personal efforts to change this attitude. Part of the problem, he argued, as did many educated Maasai I spoke with, is "the culture" that "sees girls as less than boys." He spoke of trying different methods to instill the girls with confidence to speak up in the classroom, debate boys, aspire to the top positions in class rankings, and "work hard" so that they could advance to secondary and complete school. He spoke of what he perceived to be girls' reluctance to aspire and boys' expectations that their female peers could not or would not perform. It was after 7:15 P.M. when we arrived at the Kilusu homestead. None of us lived in houses with electricity; we were all anxious to get to our respective homes before the equatorial dusk quickly dissolved into darkness. We left our conversation with an agreement to meet again and talk further about these competing perceptions of non-Maasai and most Maasai about Maasai attitudes toward education.

I offer this encounter as a way of signaling the dynamic and contradictory aspects of the daily discourse around education in the rural schools and surrounding communities involved in this study. While Maasai are not the only or the most deeply alienated communities from educational provision in Kenya, the prevalent story—that Maasai "hate" education and always have—is on the tips of many Kenyans' tongues. There is a commonsensical confidence underpinning statements like the contractor's that I heard repeatedly, as if the facts of the matter were given, and not only not subject to change but truly unchangeable. Yet the representatives of the Maasai communities where I spent time, and certainly the mothers, teachers, and schoolgirls we interviewed, have come to see school as "the central institution in which children are growing up" (Archambault 2007, 300). Even as some Maasai continue to see education as separate from and often opposed to "traditional culture," what I found echoes what qualitative and ethnographic studies of education in Maasai communities have also observed (Archambault 2007; Bishop 2007; Bonini 2006; Sena 1986): rather than standing in clear opposition to culture, in Maasai communities today "education is a cultural project" (Archambault 2007, 278).

Cherity's representative comments suggest that for many Maasai who have been to school, being different from those who have not been to school has become important for the way they think about themselves and make sense of their lives. Historicizing education discourses foregrounds the taken-for-granted systems of meaning that shape the conditions of possibility in which girls come to know themselves and help to contextualize schoolgirls' perceptions, aspirations, and desires as subjects in their own right. In order to understand Maasai schoolgirls' assertions in the early twenty-first century about the centrality of education not only for their everyday lives but also for the lifeblood of their community, we must first take a look back to the twentieth century. Maasai history is never told through the point of view of Maasai girls. If we take Cherity's insights seriously, we are directed to look back to the time when her great-great-grandparents "were made to leave [their] place," as a way of "seeing ahead" to the contours of conflicting (and conflicted) ideas and attitudes regarding gender and education that shape her future today.

Colonial Encounters, Entangled Social Identities

All of the examples of "see[ing] ahead" Cherity enumerated highlight the significant ways in which being Maasai today remains linked to dominant ideas about "Maasai-ness" in the past that continue to inform the present. Strikingly, the clearest reference to historical processes in Cherity's account is her reference to being "moved to these deserts," a reference to the forced migration and resettlement of all Maasai into a specific closed geographically bounded area. While Cherity is the only schoolgirl we talked to who made specific reference to the early colonial relocation of Maasai communities, some girls mentioned learning about their own histories through "long ago stories" their elders told them. According to Maasai elder and scholar Sarone ole Sena (1986, 28), Maasai describe the last decade of the nineteenth century as "the time when children were exchanged for food." This period is referred to as *emutai*, or "the finishing off of everything completely," or simply, *the disasters*, and I imagine that stories of this time must have been (and still are) among these oral history lessons.

"Long Ago Stories" of Disaster and Dislocation

The loss of 80 percent of Maasai livestock to disease in the late 1880s led to widespread famine, small pox epidemics, and ultimately internecine wars.[5] Maasai pastoralism, processes of social reproduction, frontier relations with non-Maasai neighbors, and spatial locations were sporadically reoriented and reorganized as a result. As pastoralism became intertwined with identity and survival (Kipury 1988; King 1971; Waller 1976) and "Maasai-ness," or Maasai sense of "ethnic identity" as a "product of shared historical experience" (Hodgson 2001b, 13) was in considerable flux as communities focused on reconsolidating their political economy and sociocultural structure.

At the same time as these critical junctures in Maasai history, nearly four thousand miles away, the General Act of the Berlin Conference in 1884 inaugurated the Scramble for Africa and allocated the whole of historical Maasai territory (including areas of what is today Tanzania) to Britain and Germany. This event marked the beginning of the territory's formal incorporation into the world economic system as a dependency of the British Crown.

Once incorporated, lands legally designated as the East African Protectorate (EAP) could be permanently leased to European settlers. Imperialist ideologies concerning modernity and progress, including capitalism as the mode of production and social reproduction, sedentarization as the foundation of civilized social forms, Christianity as a moral framework, and Western white male subjectivity as firmly atop of the social and political hierarchy all fundamentally influenced the ways in which administrators would conceptualize the earliest version of "development" policy[6] targeting Maasai life, including education policy. The codification of white settler colonialism unevenly entangled with local indigenous power structures and interests became the system of reasoning within which ideas about an essential and universal Maasai ethnic identity would be produced in the territory that would become Kenya.[7]

Making Maasailand in Kenya

In this context, the "Anglo-Maasai Agreements" of 1904 and 1911 mark watershed events in Kenyan Maasai history and illustrate how being "forced to [the] deserts," as a historical process, created "Maasailand" as a closed territory reserved for Maasai only, which effectively essentialized "Maasai" as an ethnic identity, produced Maasai as a "tribe" (Blewett 1995), and created a context for the sharpening of ethnic identities and territorial relations with non-Maasai communities (African and European) in historically unprecedented ways (Waller 1993).[8] Most colonial administrators read Maasai reorganization and survival strategies in the aftermath of the disasters as indications of social disarray, demographic decline, and the opportunity to impose order and control in anticipation of creating a lucrative colony. The fertile land in the central highlands that the British saw as a means of unexploited profit and a region that seemed hospitable for sustained European settlement was actually fiercely guarded Maasai territory. However, as nomadic pastoralists who moved with the seasonal rains, Maasai left little trace of habitation or "permanent" settlement. Although the well-watered highland pastures provided crucial grazing for cattle during the dry season in the southern rangelands, as well as sites central to collective rituals of social and cultural reproduction, such as male initiation ceremonies, the highlands were tabula rasa to European explorers, missionaries, and colonial administrators (Hughes 2006).

The 1904 agreement created two separate "reserves" in the north and the south, effectively curtailing cyclical movement between these territories. The 1911 agreement nullified the 1904 agreement, resulting in the forced movement of an estimated ten thousand people, two hundred thousand cattle, and fifty thousand sheep from the northern "reserve" to the southern lowlands, consolidating all Maasai communities in one "closed reserve" for Maasai only (Archambault 2007). This move reduced Maasai territory from fifty-five thousand square kilometers to thirty-five thousand, which was excised further between 1948 and 1964 for the formation of wildlife reserves and national parks (Fratkin 2001; Galaty 1993; Rutten 1992).[9] This process of creating "Maasailand" as a demarcated geopolitical space and "Maasai" as a homogenous ethnic category had important repercussions for social relations and cultural norms within communities, as well as in relation to white missionaries and administrators, as Maasai worked to recover from the disasters and the dislocation of the Moves while also learning to negotiate a new world order under colonialism.

Negotiating Shifting Social Structures and Social Norms

For more than sixty years of colonial occupation and well into the postcolonial period, the majority of Maasai resisted the imposition of Western education in the form of schooling, in part, because of the implications of these changes, even as these cultural structures and attendant norms have always been mutable and porous. Like any human meaning system, Maasai social formations and cultural processes are characterized by a history of dynamism and contestation, as well as dogged persistence that, to varying degrees, still frame Maasai schoolgirls' negotiations around identity today.

The organization and regulation of proper relations among and between Maasai people has historically and continues to function according to intergenerational mechanisms of order and authority based on the male age-set and age-grade system.[10] In this system, boys become men through graduated rites of increasing esteem, status, and power, beginning with circumcision (*emurata*) around age fifteen through seventeen.[11] Male status and power is therefore inherently relational and hierarchical; boys become men relative to other boys, girls, various categories of adult men (for instance, warriors, junior elders, and senior elders who are also their fathers, uncles, brothers, sons), and adult women (their mothers, sisters, wives, lovers, daughters). Once men pass through warriorhood to junior elder status through collective ceremonies, these embedded generational relations bond the men who were warriors together throughout their lives; this network of men and male relationships (the "age-set") constitutes the decision-making and governing structure of their communities and continues today (although in different ways) to frame the forms of personhood available at any given historical moment.

In Maasai social structure there is no parallel corporate system for females. Nonetheless, "women" have likewise been "made" in relation to others and remain relationally embedded in shifting social hierarches across their lifetimes. Historically girls (s. *entito*, pl. *intoyie*), were articulated into the male age-set system at the warrior stage, when groups of young, newly circumcised men gathered to live for several years in special settlements (s. *emanyata*, pl. *imanyat*,) populated also by boys for chores and herding, mothers for moral guidance, and prepubescent girls for leisure (dancing, singing) and sexual play.[12] Girls were associated throughout their lifetime with the warrior class with whom they danced in the emanyata.

With her "circumcision" (emurata),[13] a girl, like a boy, passed from childhood to adulthood. Whereas this biosocial transformation signaled boys' readiness for warriorhood, or a protracted adolescence unfolding over several years in which he learned how to be a Maasai man and after which he would be ready for marriage, emurata signaled a girl's readiness for immediate marriage arranged by her parents, including her father's consultation with other members of his age-set. Generally, girls were married to men of their father's relative age, which deepened reciprocity relations not only among men but also among families. In this way, marriage built communities and extended networks of cooperation, mutual respect (*enkanyit*), and love (*enyorrata*) (Hodgson 2001b, 29), as it still does today. A Keekonyokie elder, speaking to Sena in 1982, gives some insight into the depth of these bonds, with relations among gendered people and to land as central arbiters of subject formation and collective identity:

> *Enkop* (land) belongs to all Maasai; if the Purko want the pastures in our area we cannot deny them because they are our friends and brothers. We sometimes ask them to allow our cattle to eat the grass in their areas. We have Keekonyokie families living in the midst of Purko and vice versa. They have our daughters and we have theirs. We invite them and they us during certain age-set ceremonies. (Sena 1986, 174n1)

Girls as daughters were likewise trained, from the time they were old enough to walk, in the requirements of adult women (s. *enkitok*, pl. *inkituaak*); after emurata, they gained status, relative power, and esteem as wives (s. *enkitok*, pl. *inkituaak*),[14] taking their place among the community of adults charged with managing family and community affairs through relatively egalitarian relations with other adults—men and women (Hodgson 2001b), including caring for and gifting livestock; managing the collection and distribution of milk and leather; caring for babies and children, husbands, the physical house and hearth; managing spiritual relations between humans and *E'ngai* (God); and sustaining community relations among other families and non-Maasai neighbors through barter trade systems. A young wife's status and security within the household, as well as the larger community, increased with motherhood and the gradual advancement of her own children through the age-set structure. Thus, age, generation, and gender have always "distinguished categories of persons" and "structured their roles, rights, and responsibilities" in Maasai life, including a range of social norms—for example, ritual greetings that indicate who may greet whom with one's head or hand and relational power and authority these actions signify ([recall the scene with Sereti on the road] Hodgson 2001b, 26).

Maasai social structure and arrangements, on the rebound after the disasters, were upset again by the Moves, which not coincidentally coincided with the consolidation of the colonial state. The imposition of imperial gendered social regimes attached to capitalist state formation created, quite literally, new social categories and attendant subject-positions expressed as roles, rights, and expectations that eventually eroded the complementarity that governed Maasai social relations before colonial engagement (Hodgson 2001b). As African gender theorists and postcolonial feminist scholars have made clear, indigenous gender regimes in Africa as elsewhere were often dramatically altered in the imposition of the "colonial/modern gender system" (Lugonés 2007, 186), in which entanglements of imperial and indigenous ideas about gender, sexuality, race, ethnicity, generation, and class/caste often erased and always recast categories of power (Amadiume 1987; McClintock 1995; Oyěwùmi 1997).[15] By the early twentieth century, the strategies the British used to build a colonial settler state had fundamental implications for gender relations among Maasai men and women and generational relations among elder and junior men. For example, the administration imposed a cash economy, replacing indigenous modes of trade and wealth creation with capitalist methods. One effect of monetarizing trade in Maasai communities was the dissolution of the female-dominated barter system and cooperative networks, a move that eroded and eventually erased women's central marketing roles and public presence, as well as the relative power and status women enjoyed as arbiters of these processes so central to community life and border relations with non-Maasai neighbors (Hodgson 2001b). Moreover, the commodification of livestock and land by the implementation of taxation, which required cash payments by officially designated "household heads," further inscribed male elders into colonial logics as economic actors and inalienable patriarchs (Hodgson 2001b; Waller 2006).

Colonial (re)inscription of indigenous sociopolitical identities consolidated elder male power and privilege vis-à-vis the colonial state and therefore significantly reconfigured social relations. "The autonomy and interdependence enjoyed by men and women in the late 1800s were replaced by unequal relationships of economic dependence and political control in which men could begin to think about women as property and possessions" (Hodgson 2001b, 92). In these shifting identity structures, Maasai "boys" remained central (if also contentious) actors as soon-to-be-warriors and then junior men, while women as wives became "dependents" (Hodgson 1999; 2001b) relegated to the domestic sphere of the "household," and girls remained completely invisible as subjects at all. These processes "broadened and deepened [elder male] control over junior men and women" by extending their customary roles in the political-economic administration of community affairs to direct mediation of colonial policy (Hodgson 2001b, 65). These changes enabled and sustained the still popularly shared idea (outside of and within Maasai communities) that pastoralists are inherently patriarchal and that, moreover, girls and women have always been culturally understood as among the "property" (animals, children, material goods) men manage and control (Hodgson 2001b; 1999). These social expectations and everyday experiences have significant bearing for girls' educations today. While Maasai learned to negotiate (comply with and resist) the imposition of colonial categories in the parallel economy and culture of the "closed" reserve, the British administration worked to secure Kenya as a successful colony populated by productive and compliant Africans, which included the implementation of what would ultimately be a starkly uneven education policy, particularly in Maasailand.

Education in Colonial Maasailand

In contrast to the conventional Kenyan wisdom that Maasai "hate" education and "always have," over a century ago "one of the earliest summit meetings on African education in Kenya" occurred just after the first Move in 1905 among the Commissioner for the East Africa Protectorate–designated Maasai leaders Olonana, his brother Senetu, and John Stauffacher from the United States, the leader of the African Inland Mission (AIM),[16] an evangelical fundamentalist missionary society operating in Maasai territories at the turn of the century (King 1971, 121).[17] Despite the implications of this auspicious occasion, the AIM was relatively unsuccessful in inspiring Maasai to settle, learn to farm, convert to Christianity, and through these processes learn to read and write in missionary schools (Rigby 1981; Waller 1999). By and large, Maasai pastoralism had been resilient enough to persist and reproduce itself in the face of decades of demographic crisis wrought by the disasters and the Moves. As across Africa at this time, early converts (and therefore the earliest educated Maasai) tended to be "marginal" Maasai refugees who survived the disasters and Moves but could not recover their status as "Maasai" through conventional pastoral mechanisms,[18] or, later in the colonial period, those of mixed parentage,[19] and immigrants who were passing under the radar of the "closed district" by exploiting their claims to residency as Maasai relations (Waller 1976).

Early missionary education through the AIM was not designed as a means through which adherents would gain entry into the colonial economy through waged work (Waller 1999). Instead, those who ended up at the mission were educated in basic literacy and were required to read and teach the Bible for the sole purpose of becoming "native evangelists" (Strayer 1978; Waller 1999, 85). From the point of view of the majority of Maasai who at this time had rebounded from crises, the new way of life that Christian conversion offered was inferior to their own systems. According to Waller (1999, 92), early converts were not only "*il ashumpa* (like whites) but *isigan* (menial)." Hodgson (2001b) specifies *irmeek* (s. *ormeek)* as a Maa term first used to refer to all non-Maasai Africans, particularly those who spoke Swahili, worked for the colonial government, went to school, or were baptized; later, the term was used to "stigmatize Maasai men who went to school or were baptized" (64).[20] The missions then, for most Maasai, were understood as precarious, "foreign" places; converts fundamentally lived outside of pastoral praxis and were thus considered "aliens, not Maasai" (Waller 1999, 83). Not surprisingly, early converts (who became mission teachers and itinerate preachers) were notably male, as elders forbade girls and women to visit missions.[21] Overall, the mission did not manage to attract any supporters among the leading Maasai elders of the pre-1940s generations (Waller 1999).

Isolated but Not Actually Insulated?

As mainstream Maasai largely rejected the missionary education on offer in the early colonial period, Sena (1986, 180) argues that this popular attitude was less about the imposition of Christianity or Western education per se and more about a confidence that the "protection" created by the agreements would enable Maasai to live in a "semiautonomous" parallel political-economic (and therefore cultural) space. Although Sena (1986, 180) notes that the closed status "impoverished" the reserve, it also, he argues, "insulat[ed] and isolate[ed]" Maasai communities from the economic and political processes of colonial state formation. The production of "Maasailand" as an effect of the Moves therefore "offered [Maasai] the opportunity to opt out of educational schemes and the wage economy" (Sena 1986, 180). This sense of Maasai autonomy, ironically based on a manufactured marginality instantiated by the Moves, as well other colonial policies to curtail pastoralism, continues to be a double-edged sword for development through education in rural Maasai communities.[22] Naisula, a Maasai primary school teacher for more than ten years, like Cherity and others across the interviews, expressed frustration about these events of the past still salient in the present. To her, this confidence in the agreements a century ago looks and feels today more like a trick of history:

> Communities that accepted education from the very beginning like Kikuyus and Luos are now having a high standard of living, but Maasai never accepted it. They were blackmailed by the wealth they had in cattle. Elders were afraid if the youth [boys] went to school, they would be lost to the [outside] culture and become thugs. If girls went to school, they would refuse to be married to the men their fathers' chose for them and would want to choose men for themselves—[the fathers] would say "like a prostitute"—so taking girls to school would waste time and money. In the interior this attitude is still there.

Elders demonstrated these attitudes in 1919, when the first colonial school in Maasailand, the Government Maasai School (GMS), a three-year primary school, opened in Narok Town; they agreed to fund it under the agreement that their own children would not have to attend (Gorham 1980). The very issues that inspired leading elders to reject schooling for their own children were the same issues that kept most Maasai away at the time as well. Elders successful in the pastoral system continued to prefer cultural, political, and economic distance from the colonial state (Sena 1986), and given the sense of betrayal many felt about the Moves, communities were skeptical that colonial policy was in their best interests (Hughes 2006). Motivated by paternalistic imperial desire to control elusive pastoralists, colonial administrators saw mandatory schooling as the best means for sedentarizing, demilitarizing, and monopolizing Maasai modes of cultural and material production by curtailing and eventually dismantling what they perceived to be deleterious social arrangements, including the age-set system, warrior camps (*imanyat*), and warrior (*ilmurran*) practices, such as cattle raiding (Gorham 1980; King 1971; Waller 1999; 2006). Moreover, education policy became directly entangled with government control over the cattle market when administrators created a school quota system that targeted pastoral labor (boys and young men) and codified fines for households that did not comply. As a result, educational provision was seen by most Maasai as an imposed system designed to threaten their way of life rather than enhance it (Gorman 1980).

If the leading elders' children did not go to school, then who did? While forced quotas did motivate households to send children to school, a combination of the labor demands of pastoral production and the irrelevance to daily life in the reserve of the agricultural curriculum ensured that the best and the brightest were not chosen to attend school. On the contrary, households selected the most marginal members to fulfill the quota. The pattern of "marginal" Maasai attending school, established with the first mission schools, was repeated in the early government schools, albeit with a slightly different slant. Instead of choosing those boys and young men (girls were not considered) who were perceived to be smart and strong to attend school, the weakest boys, either physically, mentally, or both, were sent to school, and the cleverest were sent with the cattle. Alternatively, households would send any boys who were "less Maasai," by virtue of mixed origins (typically Maasai-Kikuyu unions); later in the colonial period as in-migrations of non-Maasai into the "closed" reserve intensified, Maasai would send the children of their non-Maasai employees instead of their own.

The closed-district status did little, therefore, to "insulate" Maasailand for Maasai only as in-migrations of non-Maasai persisted for various reasons, but it did effectively "isolate" the reserve from integration into the wider economy and further normalized Maasai ethnic otherness and incommensurability with the modern aspirations shaping the colonial state, particularly as no attempts were made to ensure that Maasai primary school curricula kept pace with the rest of the schools opening in the wider colony (Gorham 1980). As government primary schools were sporadically built, poorly attended (by teachers and students), and sometimes simply closed, schools in the reserve struggled to become viable institutions to meet an increasing demand for education relevant either to pastoralism or to academic matriculation to secondary schools outside of the reserve (Gorham 1980; Sifuna 2005).[23] The few educational resources in the reserve were largely utilized by non-Maasai migrating in, although Maasai funds, lands, and livestock were leveraged to build and provision schools.[24]

In its initial forms, education in the Maasai reserve was focused on "curriculum . . . to improve village life . . . [such that] whatever occupation a Native finds in a village has been made the subject of interest in a village school" with administrators noting "too great an emphasis is not laid on literary education" (Narok Annual Report, 1923, qtd. in Gorham 1980, 12). School-going Maasai and their parents, however, wanted more, not less, educational access, and they wanted the "literary education" necessary to matriculate beyond the village school. Demand focused on the opportunity to graduate from primary school and go on to secondary school outside of the reserve. However, there was no way to sit for the primary-school exam required for graduation to secondary school because none of the schools in the reserve offered all the grades necessary to qualify. In 1937 the Government Maasai School in Narok (GMSN) finally reached six standards to become a full primary school. This meant that, for the first time, Maasai students could complete a curriculum that would qualify them to take the Kenya African Primary Exam (KAPE) and attempt to continue to secondary school at Alliance High School (which had been open to students from other parts of the colony for eleven years already). In an ironic twist, the colonial Education Department decided at this time to institute an animal husbandry component to the curriculum at GMSN as a way of tying student learning to immediate needs in the reserve. School-going Maasai and other students at GMSN did not want to attend an additional year of primary school just for animal husbandry when that time could be spent preparing for the KAPE.

Contradictions Continue to Independence

By the end of World War II, through the declaration of the State of Emergency in 1952, and up to the eve of Independence in 1964, Maasai-colonial relations around school provision were deeply contentious and contradictory.[25] School-going Maasai and their parents increasingly rejected the vocational education available in the reserve; they, in large part, did not want biblical training through the mission, industrial training, or veterinary training on European highland stock; instead, they wanted advanced academic training and the chance to attend Alliance High School and then to compete for the employment opportunities in the formal economy this achievement promised (Sena 1986). At the same time, school expansion, always associated with land and labor loss, became widely understood as policy designed to further disempower and marginalize pastoralist modes of production and to transform cultural institutions, such as the age-set system. "Thus while the focus of educational resistance in the two decades before independence shifted from the content of government schooling [the focus on intensive agricultural practices inappropriate for arid and semiarid lands] in Maasailand to the consequences of educational provision, it continued to condition educational promotion until well into the post-independence period" (Gorham 1980, 2).

The complicated results of these practices were born out as history unfolded and relatively few Maasai (men) emerged among the educated Africans who began to galvanize around the politics of independence and decolonization or who had succeeded in integrating into the cash economy of the colony outside of the reserve. Moreover, as in-migrations increased over time despite the official "closed" status, the cultivating families who moved to the reserve to claim land and spaces in relatively empty Maasai government schools increasingly sidelined local Maasai in education attainment. These individuals helped to populate the "alien" enclaves that continue to marginalize Maasai to the edges of "Maasailand" and perpetuate popular assumptions and stereotypes that reify Maasai marginality, even as many Maasai (educated and uneducated) work to counter this positioning. The central paradox of Maasai-Euro relations in the colonial period—based in alliance and resistance, protection, and control—endures in the postcolony as the conflicted, contradictory, and limiting dialectic between Maasai (or, static ideas about "Maasai-ness") and the Kenyan state.

Koko's Granddaughter's Daughters

In her ethnohistory of Maasai in Tanzania, *Once Intrepid Warriors: Gender, Ethnicity and the Cultural Politics of Maasai Development*, Dorothy Hodgson (2001b) features the oral history of Koko, an elderly woman in her nineties in 1992, who recalled her *entitoisho* (girlhood) in the early 1900s.[26] Although she recalls her father's stories of the disasters, and notes that "no person ever returned to the old way of life, as before" (37), she also recalls her girlhood with fondness; she spoke of collecting wood, carrying water, caring for young children, and helping her mother with household chores, all the while surrounded by wealth in livestock, family, friends, and lovers (*ilsanjan*). She recalled "with special delight" her time spent with warriors of the *Iltareto* age-set, who were warriors from 1911 to 1929 (41). She nostalgically described how her young body was covered "almost everywhere" with metal and beaded jewelry; she recounted:

> When we were young girls [*intoyie*] we flirted with the *ilmurran*, especially those that braided their hair into long pigtails [*iltaikan*]. We would give them milk mixed with blood [*inkipot*] and they would become our lovers . . . we danced and danced . . . we would go into the shade of trees to play with *ilmurran* and sing and dance with them. Those days were really wonderful. (41–42)

Married sometime before 1916, she recalled her married life as happy and fulfilling, despite being a junior wife who sometimes quarreled with her husband and competed with her co-wives for his attention:

> I was happy [to be married] because I could move to this homestead and begin to have children. Our homestead had many cattle and we cared for them. We gave birth to some children who lived and others that died because *Eng'ai* [God] took them. And those children who lived eventually married and had girls and boys. . . . So I received many good things, since if you give birth and have your children isn't that wonderful? (43)[27]

Even though Koko was a girl about a century before them, the schoolgirls we spoke with shared similar experiences of girlhood. Most of them slept in traditional Maasai houses their mothers built by plastering cow dung mixed with water on tightly woven bent-branch frames in homesteads populated by extended families, kinship relations, and friends.[28] They collected firewood in the foothills, strapped it to their backs with leather binding, and carried it home.[29] They fetched water from distant taps, intermittent streams, or manmade dams; they cooked thick maize-meal porridge for their families over open fire or small charcoal stoves and cleaned their dishes; they washed their family's clothes by hand in plastic basins and hung them to dry on barbed-wire fences and thorn trees; they cared for their younger siblings; they helped their mothers bead jewelry for themselves, friends, and petty trade; they looked after small stock, like goats, on the weekends, and helped their mothers and stepmothers collect and distribute milk and milk byproducts.

Despite the continuities between Koko's girlhood and girlhood today, there are significant discontinuities. Koko and the other elderly Maasai Hodgson interviewed reflected on the changes they had seen in Maasai society. As one retired, venerable elder noted, "Before . . . an elder was called an elder, an *olmurranni* [warrior] was called an *olmurranni*, and a woman was called a woman. What are they called these days?" (273). What happens to popular understandings of social relations, collective identities, and individual subjectivities when the governing structures and categories themselves are in flux? As Phillip, a Maasai man and senior teacher, explained to me:

> In the culture, [the age-set structure] helps in the passage of norms from one generation to another. You see, culture is also dynamic, it is not static. It is also changing. Nowadays, we go by the school calendar. During the holiday, we hold an *emanyata* very briefly, and then we dismiss the children before the school opens so that they can go and read (study). We are also discouraging moranism (warriorhood) as a way of encouraging more children to go to school, and also moranism was part of peer influence. To discourage that peer influence, we discourage moranism. We are encouraging more children to go to school.

It is important to note that Koko does not mention school in describing her own girlhood, although she does echo the comments of Naisula and others across my interviews, that elders in her time "fear[ed]" that children "would become different" if they went to school. According to Koko, the ones who did go to school were "forced" because "no one liked [school] in the past." But "these days," she explained, referring to the early 1990s, "everyone wants to go, even if they are not chosen they volunteer themselves. Girls and boys attend school these days, and everyone is happy" (46). Now, Koko's granddaughters have grown up and are to varying degrees struggling to educate their own children, including their daughters. It is hard to imagine a Maasai girl in the case study communities today who would decline the opportunity to go to school. Moreover, schoolgirls see themselves as the beneficiaries of changed attitudes among their parents, and even in some cases their grandparents, regarding the viability and the imperative that families figure out how to make schooling possible. As Dorthea, a fourteen-year-old student in Class 6 at Enkeryian Primary School, explained, "My parents have seen development when they saw some families educating their children and the children have come back to help them. Then they educate theirs. In my parents' life they have seen that they should work hard to meet the goals they never had before." Dorthea's observation that her parents are "working hard" to "meet the goals they never had before" profoundly encapsulates fundamental shifts in Maasai attitudes—if unevenly—toward an embrace of education in the form of formal schooling for all children. Moreover, as chapter 2 will discuss, this comment captures shifts in the political economy of development tied to waged work and the attendant reinscription of gendered subjectivity and the intensification of "women's work" (and also "girls' work") to meet the demands of "life today."

Learning to Love Education

At Independence about nine hundred thousand Kenyans were in school (Buchmann 1999), and pastoralist societies had the lowest rates of school enrollment (Sena 1986).[30] A signature policy of this era was *Harambee*, Kiswahili for "let us pull together," a self-help movement designed to empower African Kenyans to take charge of infrastructural provision and economic advancement through locally elected county councils after decades of colonial policies to prevent self-determination, and educational provision expanded rapidly. Yet the decentralized nature of Harambee development led to regional disparities in the number and quality of schools. Wealthier and politically connected ethnic groups who counted more already-educated people among their ranks and had experience successfully building their own schools during the colonial period were able to build more and better-quality schools. And in a pattern established before Independence, pastoralist communities lagged behind (Sifuna 2005; Buchmann 1999, 100; King 1971; Sena 1986).[31]

While the creation of "Maasailand" with the closing of the reserve had serious repercussions for educational provision during the colonial period, the official opening of the reserve to non-Maasai in 1970 in newly independent Kenya accelerated political-economic changes that prompted the slow and uneven spread of positive attitudes toward education among many Maasai. For one thing, independence coincided with the coming to power of the *Ilnyankusi* age-set, some of whom were the products of early educational efforts in Maasailand (Gorham 1980).[32] These educated Maasai advocated for schooling for at least some children in every household as a means to protect and preserve their land and way of life in the face of interrelated external forces: the devastating effects of a drought from 1959 to 1962 (Gorman 1980); the increased pressure on land from in-migration, intensified by the opening of the reserve to non-Maasai (Sena 1989); and land loss from the increasingly prevalent practice of group ranch demarcations and subdivision, a process started in Kajiado with support from the World Bank in the late 1960s into the 1970s (Archambault 2007; BurnSilver 2009; Galaty 1992). To expedite participation, the central government put pressure on local state-designated political leaders (chiefs and local police) to enroll Maasai children in school. Within the confluence of these internal and external factors, many local leaders, by and large, agreed that education was vital to development, and certainly some Maasai families turned their sights toward school (Gorham 1980; Sena 1986).

Conversations with teachers suggest that it was in the 1970s and 1980s when attitudes about education began to change, although slowly and unevenly. The struggle for school among young people at that time seems to have laid the foundation for the parallel "love" discourse within Maasai communities initiated by post-Independence leaders that is now growing louder and more persuasive than the "hate" discourse, at least among the schoolgirls, mothers, and teachers we talked with. Stories Maasai teachers shared reflect persistent tensions attached to education as a mechanism for social change instigated (and made increasingly imperative) by processes of development that started with the colonial state and was extended by the postcolonial state. When I met Maasai deputy head teacher, Dennis, he was thirty-seven years old, married to a Maasai woman who was a social worker, and raising children of his own. He had taught for ten years in the study area before becoming the deputy head teacher for the school that served his boyhood home. He was proud to announce that he had just completed his bachelor's degree in education through a distance-learning program from a prominent Kenyan university.[33] Born in 1971, he was the youngest of five children in his mother's house; his father had three wives and nineteen children all together. Dennis started school in 1980 at age nine:

> None of my parents had gone to school. During my early childhood, schooling was not a priority; the cultural traditions were still strong. Education was seen

> to be foreign and unimportant. Moranism (warriorhood) was given the upper hand—that was the education—a way of transmitting information from one generation to the next. External pressures mounted on the parents, the government and local leaders, and they had to send someone. So my eldest brother went with the animals, the next brother went to school, my sister didn't go because they didn't want to take resources for educating girls, and the brother before me went with the animals, and I was then taken. I was young when I started looking after the livestock and then I saw that others were going to school. I never wanted to go to moranism, and with time I came to like being in school; my friends had positive attitudes. And I always wanted to be a teacher. I always wanted to write for others—neatly and smartly writing on the board and hearing praise from others. It has always been in me, and I have never regretted why I am here. My elder brother was once a teacher, but now he is the senior chief in the location.

Dennis explained that he and his eldest brother were sent to school because his father responded to "pressure from local authorities" to enroll at least some of his children in school. Phillip, Dennis's age-mate at age thirty-eight and a senior teacher at another primary school in the area, was likewise taken to school because "the police and the chief required one boy." Phillip explained, "They wanted to arrest my father, so he said, 'Take this one—he's old enough to walk.'" Phillip was almost fifteen at the time. Like Dennis, he "was interested in school because it was fun, and [he] didn't enjoy looking after cattle all day." James, a Maasai head teacher, older than Dennis and Phillip at forty-six, told a similar story:

> I looked after the cattle until I was about ten years old, around 1971. The government used elders to take children—always boys—to school by force. They came with the police during the day. There were five boys, but the older ones were with the cows and the girls were not at home, and they were younger. My parents were horrified. I cried. I remember my mother crying. I liked school once I got there. I was leading the class through primary. My older brothers never went to school; my sisters never went to school. I convinced my father to let me take my younger brother to school (a man who has since become an esteemed leader and candidate for Minister of Parliament for the area).... I am glad now because I can earn a living... my world is a bit larger than [my brothers' and sisters'] because I can read and communicate in different languages.

Unlike Daniel and Phillip, however, James did become an ilmurran. He was clear that his education in indigenous knowledge systems was important for his work as a teacher and school administrator; his deep understanding of culture, he explained, made it easier for him to interact with the parents of his students, particularly fathers, who had not been to school.

Tradition was really regarded then, motivated by the environment at that time. I became a moran (warrior) during the holiday and moved with the warriors. I do not regret being a moran [because] I know the tradition fully and I had the traditional training for life—not from schooling. I learned patience, I learned relationships, particularly showing respect, and I learned to be responsible even when I was young with property (cattle) and even myself.

Schoolgirls likewise noted significant changes in their parents' attitudes about education pinned to "the life of today" relative to the past. In all of our interviews with schoolgirls we asked them why their parents "were happy to see them in school" when, as was the case in the vast majority of girls' homes, neither their mother, their father, nor their mother's co-wives had been to school, and in many cases, neither had their older siblings. Schoolgirls indicated that their parents often had wanted to go to school but were denied the opportunity when their parents "refus[ed] to take them to school." Some schoolgirls simply noted that "there were no schools for [their parents]." There was a strong sense in the interviews with schoolgirls that because their parents had been denied opportunities, denied access, or in some cases refused education for themselves, parents today do what they can to educate their children. Many noted that their parents have "seen development" in families with educated children and wanted those "fruits" for their own families. Schoolgirls' explanations for why their parents "love" school now highlight the social and cultural effects of the schooling imperative. Echoing Cherity and Naisula's insights, according to schoolgirls, their parents see education as a primary strategy for righting the wrongs wrought by decades of uneven educational provision by missionaries, the colonial state, and the postcolonial state. As Dorthea noted:

> My father said "because I have not gone to school I will let you go to school because it was not my wish that I did not go to school. At that time there was no school, but in this time there is school. I have to put all of [my children] to school so that you will be big in the future, you will be who you want to be, a leader." My parents are seeing those people like Kikuyus are leading others, so they want us Maasai to do or be like that.

Connecting education to development, one schoolgirl's comment reflects the general sensibility among the schoolgirls when asked to explain why she sees maendeleo in her generation but not in her parents': "Then there were no schools for them. . . . They were starting to develop [then] but now we know many things which they have never known [and now] they are starting to know." Assertions that there were simply "no schools for them" emerge in conjunction with matter-of-fact statements describing cultural reluctance among their grandparents' generation to ensure a full course of schooling for all of their children. As one schoolgirl noted, "They did not know the importance of school in their time, but in our time, we can go to school." Others echoed her sentiments: "[My parents were not taken to school] because in their time Maasai never put children in school. But now they have come forward and want all children in school." Some clarified that the pastoral economy took precedence: "In their time there was no school. They were looking after [livestock]. There was no time for school then." Most everyone we talked with among schoolgirls, mothers, and teachers in some way indicated that "in the world of today," it is no longer possible to even subsist much less grow wealthy by pastoralism alone. As one schoolgirl noted, "Long ago people did not go to school. . . . Fathers only knew about cows. These days it is not enough. . . . Someone can come looking for people to do a job. Only those who have gone to school can get that opportunity."

Although schoolgirls repeatedly indicated that there were "no schools" for their parents, educational provision did accelerate in the districts created out of the reserve—Kajiado, the site of the case study, and Narok.[34] As soon as the first secondary school was built in Kajiado Town in 1965, children crowded into primary school classrooms hoping to realize a full course of schooling that would enable formal wage work in the new national economy. By 1969, the number of primary schools in Kajiado had almost doubled and enrollments were more than seven thousand. Forty percent of these pupils were girls, although most were not Maasai but rather the daughters of in-migrating non-Maasai who anticipated the formal opening of the reserve in 1970 (Gorham 1980). By 1972, there were more than ten thousand students in fifty-three primary schools in Kajiado district (Gorham 1980), although the ethnicity of these students is not clear.[35] By 1979, the Maasai school-age population attending school in both Kajiado and Narok districts was about 40 percent as compared with only around 13 percent in 1962 (Sena 1986, 92). As schooling participation increased, however, by the late 1970s it was already difficult for primary school graduates to find employment for which they had previously been qualified (Sena 1986).

Everything We Do Is about Education

In 1990 the benchmark World Conference on Education For All (EFA) in Jomtien, Thailand, set the stage as the "decade for education" and "marked a new start in the global quest to universalize basic education and eradicate illiteracy" (UNESCO 2004, 90). Kenya arrived at Jomtien "a success story, having achieved universal primary education" on its own, based on internal demand for schooling (Commonwealth Education Fund 2003, 4; Chege and Sifuna 2006).[36] Yet by 2002, when President Moi's twenty-four-year reign ended and Mwai Kibaki became Kenya's third president, gross enrollment was 85 percent, and more than three million school-age children (11 percent of six-to-thirteen-year-olds) were not in school (Commonwealth Education Fund 2003; Swadener et al. 2008). Positioning itself as an early beneficiary to the Fast Track Initiative (FTI), considered the first global contract on education, was a politically attractive way for the new regime to secure legitimacy with foreign donors and the Kenyan public. In 2003 the state declared a full course (standards 1–8)[37] of free primary education (FPE) to all Kenyans in all districts, a move that signaled its commitment to achieving universal primary completion to funders and its capacity to make the dream of schooling a reality for everyday citizens. The policy attracted historic levels of funding (Chege 2006; Fast Track Initiative 2006).[38]

Kenyans responded positively to FPE as a policy that seemed designed to relieve the burdens of the more than thirty years of turbulence in education policy and provision. Demand was registered instantly; by 2004, 22.3 percent more children were enrolled in school, an increase of more than one million children, for a total of 7.2 million children enrolled in school (Republic of Kenya 2007; Sifuna 2005). The government abolished local school committee levies and tuition and agreed to cover the cost of basic teaching and learning materials, activities fees, government-trained teacher's salaries, and critical nonteaching staff salaries, as well as subsidizing every child in primary per year with 1,020 Kenyan shillings (Ksh).[39] Parents would be required to supply uniforms and to refurbish existing classrooms and activate local resources for space, like churches and social halls, to accommodate larger enrollments. National gross enrollment rates, however, hid deep disparities within regions in Kenya. Comparative studies reveal that as most Kenyans were enrolling in school, pastoralists continued to be on the margins of widespread social change (Sifuna 2005).

Sifuna (2005) found FPE had a strong impact in the six predominately pastoralist districts of the ASALs he sampled.[40] Increases in enrollment were around 28 percent on average, well above the national average. However, he also found that FPE seems to have had more impact on boys' enrollment than girls' in his sample districts. In Narok, a predominantly Maasai district contiguous with Kajiado, the enrollment trends from 2000 to 2003 show an increase for boys by 30.2 percent, whereas girls increased by a mere 3 percent. Moreover, despite the initial increased enrollment, dropout rates for both girls and boys were high, and glaringly so for girls.[41] The biggest obstacle in the ASALs and in all economically vulnerable regions was then and continues to be the direct costs of schooling. Free public education did not necessarily reduce costs (Sifuna 2005). By the time of implementation in 2003, the average annual cost to send one child to school is estimated to have been approximately 4,000–5,000 Ksh (Sifuna 2005). The government subsidy of 1,020 Ksh did little to mitigate these costs for the poor. Moreover, in the ASALs, as across Kenya, dramatic and rapid enrollment increases in an already-overburdened, gender-disparate, materially inadequate system resulted in overcrowded classrooms, teacher shortages, increased fees (parent associations started to require small user fees to hire extra "parent-paid" teachers to offset government-paid teacher shortages, and this remains common practice in the case-study area), insufficient supplies of teaching materials, reduced/compromised quality of instruction, increased frustration, increased dropout rates, decreased completion rates, and decreased new enrollment.

Since independence, access to and participation in formal schooling in Kajiado County has moved in fits and starts, largely in tune with the rest of the country, if several paces behind, particularly in the arid and semiarid areas of the county. Maasai, like all Kenyans, were swept up in the process of decolonization, which was itself a contradictory process. Kenyan movements for self-rule and independence were deeply rooted in the very worldview they sought to and fought to overcome, including a faith in education and an embrace of education as the singular path to modernity yoked to economic growth. Despite the challenges of going to school in most Kenyan contexts and certainly in Maasai areas—fluctuating gross enrollment rates, the hidden costs of "free" primary education and the often-exclusionary costs of secondary education, poor infrastructure, teacher shortages, insufficient instructional materials, gender disparity (even if gender parity in enrollment has been achieved at the national level), and overcrowding—these days, most schooled Maasai make clear, and most unschooled Maasai agree, education is the future (Archambault 2007).

As Nasarean, a secondary-school student I met while she was home in Loodariak for the December holiday, stated, "Because of the world of Kenya that we are in now, everything we do is about education." In a 2005 survey of 390 residents of Maasai homesteads in an area near Kajiado Town called Enkop, Archambault (2007, 14) found that 99.7 percent of her respondents declared education to be important. Only one woman and seven men of the 390 said that education was not important. In my interviews, all of the mothers, schoolgirls, and teachers we talked too agreed. Paradoxically, because the "hate" discourse is still operative, Kenyan authorities can continue to rely on distorted assumptions about "being Maasai" in order to justify the enduring lack of provision in Maasai areas of the country, while continuing to engage in land alienation, extractive industries, and international tourism at local peril.[42] As in the past, Maasai relationships to education today are more than liking or hating; this relationship is embedded in a matrix of social, economic, political, and historical relationships that condition access and responses to education as an imperative of economic development. And because the "terms people use to organize their lives are not simply a gloss for universally shared assumptions about the world in one's place it, but are actually constitutive of different forms of personhood, knowledge, and experience" (Mahmood 2005, 16), these entanglements are registered within negotiations over individual and collective subjectivity and belonging.

Conclusion

As Cherity's comments suggest, history is not simply in the past but continues to unfold in the daily lives of rural Maasai communities struggling to preserve and innovate sustainable livelihoods and for whom education has come to represent the best path to ensuring the future. Cherity's insights have directed us to "look back" as a way of "seeing ahead." How is the contemporary "hate" discourse (and its attendant "love" discourse) seeded in a much deeper past? In my reading of these historical processes, the Scramble for Africa in conjunction with the emutai gave momentum to an influential set of discourses in the dynamic formation of Maasai contemporary collective identities seeded in the earliest days of European contact, identities refracted in, for example, Cherity's understanding of her community's contemporary marginality. Her characterization of Maasai otherness as the incapacity to leverage generations of educational access and participation necessary for "development" and belonging poignantly demonstrates how the historical production of Maasai marginality to the colonial and postcolonial state is dynamically present. Cherity indicates the ways in which "being Maasai" has been, and continues to be, associated with both a refusal to participate in a modern Kenya and the incapacity to participate despite a desire to do so. Like Hannah, young Cherity sees an existential link between "being Maasai" and "being educated"—taken together, these elements of contemporary subjectivity enable, for her, access to personhood and citizenship with participation in formal schooling as the arbiter of both.

As ideas about "being Maasai" have been and continue to be dynamic, ideas about being gendered people—and specifically for the purposes of my analysis, being Maasai "girls" and "women"—are also in flux. The continued unfolding of the historical processes of empire complicated by "development" as a mixed bag of imperatives, incentives, and aspirations continue to frame contemporary schoolgirls' everyday negotiations of their gendered identities within Kenya today. Normative rules for acceptable feminine behavior and ways of being are defined relative to and in opposition with normative rules for proper masculinity across the life course, even as practices of the male age-set system that have historically created "men" are changing in the case-study area. Contestation over who a "girl" and "woman" are or can be and the configurations of personhood and subjectivity these social categories contain and confer are often understood relative to schooling. Although contestation and change characterize Maasai social organization historically, contemporary popular recourse to these gendered and generational structures as timeless and stable enables the tendency among Maasai men and women (girls and boys) to reify dichotomous and hierarchical gender relations in which men are seen as the principle economic and political actors and women are in charge of and associated with the home and children. Ethnicity and generation as intersecting categories of power cannot be divorced from girls' experiences of gender.

These ideals persist even though "now is not life before. The world has changed." In the face of crises generated by historical as well as contemporary political-economic restructuring policies such as land reform, women are increasingly involved in income-generating activities outside of pastoralism (Archambault 2013; Hodgson 2011), as well as often contributing more labor to livestock production than men, as loss of pasturage has prompted "grazing close to the *boma*," transforming much pastoral labor into "women's work" (Wangui 2008, 372).[43] Nonetheless, Maasai parents continue to make decisions about schooling in the context of the traditional pastoral communal-household economy. Schoolgirls' comments indicated that for many of their parents (and sometimes grandparents or elder uncles), it remains unthinkable to lose livestock labor (boys) and reciprocity linkages (girls as brides) entailed by choosing education for every child. Yet since the 1970s many Maasai (educated and uneducated) have also sought integration into the cash economy through education (or responded to pressure to integrate) precisely for the purported access to development that belonging to the postcolonial nation-state continues to promise.

"Education for All" and the specific centering of girls' education as a "key" to overall community uplift and "development" present powerful antidotes to pervasive political-economic marginalization. Another head teacher, Njoroge, a non-Maasai man, echoed all of the teachers I talked to: the purpose of education is to "change one's life," and for a girl this means being seen as an asset to her community. He went on:

> Even without education, life is there, but nowadays it's better with education ... before [in the past] if girls went to school it was only to be literate, but not to become professionals. Now, we have different needs. We all need to depend on ourselves whether we are married or not. And being a professional makes a girl become a woman who is profitable to her community.

Dennis's comments likewise position girls' economic and productive potential as a central rationale for girls' education:

> These girls now, when they come to primary school and continue to secondary, they complete that cycle. If possible, let them then go to university. They say educating a girl is educating a community but educating a boy is just educating a family. I've seen girls help the entire community. This is easily translated to society because the way she manages her home, her children, and her community affairs will make her an important asset within our society. We will all have a better community in terms of health [and] economic and social bargaining power.

Both men's belief that educating girls multiplies the benefits of education beyond the individual girl or her family are echoed in local and transnational discourses regarding school(ing) girls, including the use of economic idiom (profit, assets, bargaining power) to describe girls' bodies and contributions to social life. As I discuss in the next chapter, although the Maasai schoolgirls, mothers, and teachers I talked with had never heard of "the girl-effect dividend" per se, girl-effects logic was alive and well in our interviews and informal interactions. These ideas help to shape the contours of schoolgirlhood in which the continued unfolding of history politicizes the transnational discourse of girls' empowerment as a locally salient and embedded social construct that creates conditions of gendered possibility for girls who go to school.

CHAPTER 2

"I see that when I am in school, I will have a good life."
Producing and Performing Schoolgirlhood

> School serves as site in which another kind of global export occurs; it is a key mediator and arbiter of globalized cultural scripts and sub-scripts about modernity, women's empowerment, girl-power, and economic independence.
> —Sanyu Mojola

The group of sixteen schoolgirls gathered under the Kenyan flag in the front of the Embolei Primary School arranged themselves in two single-file lines and walked toward the classroom where the desks and chairs had been cleared and the cement floor swept clean to create a space for their performance.

The girls entered the classroom in a burst of color and sound. Although women all over Kenya and elsewhere in east and southern Africa commonly wear cotton wraps colorfully decorated with elaborate designs and proverbs written in Kiswahili, Maasai girls and women wear *shukas* in a distinctive way by crisscrossing two of them and tying the ends at each shoulder to form a sleeveless dress.[1] Girls usually wear a t-shirt under this sheath, whereas women tie a third shuka around their bare shoulders like a shawl. A solid-color skirt (often blue or red that may or may not be beaded) falling mid-shin is worn underneath. By tying on this colorful sheath, schoolgirls transformed their everyday short-sleeved, red-and-white gingham school uniforms into iconic Maasai "traditional attire." A leather belt elaborately hand-beaded with Maasai colors and patterns around each girl's waist accessorized and secured each ensemble. Layers of similarly colorful and hand-beaded necklaces adorned their necks and wrists, and sometimes headpieces finished the "traditional" look. Their belts and jewelry were all trimmed with dangling dime-sized silver disks that jingled and chimed as they walked in unison into the center of the room.

Once assembled, the schoolgirls sang and danced a call-and-response choral composition titled "Give Me Education," written and arranged to traditional Maasai rhythms by Abraham, a teacher in the school and also the choral director. The girls were practicing for an upcoming county choral competition, and since Maria and I were interviewing in the school for a few days, Abraham invited us to watch them. Abraham translated the Maa lyrics to English for me. The Embolei schoolgirls' song went like this:

> My father, my mother.
> The two people I love most.
> To you I make my request:
> Give me education.
> I want to become a teacher or a pilot.
> I want to become a manager or a journalist.
> I want to become a lawyer or a judge.
> Give me education.
> It is the light of the world.
> It is the key of good futures.
> It is the blessing I want from you, mother.
> It is the inheritance I want from you, father.
> Give me education.

Drawing on the tradition of ilmurran singing "praise songs" of warrior exploits, Abraham explained that the song was designed to "praise" girls' education. The lyrics indicate the intended audience for the song are those Maasai parents who still needed convincing that education is "the light of the world" and, particularly for girls, "is the key of good futures" symbolized by employment as a list of job titles impossible to realize without education. The lyrics make clear that Maasai girls want access to formal employment. Moreover, they insist, girls love and respect their parents and, by extension, their culture, and it is from this relational position that they make their "request." The lyrics argue that girls' education is not outside of Maasai meaning systems but is rooted in local ways of thinking by invoking a mother's capacity to pass on her blessing (Hodgson 2005) and a father's power to pass on his wealth.

In each instance, education is presented as an endowment bestowed by the girl's family. The choral performance thus becomes a culturally legitimate way to broadcast support for girls' education using schoolgirls' actual voices to emphatically sing out "Give me education" to those with the authority to alter conventional expectations for girls.

This performance is emblematic of the songs I have seen Maasai schoolgirls rehearse for public events during various trips to Kenyan Maasailand over the past several years. In each instance, the performance is strikingly similar: schoolgirls dressed in "traditional attire" layered over school uniforms sing praise songs extolling the wisdom and benefit of Maasai girls' education. As Abraham explained: "We no longer sing of cows or lions or praise songs of warriors. We write new words for the new messages of today. Now we praise education and criticize those vices that are here now, like smoking and wearing incorrect clothing like miniskirts."[2]

Abraham clarified that he composed the lyrics not simply to praise girls' education (and at least in this case, not necessarily to praise girls themselves) but to publically articulate "new messages" using "new words" that resonate with contemporary constructions of needs, desires, and gendered regulations for girlhood respectability.[3] In the choral performances I have observed, it is significant that the girls singing were always already students.[4] Their parents, or someone with the means, inclination, and authority, had already been convinced of the benefits of schooling for their girls, at least for the time being. The intricate gendered and generational social relationships embedded in the choral performance are examples of cultural configurations of schoolgirlhood as a new kind of gendered childhood reserved for girls who go to school in which new possibilities (such as professional employment as a girl's "inheritance") are paired with conventional beliefs regarding love, respect, proper feminine comportment (including "correct" clothing), and embedded relations of power—of meanings and people. I have never seen a group Maasai girls of the same age cohort (ages ten to twenty) who were not in school perform in this way. This is because, despite their ages, they would not be seen (and may not see themselves) as girls, but as rather women, new wives, and, often, new mothers. Social relations and functions like marriage and motherhood are more salient for the local production of social categories and subjectivity than age, particularly outside of institutions like the school. Relatively new shifts in gendered conceptions of who girls are and can be in Maasai social life are thus directly hinged to any given girl's relationship to schooling. The presence or absence of certain girls in the performance of "Give Me Education" provides a clear example of the power of school as an institution for the production of gendered personhood—for those within it and outside of it.

Girls who are already students must be the ones to perform these "new messages" about Maasai girlhood because schoolgirls are socially legible as "new" kinds of girls. In this scene, the words of the song, the location of the performance in a rural classroom, the culturally adorned bodies of the singers, their impassioned facial expressions and hand gestures, their soaring voices, the dust in the air, and the hot sun on the corrugated metal roof all came together to conjure, call forth, and reiterate the girl who is Maasai and who goes to school as a "blessing," a gift, and a promise for the future. The "Maasai schoolgirl" as a social category and subject-position, and schoolgirlhood as a cultural space are thus composed and configured through the confluence of teachers' and parents' expectations for schooled girls' behavior and the choreographed, rehearsed, and embodied expression of girls themselves. As a performance of subjectivity, the schoolgirl as the ideal subject of development investment comes together with actual schoolgirls' enactment of girl-effects discourse as it comes to them through community expectations and desires.

In chapter 1, I argued that ideas about "being Maasai," sedimented over the course of the twentieth century but seeded in its first fifty years, continue to animate the persistent belief among Kenyans (and outsiders, including agents of development) that as pastoralists, Maasai necessarily resist and tend to reject education and "always have." Despite the durability of this belief and evidence of continued resistance among some Maasai to "education for all," there is also a parallel and increasingly urgent discourse in which rural Maasai communities are interested in "new words for new messages" relevant to and resonant with the "world of today." In this chapter I consider how circulating transnational discourses about who the schoolgirl must be for development are taken up, as well as generated, by schoolgirls themselves as the targets of this discourse along with some of the adults in their communities. As I hope to show, schoolgirls, mothers, and teachers actively shape schoolgirlhood as a cultural space and the "schoolgirl" as a social category within the increasingly pervasive (and persuasive) logic of educating girls as the solution to ongoing economic structural crises and ethnic marginalization.

Repackaging Girls' Vulnerability as Empowerment

A Nike Foundation video titled *Girl Effect Rising* captures and narrates the debut of the Girl Effect campaign at the World Economic Forum in 2009. In the video, the United Kingdom's former first lady Cherie Blair's answer to the question "Why invest in girls?" provides a striking example of the paradox of girls' empowerment at the center of girl-effects logic as a paradigm for development:

> We're talking about the strongest people in their society. They're people used to dealing with a crisis . . . because their entire life has been about being undervalued yet somehow managing to still make a difference. We should have absolute confidence in these girls. It makes absolute sense to invest in them. . . . They're not asking us for our pity. They're just asking for us to enable them to do what they're already doing, but they could do so much better with our help.[5]

This contradictory logic in which the "undervalued" are heralded for their newly discovered ability to transform vulnerability into heroic capacity through external investment is presented as an implicitly feminist reformulation of the abject "girl-child" as "the strongest [person] in [her] society." However, this repositioning can also be seen a function of interpretive power ascribed to development actors from the Global North. Conventional "faith" (Rist 2002) in development as the unfolding of modernity in the form of Western models of capitalism and democracy is premised on gendered assumptions about women as "enterprising subjects with limitless capacity to cope" (Wilson 2013, 87). In Blair's twenty-first-century version of liberal feminist discourse, girls (rather than women) are "unleashed" from conventional gendered expectations that immiserate them such that they become a more efficient and effective version of themselves in order to "[stop] poverty before it starts."

According to girl-effects logic, targeting adolescent girls (and women) in Kenya, as elsewhere, for their reliability (and thus predictability) as biopolitical investments promises great "returns." There was no shortage of hard work among the schoolgirls, mothers, and teachers I talked to in KCL. Nearly all the "modern-sector" wage earners I interviewed in the case-study area, which is to say all the teachers and NGO staff members who facilitated my research—men and women—supplemented their formal income with informal work. Maasai men, for example, were also livestock owners and traders, even if they were not the actual agents buying and selling in the marketplace or herding the animals; others looked for "contract work" with the government (at the time, many worked as enumerators for the national census or campaigned for local aspirants in 2007 election), all while teaching full time.

Nearly all of the Maasai women had some informal work on the side as well; many produced beaded jewelry for local and tourist markets. Some operated dukas; others, like the men, sought out contract work. Some women managed all of these strategies on top of full-time teaching. One of the two accountants (who were both women) for the Maasai NGO that facilitated my research also owned a beauty salon; the other managed small-scale milk-and-vegetable production for local markets in her family compound. People who did not have "side jobs" were looking for them, or they were working toward second diplomas (associate's degrees) or master's degrees through distance-learning programs. While both men and women shouldered the burdens of formal and informal work, professional women continued to be responsible for the work of caring for children, as well as the homestead itself (including livestock) either by doing it themselves or organizing other women (often uneducated family members or neighbors) to do it for them/with them. Many of the mothers I interviewed (those who had a few years of primary school and those who had no schooling) were engaged in micro-microenterprises, such as charcoal production, jewelry and handicraft production, or running a small tea shop (sometimes just under a tree for a few hours a day), as well as taking over pastoral labor, such as herding, because their children (a household's traditional labor force) were in school.

Localizing Girl Effects

Ideological and financial investments in girls' education as "smart economics" has been taken up at the level of the state and integrated in Kenyan development policy. The rapid and overwhelming response to the Kibaki regime's 2003 FPE policy effectively situated Kenya as a country committed to the global compact on universal education, EFA, and thus the Millenium Development Goals (MDGs). This global discourse regarding the linkages between educational access and economic development and the purported multiplying effects of investment in gender parity in education, particularly at the primary level, solidified mainstream economic assumptions about the centrality of girls' education for reducing poverty and creating growth. In Kenya, the rise in enrollment rates was accompanied by sharpening gender disparities in retention, transition to secondary, and completion (Republic of Kenya 2007; UNESCO 2006).

In an effort to both counter these processes and keep pace with global policy, the Ministry of Education, in collaboration with donors, created Kenya's 2007 *Gender Policy in Education* (GPE). This policy clearly reflects the central arguments articulated by several key multilateral agreements, including the Beijing Platform for Action (BPfA) and the Convention of the Rights of the Child (CRC), as well as EFA and the MDGs.[6] The GPE's authors state that "education is widely recognized as the key to national development.... Attainment of gender equity and equality in education ...

is a core development issue and goal in its own right" (Republic of Kenya 2007, 1–2). Despite the irony of drawing on the authority of the World Bank given the deleterious outcomes of bank policies during the 1980s that still have intergenerational repercussions more than thirty years later, policymakers then cite former World Bank economist Lawrence's statement from the early 1990s as a self-evident justification for specific allocation priorities: "Investment in girls' education may well be the highest return on investment available in the developing world" (2). They go on to repeat and reiterate the standard rhetoric of the individual, community, and national ripple effects of girls' education (articulated by "educated women") that continue to animate girl-effects logic:

> There is adequate evidence that educating women is beneficial at the national, community, family, and individual levels. With even a basic education, individual women engage in economic activities and thus contribute to a greater national productivity. At the family level, educated women have reduced fertility rates, brought up healthier, better-educated children and families, and reduced infant and maternal mortality rates. At the society or community level, educated women participate more in development activities, as well as in political and economic decision-making processes. Further, educated women enter the labor market and earn income through engaging in productive economic activities. This enables them to attain financial independence, reduce poverty, and enhance gender equity and equality. Educated women are also in a better position to protect themselves and their families against HIV and other infections. (1–2)

Kenyan educational policy discourse has, since Independence, linked education to economic development through theories of human capital investment as the prime driver of human, social, and political development (Republic of Kenya 1964/1965). In the GPE, policymakers officially "mainstreamed" gender as a national commitment by rearticulating global discourse regarding girls' education (coded as "gender and education") into already existing development frameworks. Similar to the slippages in transnational circulations of girls' education policy by bi- and multilateral agencies (Monkman 2011; Monkman and Hoffman 2013), here "gender" is conflated with sex and means "women" (which subsumes and implies "girls"); correlations are presented as causality with no cited evidence, only self-evident assertions; and justice claims are sutured to utility claims such that ethical imperatives are entangled with economic logic. The GPE reiterates the ideals and interests reflected in global agendas and "formalizes the rights and responsibilities of all people involved, directly or indirectly, in the education sector" to "contribute to the elimination of disparities" (Republic of Kenya 2007, vii), including "local communities, parents, boys and girls" (5).

Although the policy indicates that gender equity and equality in education are "goal[s] in [their] own right" (1), the predominating thrust of the argument for a national gender policy in education is the purportedly incontrovertible link between educating females and national economic development. From the perspective of "smart economics," prioritizing investment in girls' education is not only the "right" thing to do, it is the "smartest" strategy for realizing "returns." Yet postcolonial education policy and experience has been and continues to be characterized by the inability of the Kenyan state (via donor funding and multilateral financing) to meet the overwhelming demand for formal schooling for everyone, much less more girls. Historically neoliberal macroeconomic reforms tied to external aid for education, as well as internal political corruption broadly and in the education sector specifically (Bloch and Swadener 2009; Unterhalter and North 2011; Unterhalter et al. 2011), have both driven education reform and destabilized educational provision. That the GPE came with actual development aid and other forms of political-economic currencies, such legitimacy as a state willing to invest in education and specifically in policies and legislation designed to increase access and accommodation for girls (Unterhalter 2012)[7] has intensified ideological and material imperatives to educate girls. In economically vulnerable communities in Kenya, such as pastoralists, this desire to educate all children, including girls, is met with the decline in capacity for many families to do so.

Neither Maasai schoolgirls nor their mothers or teachers gave detailed accounts of crises in social reproduction and pastoral livelihoods, but they did consistently refer to the problem of poverty, specifically to obtaining school fees, along with the implications of drought on household capacity to send all children to school (see also Kristjanson et al. 2010). As the Embolei choir prepared themselves, I observed a mother talking with the deputy head teacher about her struggle to get the 25 shillings her child needed to cover the fee for taking an upcoming exam. While 25 shillings is a very small amount of money, Maria explained, "if you are doing nothing to earn money, you can't even get five shillings, much less five times that. That mother has no access to funds of any kind."

The persistent and ever-mounting crises of pastoralist praxis has been and continues to be a prime motivating force in the turn to education in rural Maasai communities (Archambault 2013; Galaty 2013). Through processes of land alienation by colonial annexations and forced migrations, conservation procurements (national parks and wildlife reserves), privatization, and encroachment by elite (Maasai and non-Maasai) Kenyans (Archambault 2013; Galaty 2013), Kenyan Maasai are now semi-sedentary, employing a modified version of pastoralism within a markedly constrained geographic space (Wangui 2008). Since the colonial period, pastoralist communities have been both marginalized by and targeted for market-centered development interventions. Various attempts funded by the World Bank, among others, to manage pastoralism as an economically productive enterprise have had largely negative, and still unfolding, implications, particularly the imposition of group ranching schemes (collective title holding) in the late 1960s and the shift to privatization (individual title holding) in the 1980s (see BurnSilver 2009; Galaty 1992). Recurrent drought conditions and shrinking pasturage in Maasai areas combined with the effects of neoliberal policies throughout Kenya, including rising food costs, an overall increased cost of living, rising population rates and consequent labor supply, stagnant average formal-sector earnings at all levels of education except university, and massive expansion of the informal sector, has severely undermined resiliency to recurring shocks (Archambault 2007; Kratli and Dyer 2006; Kenya Food Security Steering Group 2008; UNDP 2013).

As the insights of the participants to this study suggest, much of the recent embrace of formal schooling for all children is rooted in real fears concerning entrenched intergenerational poverty related to these transnationally implemented, structurally induced crises across Kenya and with specific implication for the demise of pastoralism as a mode of production and a way of life in Maasai communities (see also Archambault 2009, 2013; Sena 1986). Mothers see education as a future investment in livelihood as well as lifestyle diversification (BurnSilver 2009). In this sense, all children's education held the potential promise of future well-being as pastoralists with options to improve pastoralism as well as augment it with other kinds of more lucrative economic activities than the low-skill options already on offer, such as collecting and selling firewood or selling *chai* and *chapati*.[8] Education as formal schooling is therefore seen as the only path to cultural change *and* cultural preservation.

Maasai are thus engaged in daily discussions about who goes to school, when, where, for how long, with what means, and to what end(s) because while "education for all" may be aspirational, for rural Maasai communities, it is by no means a reality. Sifuna (2005) argues, echoing Sena (1986), Carr-Hill and Peart (2005), Leggett (2005), and Archambault (2007), that pastoralists, Maasai included, "do not have less interest in schooling for their children than parents in largely agricultural groups," and more pastoralists will choose schooling when costs are reduced. Given the direct and indirect costs of schooling, sending more than one child to school is often more than many households can bear. As all of my interviews made clear, within any given household, it is increasingly the case that some children are sent to school while others are kept at home (rather than no children attending school at all as a result of culturally sanctioned refusal; see also Warrington and Kiragu 2012). Schoolgirls could list among their siblings who was in school and who was not, but they often could not explain how these decisions were made. When they could, the explanations came down to "*he* was kept with the cows" and "*she* was married." "Contrary to an approach based solely on the rights of individuals," decisions about the education of pastoralist children, girls and boys alike, tend to be oriented toward the collective good of the household "based on their parents' best judgment of what is in the best interest of the family" (Leggett 2005, 137), and these judgments are taken within individual and collective gendered generational expectations.

Maasai mothers, particularly uneducated mothers working exclusively within the pastoral economy, have struggled to manage the results of structurally generated crises, including recurrent drought, male outmigration, and the intensification of their own gendered labor well before the proliferation of girl-effects discourses. Yet the increasing value of girls' education encapsulated by the often-heard adage, "Educate a girl, educate a community," garners its power not only from the gendering of crisis response for the past twenty-five years (evidenced by mothers' progressively increased burden to mitigate poverty) but also from the *girling* of gendered expectations to interrupt intergenerational crisis. Development policy and practice are never fully determinative of how people will come to see themselves and come to be within subject positions; nevertheless, the actual people targeted for and by development can and do take up, internalize, sometimes resist, and otherwise engage with the new meanings assigned to them. Maasai schoolgirls, mothers, and teachers' perceptions of girls' education often reflected girl-effects logic, but their narratives also indicate everyday negotiations with the operational edicts of transnationally scripted neoliberal girl-power, locally embodied and experienced.

Performing Schoolgirlhood: A New Kind of Gendered Childhood

The opening scene in Embolei illustrates an example of the ways girls' education is often evoked and invoked in public discourse across Maasailand. The palpable "hunger" for education, personified in the girls' performances of themselves as dutiful, respectful daughters *and* schoolgirls was repeated in formal interviews and informal conversations. A prevailing faith in education as an important cultural good permeated every interaction I had. Not one person we spoke with could—or would—explicitly comment on any negative repercussions of attending school for girls; everyone adamantly argued that for girls, schooling is a "right," or as the choral lyrics indicate, a "gift" so valuable that it could be symbolically framed as an "inheritance" bestowed by a father on his girl-child, replacing, at least during the space of the performance, the idea that a father's most valuable gift to his daughter has historically been limited to her marriage arranged to a carefully chosen husband.

As ideas regarding girls' education for development circulated among community members who gathered around hearths and under shade trees to "chew words" and added urgency to sermons in churches and agendas at NGO meetings, they gained momentum and collected authority as they reverberated through communities.[9] As mothers' and teachers' comments made clear, this faith in schooling for development motivated the will to improve—self and society—that characterized the prevailing systems of meanings in which schoolgirls came to know themselves, and it animated dreams of "becom[ing]" lawyers and journalists, although none of the schoolgirls we talked to knew anyone who was a lawyer or a journalist (Frye 2012). Adult expectations for the distributive effects of girls' education as a buffer against entrenched poverty shaped schoolgirlhood as a space of possibility created through the intensification of discipline and responsibility.

Education as Gendered Independence

Hannah, the widow who shared the "joke" from the introduction, supported four of her five children in school with a combination of the proceeds from "The Hilton" (her one-room café) and through pastoral production involving cooperative arrangements with extended family and friends. She explained that prioritizing her children's education was important for her on multiple levels:

> I am now living with poverty, but I know the only people who will get me out of poverty are my children. There are many things I want to do in life, but due to lack of education, I can't do them. . . . I could have been having my job, a well-paying one. I could have been educating them with my own money and not depending on anyone. I am happy to see my children in school because they will be able to do whatever I have not been able to do because of lack of education.

Hannah believed that her children would be ones to positively change her own personal situation by "getting [her] out of poverty." Moreover, she suggested that had she been educated herself, she would have been in a better position to take care of her children and would not need their help. As previously noted, Hannah believed that "education gives you value"; part of this value is a certain degree of autonomy thought to come from earning money in the wage economy. By virtue of her children's educated status, Hannah imagined that they would have opportunities she never had, including the chance to educate their own children with resources generated by their access to paid work. As she goes on to say later in the interview when we asked her what her dream was for her daughter in Class 7, she said: "I want her to continue learning so that she will be able to help herself."

Mothers were adamant that educating girls was the mechanism for independence from certain patriarchal claims, specifically the often-stated norm that fathers and husbands were the ones to make decisions for and about girls and women. Connected to the belief that educated girls would have more autonomy in their personal and community relationships is related to a refrain regarding the persistent danger of drought to "wipe away" wealth in cattle. While no one suggested that Maasai should cease to be cattle keepers, the adults I talked with all seemed to agree that education is the key to livelihood diversification as a buffer against the devastation of drought compounded by land loss and severely restricted access to pasture. Mothers unanimously agreed that education provided independence from certain pastoral claims. That is, mothers indicated that relying exclusively on the pastoral economy controlled by men in which women have been positioned as dependents was a primary reason girls should be taken to school. Not only could educated girls grow into "independent" women, they could more effectively contribute to the household (and thereby bolster pastoralism), which was primarily articulated as ensuring children could go to and stay in school. As one mother of eleven children and one of four wives explained:

> People have changed and got the knowledge to know that school is important. Before girls did not go to school. . . . My daughters who did not go to school have problems now because they were married into poor families. They come to us for help now, but if they had been in school they would have something to support themselves and their children. Even the boys, they were being circumcised and went to moranism (warriorhood) and wasted time. This moranism will come to an end. He will retire from moranism. His job [then] is only to look after cows. But the one who was in school will still be working. School will not end. If they stay in school they will help their families because the Maasai people are people who have a very hard style of living, only depending on cows, which the drought can sweep away with no money to replace them. We now see education is good because it is not taken away by drought.

This mother believed that had her daughters been educated, they could draw on their own resources to "have something to support themselves and their children" rather than relying exclusively on their husbands and, in this case, their parents. Agnes from Embolei, one of three wives and birth mother to four children, explained why she, her co-wives, and husband, none of whom had ever attended school themselves, had taken all of the children in the homestead to school:

> We have seen that other people have taken their children to school and their lives are good, so we have agreed because at long last there will be something good for us and them because later it pays. Education is important because when you are in school and learn you will have money, and you can store your money in the bank, and you can use that money to build a house. People who have not gone to school don't have knowledge to put money in the bank. I only have that knowledge to look after cows.... When I was young I did not have that mind of school, but now I wish that I went to school. The drought can sweep all, but education cannot be swept.

Sacrifice and Possibility in the "New World"

Mothers spoke of the sacrifices they had made in order to privilege at least some (if not all, in some cases) of their children's education. A Maasai man who had been teaching primary school for fifteen years when we met and who faced his own battles in the struggle for school, explained what the future might hold for those families who relied completely on members who had not gone to school:

> [They] do not rely on what people who are educated think of as the future. ... To them, there is no future. They just live day-by-day. They don't have that vision that you are saying is the future. They don't. As long as they have some little animals—a few cattle and goats—that is their future. Their future is the present day. They don't know of tomorrow.

This teacher's characterization of "those in the village" as shortsighted reflects a shared understanding among teachers and schoolgirls that those who have not gone to school not only do not think of the future—as the girls would say, "looking ahead"—they also do not have the capacity educated people would have to intentionally plan for the future. Yet these attitudes contradict mothers' comments suggesting that uneducated and undereducated parents are keenly aware of and plan for the future. Scholars interested in livelihood diversification strategies (BurnSilver 2009; Nkedianye et al. 2009) and the relationship between education and social change in Maasai and other pastoralist communities (Archambault 2007; Sena 1989; Bishop 2007; Bonini 2006; Lesorogol 2008; Carr-Hill and Peart 2005) have documented how decisions regarding education clearly entail an intimate calculus of costs. These families had considered the indirect costs of loss of household labor, the loss of bridewealth (at least in the short term), and the direct cost of schooling, and they decided that the benefits would outweigh these costs.

For instance, when I asked a mother named Rose if she worried about her children losing aspects of their culture as they learned other languages and other knowledge through school, she suggested that development, or "seeing ahead" and planning for the future, is not a concept tied only to school knowledge and schooled behavior. Rather, for her a way of considering the relationship between the present and the future is through the transmission of "good culture," or the elements of culture that have been in place before the widespread, historically produced desire connected with the economic need to attend school. These aspects are consciously preserved. She elaborated:

> It's hard to lose one's culture. But what we need to know is that culture is timeless. We should preserve what was important before even now. Should we throw away respect? Or how to take care of our cows? Or anything that brought us development? Or knowing how to sit down and plan for your life? Those are things that bring development. But if there is anything that doesn't elevate or bring development to people, then those are the things we should leave out of our culture. But what helps is if somebody has a good vision, if those people in a home . . . have respect and love others and know how to work together, including the wife helping the husband with taking care of things together and taking care of their children. In our culture we said one person should take care of this while another takes care of that, instead of being forced. Isn't that good culture? If you have good culture, you will go far.

Likewise, Yvonne, a mother who lived in Narok but was staying for a while with a family in Loodariak, noted:

> At home, the first thing we teach our children is respect. To have respect even when you go to school, to have respect even when you see other people, and listen to what you are told, and to listen to what you are told in school and at home, and when you are home you should take care of things [property] at home because that is what you were raised with.

A deeply held sense of respect felt as responsibility and obligation to family and future outlined the parameters of schoolgirlhood for mothers in part because they wanted to redefine some elements of womanhood for their daughters while preserving others. For instance, I asked Agnes from Embolei if she had ever considered taking advantage of adult education classes offered by a local indigenous NGO. She explained that she was interested, but she was too busy maintaining her household and "looking after" livestock in order to afford school fees to attend classes herself. Land loss from privatization (which often involves fencing) and other processes has forced pastoralists to herd animals relatively close to the homestead, and because most children are in school, women are expected to step in and herd during the day and then be back home in the evenings to feed and care for everyone, including the animals (see also Hodgson 2011; Archambault 2013, 2016). Agnes's roles in the pastoral economy have multiplied and so has her obligation to "share" the responsibility not only to earn cash particularly for school fees but also for food, healthcare, and clothing. While Rose indicated that men and women have always shared responsibility for households, although perhaps in gender-segregated ways ("one person should take care of this while another takes care of that"), Agnes, echoing other mothers, suggests that expectations for mothers to have access to cash has intensified. As Hodgson (2011) has argued based on her research in rural Tanzanian Maasai communities, as Maasai men struggle to keep pastoralism economically viable and often migrate to cities for work when they cannot, pastoralist women face "increased workloads and responsibilities" that are "rarely matched by increased rights and decision-making control" (146). Agnes explained that she and her husband now "help each other" with school fees because "maybe your kid comes home and needs only 20 Ksh for fees, you cannot ask the husband to come just to pay that fee. You also have to contribute." The expectation that she "contributes" is not necessarily articulated as a choice or an "empowering" force but rather a duty to her children and the family. By realizing her gendered obligation to her children, she gets that much closer to ensuring the promise of the distributive effects of their schooling to the household. Like the mother who struggled to "find" 25 shillings for her child's exam fee, Agnes "cannot ask [her] husband to come pay that fee," as it is her obligation to procure funds for her children's schooling, yet she does not suggest that any commensurate rights or social power come along with this responsibility.

That fathers are no longer the only ones expected to contribute to the household economy was most often attributed to pastoral crisis generally and drought specifically. Interviews with mothers suggest that as the pressure mounts for more children—indeed "all" children—to step out of the pastoral economy and go to school, the women feel new burdens to earn income on top of conventional expectations that they judiciously manage household resources allocated to them by men to ensure social reproduction. Both schoolgirls and mothers express an increasing ethos of self-responsibility and individuation (as individuals, and as families and households as individual units) as both groups imagine education and the waged work that one obtains as a more reliable safety net than pastoralism alone.

For example, Hope, birth mother of seven children in school in Oltepesi, sold hot tea by the cup under the weak shade created by a makeshift structure of sticks and thin blue plastic bags assembled by the side of the tarmac road. She said, "It's hard to keep the children in school. Right now I am doing a little business. If God helps me and I get a little something [cash from selling tea] I take it to the school to pay their fees." An earlier drought had devastated the area, but she was proud that all of her children survived and had stayed in school.

> Yes, [when the drought was here] I was affected and it took the cattle. But the good thing is that it didn't take any of the children, and the children did not stop attending school. . . . All the homes in this area were affected because the cows and goats [died]. But not the children because their parents were there for them.

I asked her how she managed to the do the work at home, look after livestock, and also run the tea stand. She explained: "We are four [her husband, herself, and two co-wives] and sometimes when we can, we employ shepherds. I trade the days with cattle and the [tea stand] so the children can't miss school." Schoolgirls poignantly understood their obligations to their natal households—the work of home they are required to do as girls—but they also realized that their uneducated mothers and older sisters were challenged to realize their additional responsibilities to "contribute," given their limitations. These observations fueled schoolgirls' desire to have "a salary," which they understood as a far better mechanism for fulfilling their obligations to supporting their natal families, as well as the ones they would create through marriage.

Mothers wanted to educate both boys and girls, but they had special concern for their daughters. They experienced the intensification of their own gendered labor and worried that uneducated daughters would be caught in the same patterns. Certainly, they did not want to see any of their children living in poverty, but for mothers of daughters, they wanted to see their daughters loosen their dependence on fathers, husbands, and pastoralism and instead "depend on themselves." A mother in Loodariak explained:

> My elder daughter was not taken to school but was married because that is what the grandfather wanted. They did not know of education by then. I want all to be educated, both boys and girls, because all of those children are mine. I don't see this one first and this one last. But for girls, girls have demands they must meet. She is now married and, like me, must depend on the husband to dress her, feed her. But my son who went to school can support himself and his family.

This mother wanted all of her children educated and claims to show no preference. Yet, she has a special concern for her daughters because "girls have demands they must meet." She suggests her son can meet his demands because his education affords him work, likely outside of the pastoral economy. Like all the educated Maasai I met, her son likely uses his salary to support his family in part by strengthening his pastoral capacity—building his herd, homestead, age-set relationships, and leadership capacity. Her daughter, on the other hand, "must depend on the husband to dress her, feed her" and her children. If the husband is unable or unwilling to provide what she needs, including school fees for their children, then she is the one to attempt to realize these obligations despite her limited means. Her observation that when her daughter became a "wife," she became "like" her mother—dependent on her husband—reverberated through mothers' comments and refracted through schoolgirls' aspirations for "a good life" as different from the lives of their mothers and older sisters who had not gone to school.

Claims fathers and husbands make on women's and girls' labor to extend the possibility of pastoralism were significant to mothers' strongly held beliefs that girls would be better off—as would their families—if schoolgirlhood could be a protected space in which girls could (and would) work to ensure their own survival along with their immediate families and greater community. Dorcas, an elderly grandmother in Loodariak, was an adamant proponent of *emurata* for girls but felt strongly that denying girls education was "foolishness of the highest order." She saw girls' education as fundamental to girls' decision-making power and capacity to "help" her natal family as well as the family she created with her husband:

> [Girls who have been married without attending school] live far [away], and they may not help their parents. Really, those who are not educated may not help at all [despite where they live] because they are just the same as their mothers—they are under the husband. But those who are educated help even if they are far because they own their own properties so they can help.

When an uneducated girl becomes a "wife" she has no choice but to be "the same as [her] mother," subject to her husband's decisions. As Hope explained in her interview, Maasai now live in a "new world" governed by access to cash and credentials. For mothers (as well as teachers and schoolgirls) the only way to mitigate patriarchal claims on a girl-cum-woman's body, time, labor, and autonomy is access to self-earned income that, as Dorcas suggested, enables negotiating power. According to this logic, an educated girl-cum-woman has the capacity to decide for herself how to allocate her own resources ("properties," which often meant livestock but could also mean "salary") in order to assist her natal family. Educated children do more than help themselves; they can step in to help parents who are limited in their capacity to participate in the cash economy, and mothers suggested that parents rely on this future promise. As another mother explained, "If you were not educated and your child is and they get good work, it's almost like you also went to school." And another, "When the parents don't have the strength to elevate their child, education helps." For mothers, schoolgirlhood protects schoolgirls from *some* of the work of home in order to enable the work of school. Interestingly, the work of school—performing well, persisting from class to class, and avoiding "distractions" in the form of sexual pressure and harassment—is required in order to ensure a different (easier) kind of "home" work for educated women.

"If You Don't Want to Be a Slave, Learn!"

The only female deputy head teacher at the time of my interviews had been teaching for twenty-six years when we met. Her experience bore out mothers' expectations and assumptions.

> Education brings changes. For example, a woman must depend on a man for ideas and materials for her life. If you are educated, you can have an educated life—you will make your own choices and live the life that you want. Many people suffer because of drought and loss of cattle, but you will be employed, you will have jobs. You will assist your communities to have new visions. I also assist my relatives with money and ideas. I can assist them to think through what they need.

Of all the teachers I talked with, she used the strongest language against what she referred to as "traditional ideas":

> Psychologically the women at home are tortured. My own age-mates, some are dictators in their own homes and their attitudes can't be changed because they see women as slaves. In the tradition, women were ordered to follow. But now, even through whispering, women are speaking our own minds. And the girls have been listening. I tell them, "If you don't want to be a slave, then learn!"

The head teacher of the same school, a local Maasai man, reinforced her comments when we spoke later that day. He noted: "Girls are marginalized from the home level. Through informal education in the home, we are trained to believe that women can't do anything, that they don't have any potential, so the thought often is, even if you educate her she can't do anything." His colleague, a younger Maasai man and deputy head teacher at another school, explained further:

> In the traditional system, boys received very organized education through moranism (warriorhood); they were trained to be leaders in their homes and community. There was no similar institution for girls, it was ad hoc, only the practical education from the grandmother—how to care for children, the husband, and the husband's property. Girls were trained to become submissive and absorb social expectations.

Despite these descriptions of hierarchical gender norms, these teachers argued that the purposes of education are the same for boys and girls. They emphasized that girls do have potential that needs to be recognized. The head teacher stated: "We need girls to be independent. They are born only to marry. We want to move away from this and for them to have their own lives and a position of respect in the community as women."

Maasai teachers absolutely expect girls to live and perform "changed" lives as changed persons. A teacher for ten years at Ensonura Primary School, Naisula's vivid imagery was reminiscent of images of the bifurcated paths of home ("tradition") and school ("modernity") redolent in girl-effects discourse:

> When you get learned it will change your lifestyle. It is easy to develop your house, your home. Your lifestyle will be modern. Your education will get you a job. You will be independent and take care of yourself. You'll be in a position to give advice to others. You will marry, maybe, and have your job. It also helps to see that old traditions are not now important, because once you are in school you will see different things. It enlightens your mind. If you are at home with others who are at home, that culture is all that you see; you don't want to be the odd one out. Your path is to be born with cattle and marry with cattle. With schooling, you aren't locked into this channel; your mind is wide. You can even invent some things for yourself. You learn that even if you don't follow cultural rules, it's of no harm; for example, I am not afraid of curses because I don't believe in them.

As another head teacher explained, reflecting the language of human capital investment, "We all need to depend on ourselves whether we are married or not. And being a professional makes a girl become a woman who is profitable to her community." Also linking an educated girls' value beyond her own to that of the larger community, Jocelyn, a teacher from Innyonyorri Primary School, hoped schoolgirls would come to "depend on themselves. Not like the villagers, no. We want them to be changed people. People the community can depend on and who can develop the community and Kenya at large."

Performing Schoolgirlhood: Girling Education as Development

Teachers' and mothers' comments across the interviews suggest that schoolgirlhood, as a new kind of gendered childhood in which girls grow up in school rather than in marriage, is the only way for girls to become women who "have their own lives and a position of respect in the community as women." The schoolgirl subject-position and social category is enabled, normalized, and positioned as aspirational because affirmative discourse regarding the redistributive potential of schoolgirlhood circulated as powerful "new" ideas about girls' potential. As elsewhere, in the case-study area what we can call empowerment is a continual, nonlinear process embedded in social relationships.[10] As the deputy head teacher remarked, "now, even through whispering, women are speaking [their] own minds. And the girls have been listening."

Schoolgirls' comments indicate that they had in fact been listening and learning that the "new world" demands girls become women who must do all that their grandmothers, mothers, aunts, and older sisters have ever done consistent with expectations for women's labor and duty with the added burden—and the "blessing"—to earn cash income, preferably in the formal economy. "Education for all" in the context of neoliberalism is linked to generating a literate, gendered workforce that will learn to "manage" its own poverty through multiple and more or less precarious livelihood strategies that incorporate them into the global economy. As schoolgirlhood as a possibility was produced through localized responses to these forces, it was also actively embodied and performed by schoolgirls through the self-making, family-helping, and future-ensuring aspirational "hard work" of school. Schoolgirls had internalized the pressure for the intensification of gendered responsibility and obligation that characterized mothers' experiences, as well as community expectations.

Working Hard for the "Good Life"

Dorthea was in Class 6 at Enkeryian Primary School when we met for her interview in the head teacher's office. While all the schoolgirls we talked with articulated a version of her sentiments, her comments perhaps most clearly reflect an ethos of self-responsibility that relies on Maasai social expectations around respect and discipline attached to "new world" imperatives ordered by the "new world" economy. Dorthea conducted her interview mostly in English, deferring to Kiswahili only occasionally. When I asked her how she felt about being in school, she said, "I usually feel well about school because when I come to school I like making a practice of myself." She explained that when she "make[s] a practice of herself" she is "working very hard in school." Working hard, practicing herself, and perfecting her performance were, she suggested, critical for her present and her future. She also noted that although her parents never went to school and had grown up only imagining themselves as cattle keepers, they decided to take their children to school because they realized that they "need[ed] to work hard to meet the goals they never had before." The idea that parents have "goals" that they "never had before" that can only be met by "hard work" related to schooling reflects mothers' hopes and worries about the future. When I asked her what her goals would be if she were to become a Minister of Parliament, her aspirations for herself were ambitious and impassioned. She said she would build her father and mother a house; build boreholes to address "the shortage of water"; install solar lighting so that "children can come to school early to read (study)" before dawn; talk to Maasai parents about girls' rights to education; and educate "all Maasai girls" so that "none are lagging behind."

The idiom of "hard work" reverberated through my interviews with schoolgirls. Dorthea explained that when schoolgirls leave school because of pregnancy, most do not return to school "because in our community, when a girl drops out of school, there is no way of her going back to school. They [her parents, elders] say, 'We have taken you to school and you have not done what we took you there to do. Go then and do the work you have chosen for yourself.'" There are likely many reasons schoolgirls do not return to school after the birth of a child, but for Dorthea and many of her cohort, the disappointment and frustration parents feel have less to do with sexual indiscretion (although for many families this is also an issue) and more to do with schoolgirls' choosing not to carefully "make a practice of [themselves]." Her comments imply that in choosing to engage in sexual activity (that some girls may not "choose" is occluded), some schoolgirls chose the "work" of motherhood and (arranged) marriage. This idea was dismaying to her. For her, the "hard work" of school was vastly preferable to the "hard work" of home, which was synonymous with the work of wives. Without the hard work of school, schoolgirls see no possibility for a "good life."

As Josephine, a thirteen-year-old student in Class 6 at Olepolos Primary School, explained, echoing a prevalent pattern in the interviews:

> I am seeing that when I am in school, I will have a good life. But if I am just at home, no, that life is not good. A Maasai girl who is not in school is married off, and you won't know the person you are married to. You will be harassed by

the husband. If anything gets lost, he can beat you."¹¹ If you have your children and they need money for school fees, you will not go to see the goats, you will use your salary.... [You will] hire someone to look after the cattle, not you or the children.... [Also] you can communicate in other languages at the *soko*,¹² ... [and] those who are home make their house with cow dung. After school we can make our houses well.

Similar to the mothers and teachers, Josephine explained that those who have not gone to school have "not changed their life." For her, school is the place, and education is the process whereby she can "see the many things that you are supposed to change ... in school. You will know what change is important and which changes are not important." The greatest changes that were important to her had to do with transforming gendered work, specifically women's work. She imagined reallocating household herding labor from children and "mothers" to hired shepherds. She imagined this is how things would be structured in her future family. She also noted that the "help" she would give her parents once she had a job and a salary would be to provide school fees for younger siblings and food for the whole family. She also associated the "good life" with her desire to choose her own husband, earn her own "salary," and freely use her income to mother differently (and in some ways, she implied, better) than those mothers who had not gone to school.

In schoolgirls' descriptions of school as a place full of meaning and promise for the "good life," education accumulated a certain kind of value that deepened attachments to the promise of school and animated schoolgirls' ardent desire to be in and stay in school. In this sense they aligned themselves with "the educated" (Lesorogol 2008; Stambach 2000; Vavrus 2003) and the "virtuous identity of 'one who aspires'" (Frye 2012, 1565). Echoing one mother's specific contention that her educated brother had "school knowledge," which was more valuable than her "Maasai knowledge," statements from nearly every interview with schoolgirls show investments in "school knowledge" as key to not only igniting "changes" in individual capacity in order to belong in a world increasingly defined by relations beyond the homestead but also to being able to look and plan ahead to make changes: "I know how to read and write my name"; "When someone talks to me [in English or Kiswahili] I can talk because I am educated"; "I can speak to a teacher or a grown up person"; "At home we have no books, but at school we have them and we read them"; "I like doing mathematics. When you have money you will not need to find someone to count for you." As one schoolgirl noted, schooling fundamentally enables girls or anyone to "avoid being foolish ... like for example someone gets a letter and cannot read it correctly."

Moreover, schoolgirls argued, the "good life" is connected to "good behavior" thought to come as an effect of education. Catherine noted that "behaviors are different at school. At school we are taught good behaviors, but at home they don't know good or bad behavior." Although mothers outlined what they understood as "good behavior" in keeping with teachers' comments, teachers often noted the ways parents and "those at home" could not (or would not) properly educate children to succeed outside of the homestead. Schoolgirls thus negotiated their expectations for themselves within emerging norms for schooled behavior. In this sense, schoolgirls tended to see home and school as spaces in which one's behavior and knowledge was differentially valued.

Bodily presentations of good behavior ascribed to the educated thus normalized the schoolgirl subject-position and social category associated with the potential for the good life. Across the interviews schoolgirls consistently emphasized speaking English and Swahili and therefore functioning outside of homogeneous Maasai social spaces; wearing "clothes" as opposed to shukas, including a school uniform, and therefore enacting modern comportment (see also Lesorogol 2008); living in a *mbati*-and-concrete house[13] instead of an *enkagiti* made of cow dung and therefore displaying "developed" lifestyles; spending one's time "reading" (an activity that exceeds the act of reading to connote all school-related "work," including homework and taking exams), writing, and calculating figures and therefore honing habits integral to getting "high marks"; knowing how to "look ahead" and therefore intentionally planning for the future rather than living in the now or day to day; discerning what is "good" about culture to keep and what should not be kept and therefore actively shaping Maasai culture—these were all seen as the performance of norms associated with schooling. As schoolgirls took up the norms of "the educated," they daily produced the schoolgirl subject-position as an effect of the performance. To hear her speak, write, dress, engage with others, and take actions toward her future is to know that she is a schoolgirl.

With these skills, as well as new or different habits of mind and body than those who had no schooling, schoolgirls saw themselves as engaged in the daily work of maintaining schoolgirlhood. "Categories of schooling and of nonschool institutions provide an anchoring rationale for defining differences" (Stambach 2000, 110). The argument that they were "doing something"—as opposed to "nothing"—with the future goal to "help" their natal families and to enable their community to "move ahead" was key to structuring the discursive, psychosocial, and material parameters of schoolgirlhood. Part of this maintenance was the repeated differentiation between who they were, how they behaved, and what they knew, and those who had not been to school. Schoolgirls reiterated that "at home we knew nothing; school is good because we know everything"; "At school it is only learning—home is not like school"; "Home is different from school. [Over the weekend] we do wish a Monday to come so that we can go back to school." All the schoolgirls in the study worked alongside their female kin to reproduce social life every day in the homestead by "looking after" livestock (including herding close to the homestead on weekends, as well as feeding and milking), fetching water and wood, cooking, cleaning the house and homestead, washing clothes and dishes, and caring for children and the elderly, as well as often helping their adult female family members maintain the physical house and social relations through reciprocity and collective efforts. Yet schoolgirls repeatedly characterized this work as doing "nothing," whereas the work of school is seen as meaningful for the present and essential for the future.

Schoolgirls' (and mothers' and teachers') comments also indicate a sharpening of class-based distinctions regarding "educated" behavior" between families with educated members and those families with no or few educated members. As Nanka noted, "At home you will just be looking after [livestock] from morning through the whole day, but after schooling you can have your job." Echoing Nanka, Catherine argued that for those at home, "their work is just to look after [livestock], and they can't think beyond that, but when you are in school your mind opens up and you can see ahead." Schoolgirl subjectivities slipped between home and school in which all that female people are required to do "at home" is collapsed into "nothing" (even the work schoolgirls do) and the work required not only at school but as a result of school (one's "job" that renders a "salary") expands to include everything that is "something."

Ann's insistence that her younger sisters see beyond the present to consider the future underscores her associations among current work, future planning, and the possibilities enabled by school:

> Home and school are different. In school we learn. If you are at home you will just be circumcised and married. In school you will not . . . [this is why] I also teach my sisters to complete school because the world is bad for them if they will not complete school. In school you know that in some years to come you can be doctor. But at home you can only say "maybe in five years to come I will have a family."

As Jackline clarified, "If you are a girl and not in school, you will be married easily because you are not doing anything. But if you are in school, you will be given that chance to complete school." A few schoolgirls did acknowledge that at home "you will do a lot of hard work," whereas at school "it's only learning and understanding." As Margaret noted, "At school we don't do the hard work of home; it is just to learn and eat"; and Lorna offered: "Right now at school we are playing on the fields, but at home they are not playing. Do you see that [school and home] are different?" Despite the few schoolgirls who recognized the "hard work" of home, the overwhelming sense from the interviews is the idea that school is a place where "something" gets done through hard work; in other words, the results of the work of school—knowledge, skills, behaviors, credentials, and access—was seen to render something beyond basic survival—that is, the daily mundane work of ensuring life. The hard work of home, when acknowledged, was positioned as doing "nothing" except social reproduction—the work of cooking, cleaning, and herding livestock. Understood as "nothing," schoolgirls do not associate the hard work of home with work that enables them and their families to "move forward." Rather, they see the work of home as requiring them to stand still or, perhaps, stay one step ahead of falling behind.

"A Boy Depends on Himself. I Want to Depend on Myself."

Within this ideological as well as material context, schoolgirls saw earning "some little money" outside of subsistence pastoralism as imperative for women. Peris speaks of "we Maasai," but only Maasai women and girls make beads: "We Maasai, most of the time if we want to get money we make the beads. But in school we will read, and after completing school you will have your job." As Mashenwa notes, "The one who is left at home, when her children are depending on her, for example if they need money, she can only sell her things (like beaded jewelry) to get that money. But the one who has gone to school can depend on her salary." According to schoolgirls, girls who grow into women who are not educated only had the options of making "beads"—traditional Maasai beaded jewelry and other beaded goods, such as men's belts for local and tourist markets, as well as some products for sale only to tourists—and other forms of petty trade, like making and selling charcoal as Cherity's mother did, selling tea in makeshift tea shops as Hope did or running small cafes like Hannah's, whereas they saw educated women as having unprecedented options. For instance, when Faith declared that she planned to own her own land, we asked: "Can a Maasai woman own land without a husband?" She replied without hesitation: "Those who have not gone to school cannot but those who have been [to school] can." Schoolgirls knew what it felt like to "sleep without eating" in households with only one or two goats. They strongly believed that when they "finish[ed] [their] education, no one can sit without eating."

Moreover, part of doing "nothing" at home as opposed to the "something" of school, as Ann's and Jackline's comments suggest, is "waiting" to be married, a behavior anathema to schoolgirls who adamantly refuse the idea that their marriages could be arranged before they complete school (and ideally, after tertiary education). The work of home—the work of women—is also the work of wives (and mothers); schoolgirls see the work of school as integral to the work of the kind of women (and wives and mothers) they want to be in their futures. As Stambach (2000, 108) found in her study of gender and schooling in Chagga communities in Tanzania, "it is not the content of the lessons that empowers" schooled girls to think of themselves as empowered, autonomous women but "the symbolic wealth and cultural capital that schooling provides as a discursive, symbolic system." No schoolgirls we talked with rejected marriage or motherhood per se. To the contrary, they imagine themselves better Maasai wives and mothers because the "hard work" of school portends not only different work for educated women (many noted, for example, they wanted to work in offices) but also different meanings attached to different work as well as different (and better) rewards.

Schoolgirls' attitudes and aspirations reflect that of their mothers and teachers in this regard. As the adults argued, schooling is the only path to independence rather than dependence for a Maasai girl-cum-woman. As one schoolgirl explained, education is the only process through which "you will get knowledge of doing your own things." This independence, as implied in the opening choral practice, is associated with the "right" to school and the promises and protections it portends: "In school you can be taught the rights of a girl-child, but at home you will not be told because they don't know." Moreover, the right to aspire is associated with the possibilities of autonomy implied in professional wage work. The deeply held belief that education is the surest path to formal wage work is endemic to schoolgirls' embrace of education for themselves and their communities. For Maasai primary schoolgirls, "having your salary" is a primary signifier for belonging in the larger Kenyan community of persons who have "value." It distinguishes them and their life prospects from those in their immediate communities who have not gone to school and as a result have, as they see it, far fewer choices for earning an income. Girls who go to school imagine growing up into women who can provide differently for their families.

"Life of someone who has not gone to school is difficult," Joyce explained. "In school we learn about dreams. If I didn't come to school, I could not have that dream of becoming a doctor." Senewa, age sixteen and in Class 5 at Olepolos, asserted that school is important to her because "when I get my job I will not be depending on anyone. I want my own life and even [the ability] to save other people." She explained that while some parents might see arranged early marriage as the best way to care for daughters, being married into a poor family only repeats patterns of dependence: "You will not be independent if you are given to a poor family. You will still be depending on your [husband's] parents even for food." This "social projection" that as an educated woman Senewa will be in command of family resources, even in a patrilineal framework, "reflects a careful calculation of gender against education . . . [the] fascinating cultural process whereby people sometimes translate the value of schooling into social reproduction" (Stambach 2000, 94). Schoolgirls understood that shifting gendered relations of power required a degree of decision-making power that girls usually did not have but would have, they thought, if they stayed in school. Lorna, a fifteen-year-old Class 5 student from Innyonyorri, used the example of schooling to explain these relative degrees of difference between boys and girls (and presumably between men and women). She clarified that when it comes to school, a boy can choose for himself if he wants to go to school or stay home, but for girls this decision is made by the father, because "a boy depends on himself but the girl-child must depend on the father." In her experience, even boys who were also told they could not go to school simply disregarded the father "and were not told anything else." But girls, she said, "do what they are told."

Lorna was clear that she liked school because she felt being educated would shift her dependence on her father to herself, and like a boy she would be able to make her own decisions. She stated simply: "A boy depends on himself. I want to depend on myself." Although conversations with adult Maasai men about schooling decisions in their childhood homes suggested that boys too are beholden to generational patriarchal decision making, Lorna's position that boys could more easily push back against patriarchal authority makes sense if the "boys" she refers to might actually be "men" by virtue of circumcision status and therefore culturally expected, as well as entitled, to make relatively independent decisions "like men." Circumcised schoolgirls, on the other hand, enjoy no status upgrade. They return to school physically different, but the sociological promises attached to emurata for girls who go to school does not change how they see themselves or how most people see them. As every girl made clear, they are still "just girls." As I will discuss further in chapter 4, while schoolgirlhood carves out social and culture space for a girl to grow up in school, her "empowerment" is effectively deferred to adulthood. Her aspirations for a better life as the result of schooling are often challenged, even thwarted, by the social contradictions ascribed to her actual body. As circumcised children, a paradox in Maasai social relations, schoolgirls both benefit from being not-girls/not-women and face conflicting social messages about their embodied potential.

Maasai girls have internalized the gendered intensification of responsibility for and obligation to not only their own immediate success but also to complete school and enter the formal workforce for the betterment of their families, the Maasai community broadly conceived, and, for some, the nation. Maasai schoolgirls want to be exceptional—they want to be exceptions to the rule that girls are not taken to school, girls do not perform well in school, girls do not take school seriously, and that ultimately investments in girls are lost to her father's family and gained by her husband's family. While schoolgirlhood enables girls to sidestep some patriarchal claims on their bodies, interests, time, and labor, commensurate substantive rights are deferred until adulthood, and even then they are difficult to realize for many women, educated or not.

Conclusion

Girls' economic empowerment through education is heralded for the far-reaching positive ripples it can affect. Anne, a Class 5 student at Loodariak Primary School, was adamant that she "cannot get any education without school." This fundamental contention was echoed across the interviews with schoolgirls. When Warner et al. (2013) spoke with 508 girls, ages ten through nineteen, in fourteen countries as part of a study commissioned by the Nike Foundation about what they "want and need," they found that "education was the single most important issue raised by girls in the consultations, in every setting and across every age group . . . [it was] the most frequently mentioned theme across all countries, and both by girls who were in school and those who were not" (59–60).[14] An unequivocal confidence in girls' education is often repeated (and often using very similar language) among individuals and institutional girls' education advocates alike: "Leveraging education to facilitate girls' transitions to healthy, safe and productive adulthood is the single most important development investment that can be made" (Warner et al. 2013).

At the local level, the universalized schoolgirl category is fleshed out and made real within Maasai institutions and cultural norms. Maasai schoolgirls thus imagined themselves and their futures through multiple and sometimes contradictory messages and experience schoolgirlhood as multiple commitments. Everyone—particularly schoolgirls themselves—ardently believed that staying in school and performing well was the single most important "hard work" they could accomplish. As girl-effects logic predicts, they were deeply invested in the promise of schooling to change their lives. The belief that education offers the only path to a "good life" for Maasai girls-cum-women comes across in their narratives as less about making rational choices to resist or refuse gendered and generational norms and more about inhabiting constricting norms in novel ways. This happens, I suggest, in part because the girl-effects logic itself positively disrupts taken-for-granted social meanings about girls (and women's) roles, rights, and responsibilities. While schooling does not necessarily guarantee the clear-cut version of empowerment, current girl-effects logic predicts and therefore assumes, being in school gives Maasai girls limited agency to "voice" their own desires and imagine futures for themselves in which they inhabit inherited norms in "empowered" ways.

As the opening scene suggests, girl-effects logic is personified in the body of the schoolgirl as an instrument of development. Schoolgirlhood is most persuasively performed with the blessing of patriarchal authority and community sanction. Legitimized by the relative social power of their teacher's words, the Embolei singers were given license to publically perform themselves and their schoolgirlhood as the grafting together of cultural markers of "Maasai-ness" (distinctively wrapped shukas, beaded jewelry, dance movements, vocal rhythms, and Maa lyrics) and schooling (the gingham uniforms, evocation of careers, the classroom as stage). In this way, the girls' performance intervened in conventional expectations for girls.[15] For example, the performance challenged the still-prevalent local discourse that any investment in a girl's education is wasted for her parents, as any benefit will only accrue to her husband's family. The lyrics thereby subtly shift a girl's "value" as a young bride to that of schoolgirl who will be better positioned to contribute significantly to her natal family's well-being through education rather than arranged marriage. Further, by implication, the educated girl-cum-woman will also have greater capacity to contribute to the family she creates through marriage. Schoolgirls' performance of "new words" authorizing "new messages" allow them to insist that education is what they desire and deserve as a new kind of "inheritance," which is a powerful and disruptive idea in a context wherein a girl does not inherit from her father, as a man's property is customarily inherited by his sons.

At the same time, girl-effects logic reflects and reinforces transnational expectations for hard work that undergird theories of human capital as the gendering of development. Schoolgirls seem to have internalized the intensification of responsibility, obligation, self-sacrifice, and other-serving social (and emotional) affective attachments to family and community well-being that comes with this work, at least in part because these expectations reflect Maasai norms for successful femininity. Despite the relatively broader latitude Maasai schoolgirls have to negotiate some of their needs and desires than girls who have never attended school seem not to have, the schoolgirl subject-position functions at the limit of any kind of radical break with conventional gender norms. Persistence in school effectively delinks the schoolgirl from "traditional" expectations for early marriage, for example, but only (or only primarily) so she stays in school longer in order to get a better job in order to better care for her family—her natal family, as well as her "new" family she creates with a husband, as well as her community and, as the logic goes, her entire nation. Conventional expectations for women, marriage, and motherhood are not rejected here: they are enhanced and extended by education. The larger sociocultural sanctioning of education allows for schoolgirlhood to emerge as a legitimate kind of gendered childhood, provided schoolgirls embody and enact respect for parents, community, and culture, including gendered norms associated with propriety. This performance and others like it, then, have the potential to publically rescript the notions of who girls are and who they can be for themselves and their communities within the dictates of an appropriately hybrid subjectivity. As an everyday consequence, schoolgirls to varying degrees actively strive to meet their increasing responsibility to mitigate poverty for themselves and their families via faith in the promise of education as development to ensure new modes of "power."

The next chapter shifts the discussion from the wholesale "hunger" for girls' education and its promise of the "good life" to ambivalence regarding the changes in local understandings of gendered personhood that characterize schoolgirlhood as a contingent social and cultural space. Although girl-effects logic presents the girl-child and schoolgirl as inherently oppositional (Bent and Switzer 2016), I argue they are less frequently two distinct and divergent subject positions and more often mutually constituted social categories and embodied experiences. As Nashipae's and Felista's narratives in chapter 3 suggest, schoolgirlhood does not necessarily inoculate girls who go to school from the continued need to negotiate gendered (and gendering) as well as generational claims on their interests and desires. Schoolgirls' insights suggest tension, even contradiction, in their experiences of schooling.

CHAPTER 3

"The medicine for fire is fire."
Negotiating Schoolgirlhood

> There is no doubt that childhoods
> are changing among the Maasai.
> —Caroline Archambault

"*Elimu ni mwangaza.*"

Painted across classroom buildings, stenciled on t-shirts, and resting on the tip of everyone's tongues, this statement in Kiswahili, "Education is light," and others like it circulated as commonsense in the ebb and flow of community life in the case-study communities. Affective assertions of the power of schooling broadcast in church, at school, and at community events edified (and reified) education as essential for a changed, and changing, world. In this ideological context, the production and performance of schoolgirlhood localized the transnational logic of girl effects. As I have thus far shown, schoolgirls were quite aware of their situated positions, vis-à-vis education (Lesorogol 2008; Mojola 2014). When we asked Nasarean, one of a few secondary schoolgirls we talked to over the holiday when students were back home in Loodariak from distant boarding schools, why education was important for her life, she clarified the link primary schoolgirls made between the "hard work" of school and a "good life": "In the world of Kenya that we are in now, everything we do is about education. That even the job you get, you must be learned. You must know both English and Kiswahili. Many Kenyan jobs require certificates from primary and secondary school. Now good jobs call for qualified people."

Her classmate Jane added: "[Education] makes me learn more and understand much more about myself than I used to. It will help to get a job. Through education I will be able to communicate with different people from all over the country. It is important because you never know where you will land in life." Having successfully navigated one of most difficult transitions for poor girls growing up in communities in the Global South targeted for development—completing primary school, scoring well enough on the Kenyan Certificate of Primary Education (KCPE) to gain admission to provincial-level high schools, succeeding in securing the funds for tuition and boarding, and having the support of key adults to continue on to secondary—Jane and Nasarean had confident expectations about the positive and transformative role education would have in creating the futures they desired.

Gendered neoliberal discourse of individual achievement, personal responsibility, and readiness when opportunity for private gain arises reflected in these statements reinforces the idea that schoolgirls are single-source multipliers of development dividends. Girlpower acts as a kind of self-investment for the future hinged to individual and collective expectations for gendered work and gendered obligation. As more Maasai secondary schoolgirls like Nasarean and Jane persisted in school and the more stories of the "help" they returned to their families and communities circulated, the more confident primary schoolgirls could be about their own futures. Goldman and Little (2014, 772) call this "empowerment by example." Schoolgirls' dogged faith in their own gendered capacity for responsibility, discipline, "hard work," and "self-practice" was key to their positive projections of education in their present lives and future prospects. As girl-effects logic predicts, confident future aspirations reinforced a shared belief in schoolgirlhood as an incubator for developing the habits of mind and body required by and for development.

Inhabiting schoolgirlhood as a sociocultural space in which girls grow up in school enabled schoolgirls to imagine a very different kind of future for themselves that marks a departure from the conventional trajectory for Maasai girls. As in evidence in previous chapters, schoolgirls strongly believe that they can only become key levers for development at all scales by deferring marriage and motherhood, completing their education, and subsequently earning a "salary" with which to return their families' (and by extension, their community's) investments. While nearly all the girls we talked with do want to marry and become mothers, education is the only form of success they see as "meaningful," in part, as I have shown, because they believe educated mothers can more easily provide for their children and educated wives can more effectively support their households. Maasai schoolgirls want to be prepared to take advantage of whatever comes their way, whether they seek—or simply come across—opportunities in their lives, including in the labor market. They also want to meet conventional expectations—as well as personal desires for—marriage and motherhood, but they want to become "women," "wives," and "mothers" on what they imagine to be their own terms and according to their own timing.

Yet historically, and still for many girls today, most girls know precisely "where they will land in life": in the homestead of a husband selected by their parents in collaboration with local patriarchies in anticipation (celebratory or otherwise) of motherhood and the work of wives. In the context of girl-effects discourse, schooling interrupts conventional patriarchal social practices, such as arranged marriages. "Early" and "forced" marriages are seen to violate girls' rights and, moreover, prevent them from access to schooling that enables them to grow into "productive" multipliers of capitalist development. Schoolgirls, mothers, and teachers are invested in the positive effects of educating girls to erode and eventually replace the still-operative rationale that investing in a girls' education, through eighth grade or even secondary school (Form 4), is a wasted investment "because a girl can become pregnant at any time." According to this logic, any benefits that may come from schooling are then lost because the girl must be immediately married, and any assets she might bring accrue to her husband's family instead of her father's family, who had directly invested in her education. Interviewees referred to fathers (and male relatives) as the key decision makers regarding girls' schooling and, relatedly, their marriage arrangements, in ways that reflect simplistic depictions of patriarchal decision making in transnational girls' education discourse, such as the Nike Foundation's viral videos, "The Girl Effect" and "The Clock Is Ticking" (Switzer 2013).

Contrary to these depictions, everyday negotiations around schooling decisions are far less straightforward accounts of patriarchal oppression. Parents who may want to educate all of their children, including their girl-children, are not always able to accommodate every child; arranging good marriages for girls whom parents cannot afford to educate is locally understood as a reasonable approach to securing their daughters' futures, as well as patriarchal relations among families and among men as heads of families, and is a long-practiced pastoralist strategy for ensuring social reproduction, particularly in the face of pastoral crisis (Archambault 2011). Yet, schoolgirls' investment in the idea that schooling is the very best way for them to realize their obligations to ensuring their natal families' well-being and to strengthen communal relations that their status as daughters exchanged between families as wives has historically accomplished challenges both girl-effects logics of individualism and autonomy and parents' recourse to conventional communal strategies for securing individual and household futures.

These contemporary contestations around who and what Maasai girls could be(come) and do (or could not be(come) and could not do) revolved around purportedly sturdy dichotomous definitions of girlhood. Girls' education discourse and girl-effects logic consistently presents only two possible subject-positions for girls living in poverty in the Global South: the girl-child or the schoolgirl. In this discourse, the girl-child is in need of rescue from local patriarchy and lack of economic opportunity by the modernizing process of development in the form of schooling and formal employment. The girl-child's opposite, the schoolgirl, is girlpower personified. As a beneficiary of and promulgator of development, the schooled girl is "tapped" as a reliable human capital resource who will use her education to better herself, her family, and the entire community. Similarly, in local parlance, girls inhabited two possible positions—"a girl of the home" or, relative to her (actual or symbolic) sister, "a girl of the school" (Archambault 2011).[1] A "girl of the home" is fully subject to conventional Maasai expectations for girl-children, including absolute humble obedience to circumcision for girls, arranged marriage, and subsequent motherhood. Her opposite, "a girl of the school," is bound for school instead of immediate marriage. The schoolgirl is still subject to requirements for dutiful compliance with female initiation, but her adulthood and any plans for her marriage and motherhood are delayed until she completes her education. She is still expected to be humble and obedient, but also to excel in school, to be "disciplined" against the "distractions" of sexual relationships with boys/men (in other words, it is her responsibility to forestall motherhood as a way to forestall marriage), and to dutifully use her education to benefit her family and community. The completion of her education, rather than her initiation, signals social maturation and ignites arrangements for her marriage. She is allowed to choose whom she will marry and when, in consultation with elders and in deference to Maasai marriage practices (for example, clan exogamy).

These binary configurations of oppositional girlhoods, however, fail to account for girls' actual everyday realities as relationally embedded subjects (Bent and Switzer 2016). Maasai schoolgirlhood is formed by and experienced within gendered and generational sociocultural relations of love, respect, care, authority, status, and power that configure family and community formations. A fundamental tie that binds the girl-child to the schoolgirl, the girl at home, and the girl at school, is her status as a "Maasai daughter" (Hodgson 1996a). In this chapter, I focus on two schoolgirls' narratives (Felista's and Nashipae's) illustrative of a pattern in the schoolgirls' interviews that suggest the ambivalent and even bewildering character of schoolgirlhood that the effusive local and global discourses of girls' education too easily cover over.

I argue that the ambivalence schoolgirls feel and often express is a function of their social location as Maasai daughters negotiating "in-between" girl-childhood and the requirements of a "girl of the home" and schoolgirlhood that provide new opportunities along with reconfigured old constraints for being a proper daughter. Despite assurances of these neat binaries in transnational and local discourses, Nashipae's and Felista's stories (and Maria's story as it is embedded within Felista's) suggest the fundamentally contingent and relational nature of girl-childhood and schoolgirlhood. Their experiences highlight how gendered and generational relations of power operate dialectically to configure schoolgirlhood as an uncertain and inherently contradictory space in which girls in school are positioned by (and position themselves within) subjectivities in contention. These are schoolgirls' stories, but they are also stories about how daughters struggle within shifting understanding of girlhood as more Maasai girls go to school; they help to show how celebrating girls' education as the key to economic development relies on conventional expectations of daughters within patriarchal social arrangements while also simultaneously redefining who and what daughters can do and be.

Spaces "In-between" Definitions of Daughters

My research assistants and I talked to schoolgirls during the school day in each school compound, most often in an empty classroom or storage room, sometimes in the head teacher's office, and more than once (in schools that could not spare the space for a private meeting) in the backseat of the vehicle belonging to the local Maasai NGO that facilitated the research. We used a mini digital audio recorder to collect our conversations.[2] Schoolgirls seemed to delight in the idea of the recorder and blushed and giggled when we played their voices back for them. Despite their enthusiasm to hear themselves speak, and for many, their eagerness to answer (and ask) questions, with few exceptions, schoolgirls' actual voices during the interviews were often barely louder than a whisper. We learned early in the process that unless they held the recorder like a microphone close enough to their lips to touch and unless we gently reminded them to speak up and not to "shy off" throughout the interview, we would not be able to discern their voices when we played the audio back for them to hear or for us to work with. Their interest in expressing their strong desire for education for all Maasai children, and for girl-children in particular, in most cases could not explicitly override their learned reserve and deferential respect toward any elder (much less a foreign, white adult asking questions in a semiformal way). The reticence of their actual voices mixed with ambitious anticipation for the "fruits" of educational participation gave our conversations a contradictory tenor. Despite their resolute faith in education to alter their lives for the better, ambivalence also laced the edges of schoolgirls' optimistic answers. Equivocation colored their confidence as they struggled to adhere to a well-worn script of dichotomous girlhood generated both by ideas regarding Maasai "culture" and by development discourse. Instead, they consistently characterized the schoolgirl as occupying the spaces in-between conventional categories embedded in gendered and generational relations, particularly between individual daughters and fathers and the structural requirements of patriarchal social forms.

The "in-betweenness" (Bent and Switzer 2016; Switzer 2010) of schoolgirlhood emerged very early in the research during a pilot interview with Maria to calibrate the questions we would ask schoolgirls. When I asked her if she considered herself a "girl" or a "woman," she answered "neither" and followed up with, "I am in-between, neither a girl nor a woman. I am a student." Although Maria was not enrolled in school at the time of our conversation, having graduated from secondary the year before and waiting to hear if she had been accepted to the University of Nairobi, identifying as a "student" enabled her to prolong her schoolgirlhood as a space in-between the lack of agency ascribed to "girlhood" and the onset of marital and mothering responsibilities ascribed to "womanhood." By classifying herself as a student, Maria could leverage the possibilities invested in educated girls in order to navigate, and negotiate (sometimes successfully, sometimes less so), social expectations of her body, time, attention, and labor.

As I listened to schoolgirls talk about education and development through their everyday experiences, I heard repeated versions of Maria's notion of "in-betweenness." Even though nearly all of the schoolgirls we talked with had undergone (or would soon undergo) the right of passage that sociologically transforms girls into "women" (emurata), every schoolgirl we interviewed adamantly rejected being called *enkitok* (woman).[3] Schoolgirls strongly rejected identifying as or with "women" because, they argued, womanhood is incompatible with schooling and can *only* mean imminent marriage arranged by fathers without the girls' consent or consultation.[4] Some conceded to "*entito*" (girl) if the only choices were "girl" or "woman," but most chose instead to modify "girl" and be "schoolgirl" or, sometimes, "student."[5]

By identifying as schoolgirls and students, and thus positioning themselves as girls in the context of school relative to (and rather than) girls in the context of home, schoolgirls actively embodied a narrow new space for negotiating the shifting cultural politics of gender. A "girl of the home," for example, would have no grounds on which to deny her status as a "woman" and the unfolding of arranged marriage that follows initiation. By positioning one set of expectations (conventional Maasai gender norms for girlhood and womanhood) against another ("new" gender norms and expectations associated with school), this discursive maneuvering actively shifted the terms of recognition for who and what a Maasai girl could do or be in ways that made sense to those with power in their immediate worlds. This process of social resignification has had the practical effects of disrupting conventional Maasai gender categories, creating new kinds of persons, and galvanizing a sense of agency for those girls who persist in school despite the odds.

Yet this kind of resignification of social meanings is only ever partial and was unevenly experienced. The social categories of girl, daughter, initiate, woman, wife, and mother are all gendered according to relational understanding of the categories in the microfibers of community life in any given time and place.[6] Before the social and economic development pressure to educate girls, these categories had (and have, for those girls-cum-women who do not go to school) different meanings and produced differential practical effects (Pigg 1992, 1993). In this context, "daughter" is a social role that extends into adulthood and embeds girls and women in gendered relations of power understood as "natural" to the order of things. As a Maasai head teacher explained to me, and as interviews with schoolgirls, mothers, and teachers all confirmed, daughters are conditioned from birth to become adults who "must always give respect," whereas their brothers grow up learning that as boys they will grow into men, and men "must always be given respect." Consequently, daughters are social minors bound by *enkanyit*, or "hierarchies of respect," regardless of age and the social respect they gain as they age, to submit to the will of male elders (Hodgson 1999, 2001b; Talle 1988). Male elders are likewise bound to assume responsibility for decisions regarding all clan daughters. These relations, among others, help to reproduce and naturalize patriarchal power. Yet as more Maasai girls go to school, these conventional definitions of "father" and "daughter" are contestable as communities come to terms (sometimes using new terms) with gendered and generational social changes wrought by increased institutional access to schooling for girls. The determinative nature of being a Maasai daughter is perceptibly shifting in favor of (some) girls' increased capacity to negotiate their own needs and desires.

Dorothy Hodgson's (1996a) analysis of a young Tanzanian Maasai woman's challenge to her father's authority to arrange her marriage, and by extension, authority invested in lineage elders and clan leaders, gives a striking example of the role daughters can play in disrupting patriarchal authority. Her analysis is focused less on Aloya's "resistance" to gendered and generational power (Abu-Lughod 1990; Thomas 1996) and more on how patriarchies "must recognize and accommodate" shifting power relations "within and through which they operate in order to maintain their hegemony" (Hodgson 1996a, 120). Yet as Hodgson points out, what is "remarkable" about Aloya's case is that "all the trouble was started by a daughter" (122), given that daughters are assumed to be absolutely obedient to patriarchal authority. From my point of view and for the arguments I am making here, what is even more remarkable about the case is that all the trouble was started by an *educated* daughter. Although Aloya had completed primary school, married according to the requirements of a "girl of the school" to a man of her choosing with the blessing of her maternal uncle who had raised her, and given birth to her first child, her biological father still considered her his child as well as a clan daughter. When her father (an uneducated Maasai man) pursued Maasai means to (re)establish his authority over Aloya, she knew that she had no voice or standing in forums in which Maasai men gathered to make decisions regarding daughters. To circumvent this structural control, Aloya leveraged her differential positioning in one patriarchal institution (the state) against another (the clan and lineage structure). By pursing her case in court, Aloya used her public primary school education as an advantage against the traditional power of fathers to make decisions for and about daughters. Hodgson explains that "within the structure of the Tanzanian state [Aloya] was not a daughter, but a citizen, and she knew that citizens—male or female, old or young, wealthy or poor—ideally had an equal voice before the law" (109). Her ability to speak directly to the court in fluent Swahili on her own behalf and hear the proceeding without translation (capacities neither her father and nor the elders he called as his witnesses had) influenced the way she was seen and heard by the court *and* by her lineage fathers.

By "reject[ing] the passive role of silent assent expected of her as a 'daughter' in Maasai society" (109), Aloya's actions and the local patriarchy's reactions had implications for the stability of shared social meanings. An "assertive," even "confrontational" daughter "implied a father whose authority was no longer absolute or unquestioned" (119). Upon the court's rendering of the decision of guilty, Aloya's father utilized the only weapon he had as a local patriarch in reaction to the state's decision to privilege his daughter's position—he cursed her, yelling at the magistrate in Maa: "Take my daughter then, she is yours, she belongs to the government now. You take care of her, you marry her off, you receive her bride wealth. I disown her here and now" (118).[7]

The idiom of ownership—who (or what) "owns" daughters and is obligated and responsible to care for, as well as make decision for—came up in nearly every interview with schoolgirls who indicated that they had "no otherwise" but to submit to local patriarchal authority (their fathers, male relatives, and, by extension, all fathers).[8] A veteran head teacher and respected Maasai elder (who had also been an ilmurran) told me of a local father who wanted to remove his daughter, Helen, from school in order to "give her out in marriage." Note the similarity of language used. The head teacher explained,

> The father's plan was to move to another homestead and take the girl with him so that he could say she was not in school. Helen came to me with this information. I called the mother to meet with me, and she confirmed the girl's story. She said she could do nothing or she would be beaten. I called the man to meet with me. He was angry at first. He said to me, "She is my daughter, and I will do as I please with her!" I said, "No, she is my daughter now, and the district education officer is involved in this case!" After much pressure from the authorities and local elders, the man eventually relented. But he refused to greet me for one year. I challenged Helen to prove that she loves school. As her marks have steadily improved, everyone is happy.

Within patriarchal social arrangements, daughters' structural roles are seemingly set in stone; schoolgirls certainly gave the impression that they and their mothers have no legitimate way to intervene in or counter a father's, husband's, or male relative's decisions regarding their lives. All girls, whether they are "of the home" or "of the school," function within these affective attachments and powerful gendered and generational relations. Yet Aloya's (and Helen's) experiences indicate the ways in which schoolgirls were able to engage the state (through authorities such as the police, the court, and the school) as arbiters in their relationships with local patriarchies generally and their own fathers specifically. Girls in school (unlike girls of the home) are positively positioned to use their access to the knowledge and "power" (and power brokers) afforded by their proximity to school. Yet, to engage the state is to risk being disowned and disavowed as a willful daughter who "belongs to the government" instead of her family. As I hope to show in the narratives that follow, the girls' education discourse of individual empowerment and infinite possibility often collides with the realities of Maasai gender ideologies compounded by overall economic insecurity and unevenly experienced crises of social reproduction (Archambault 2007, 2016; Mukudi 2004; Vavrus 2003). The intimate interdependencies and inconsistencies among shifting categories of girlhood relative to the competing (and also overlapping) patriarchal structures of the home and the school created contradictions, and possibilities, which schoolgirls often struggled to navigate.

"Dawa ya moto ni moto": Fighting Fire with Fire

A fifteen-year-old Class 7 student at Embolei Primary School, Felista, spent much of her interview with us distraught over two pressing and related issues in her young life. First, she wanted our counsel on how to convince her father to buy plastic sheeting to cover her blind mother's *enkagiti* (traditional dung house) to protect her from the seasonal rains.[9] She also wanted to know how she could convince her father, who had already promised to "marry her off" at the end of Class 8, to let her continue on to secondary and postpone marriage until she had completed school. She explained that her only recourse, it seemed to her, was to cry, but when she cried, he beat her. If her mother intervened on Felista's behalf, he beat her too.

Felista did not cry, but she was tearful as she explained her predicament. When she was finished, I intentionally hesitated and did not respond. I was not sure what appropriate advice would be, but Maria had very clear instructions for Felista. When she responded, Maria's voice was low, and determined; she spoke with the gentle firmness of an elder sister or trusted teacher. Felista listened with the shy intensity that I came to expect from schoolgirls.

First, Maria suggested that Felista speak to the head teacher about her concerns. Then the heart of her advice came in the form of a Swahili proverb, "*Dawa ya moto ni moto*" (the medicine for fire is fire). This advice reveals the profound and contingent place of schooling in many girls' lives, particularly for girls in precarious situations. Maria said, "Your results matter. They will speak for themselves. When you work hard this term—you must work to beat the boys' scores—take your results to your father. Say, 'Father, I need a present for this good work. The present I need is for you to buy plastic bags for my mom's house.'"

Felista kept her eyes down as she chipped away at the peeling green paint on the school desk with the clip of her pen cap. In her other hand, she held tightly to the mini digital recorder like a herding stick.

Maria continued steadily. As far as convincing her father to postpone arranging her marriage, Maria was unequivocal: Felista held the solution to her problem in her own hands. If she wanted to fight her arranged marriage and stay in school, her best defense was school; she needed to show her father good grades. Maria continued, "When your results are good, even the government will be involved. You will be given a letter inviting you to secondary, and your father cannot refuse you."

Maria's tenacity and resolve were palpable, but Felista was not assured. Piling green paint slivers over the new bare spot on the desk, she wanted to know how she could "study and perform well" when she had "no paraffin at home."[10] Clearly for Felista, a real element of her (and her mother's) vulnerability and insecurity was her family's material poverty. Maria did not hesitate. She had a strategy to handle these obstacles as well. She said, "Move home directly from school, and do your chores quickly—prepare *ugali*,[11] gather the water, gather the firewood, wash the utensils, everything you are expected to do. Sleep early. Come to school at six in the morning and study until eight. These small sacrifices will be worth it." Felista wiped the corner of her eye with the back of her right hand; streams of sweat dripped off the corner of the recorder from her palm. Maria was firm and resolute: "Don't even think of getting married after Class 8—leave it! Your marks will speak on your behalf and your father cannot refuse you."

"Your father cannot refuse you" are strong words in a context in which fathers routinely refuse daughters. The idea that Maasai men, particularly fathers, refuse, resist, or sacrifice their daughters' education was evident in nearly every interview with schoolgirls, if not about their own fathers or male relatives, then about Maasai men in general. It is also evident in practice that someone—fathers or elder male proxies (often the mother's brother) were usually named—kept children, and particularly girls, out of school or cut short girls' education by arranging their marriages toward the end of primary school. The reasons for keeping girls out of school vary and may often have more to do with economic constraints and imperatives than cultural ones (Archambault 2011). Nonetheless, the popular discourse was that more boys than girls go to school because "Maasai men want only cows" and boys bring cows by earning money in wage-sector employment to enhance pastoral practice, whereas girls, they say, produce cows by way of bride wealth. Yet, unlike the girl-child desperate to attend school, Felista was already *in* school. Given the neat dichotomy often invoked between the girl-child and the schoolgirl, we might expect Felista to take better advantage of her relatively privileged position vis-à-vis "those girls at home" who had been chosen for marriage, not school. In her uncertainty and real concern, Felista came across as a girl at home longing for the safety and promise of school. Her trepidation suggested that she had not yet learned to leverage her schoolgirl subjectivity, or perhaps she had (she did take the opportunity to bring up her serious concerns during our interview), but unlike Maria, she did not (yet) know how to invent space for negotiation, even possibility, to craft her own future. Girl effects and the logic of the self-making girl-powered-girl serve to frame Felista's uncertainty not as evidence of the failure of schoolgirlhood to empower Felista but rather Felista's failure to make the most of her schooling. Instead, she came across as a girl-child and a good "Maasai daughter," silent in the face of a father who came across in her narrative as a stock character in a predictable drama. Felista expressed uncertainty and fear about her immediate circumstances and powerlessness to change her mother's situation or her own.

Maria, on the other hand, was a seasoned schoolgirl who, against her own great odds, had successfully completed high school. Her father had never gone to school and had worked exclusively in the pastoral economy. He had four wives (none of whom had gone to school) until Maria's mother died "due to sickness" in 1999 when Maria was in Class 5. She is one of six children in "her mother's house" and the first child to be educated among her father's twenty children.[12] She explained, "Because of culture, and the very strong respect that is mixed with fear, girls cannot be close to their fathers." By "close" she referred to a cultural taboo regarding physical closeness between fathers and daughters. She explained, for example, that it is still common practice that when a man enters his wife's house, the girls in the house (his daughters as well as other girls) must greet him and leave.[13] If he sleeps in the house (polygamists sleep in the houses of their wives at different times), then girls must find another house in which to sleep (usually with a grandmother or a stepmother, but if these spaces are not available, they may sleep outside on the ground).[14] In this context, Maria explained, it is not socially permissible for a daughter to sit and communicate directly with her father about what she might need.[15]

By "respect" Maria refers to *enkanyit*, which is translated also to "discipline," which she explained is a "mixture" of fear of authority and deference Maasai children are taught to feel for their parents and all social elders, particularly all fathers, including their own (Archambault 2009; Pratt 2003). Nonetheless, in Maria's case, because she lost her mother so young and her relationship with her stepmothers was not good in the beginning—they "treated [her] like someone else's child," but then she "grew up and learned to fight for [her] rights [so] they turned to [her] side"—she was emotionally "closer" to her father than most girls she knew were to theirs. She would find permissible ways to talk to him (for example, by standing at a distance to wash the dishes while he sat under the tree). Most girls, like Felista, expressed their "respect" for patriarchal authority as strong avoidance of their fathers and complete obedience to their decisions. Maria, on the other hand, believed that girls needed their fathers' guidance and advice and could, and should, seek appropriate and respectful ways to negotiate with fathers.

This atypical "closeness" with her father born from the need to solve her own problems and "fight for [her] rights" from an early age no doubt in part emboldened Maria's adamant advice to "fight fire with fire." Nonetheless, this advice also suggests that successful schoolgirls have learned that the resources for securing a future in uncertain situations must come from an individual reserve of personal resolve, including the courage to mitigate risks in one arena by self-sacrifice and self-work in another. Maria had herself won the struggle for school by leveraging her own inherent intelligence, ingenuity and willingness to "improve herself" by drawing on Maasai notions of personal struggle, duty, respect, and hard work. She told me stories, for example, of being assigned in upper primary school to share a desk with the "top student" in math, a boy known for his cleverness. She said, "I made him my friend, and we would read [study] maths together." When the KCPE scores were announced, her deskmate was, as usual, the "top boy," and she was in the "second position," bumping the boy who had usually held the second position to third. She said the boys and her teachers were amazed and impressed with her "hard work."

But before she was a schoolgirl, Maria was also a girl-child and subject to the range of obligations girl-children experience. All schoolgirls were required to do "women's work" like washing clothes, preparing food, gathering water and wood, cleaning the house and compound, milking, and caring for smallstock, as well as caring for young children. However, unlike their mothers and older sisters—all of whom had been chosen as "girls of the home"—on top of their domestic chores and community obligations, as girls chosen for school, they were also obligated to the work of school. All girls we talked with felt the pressure and the desire to "work hard," "perform well," and "improve themselves," yet not all girls are equally positioned to excel in school. They all worried about finding the time to study, as well as a place to study, as none of the girls had electricity at home; and as Felista's story indicates, some families struggled to have paraffin lamps, much less flashlights. All families struggled to some degree with the impending drought and the need for men and boys to migrate with livestock, and as households were consolidated, in some cases food insecurity disproportionately affected girls. Like Felista, some schoolgirls explicitly expressed worry about earning poor marks on the national exam and being "married off" after Class 8 or not raising the funds to attend secondary school even if their marks were good enough to be eligible. Even schoolgirls like Maria—who were subject to this range "unfreedoms" (Warrington and Kiragu 2012, 303) but also in some ways protected from them and likely would never have been pulled from school and "given out" to marriage—functioned within a context of this possibility.[16]

Nevertheless, as Maria grew up in school, in addition to English and mathematics, she also learned to navigate and manipulate the contemporary cracks in the gendered and generational veneer of Maasai social structures, in part by relying on her own sense of obligation to be a good daughter. As a schoolgirl, Maria learned the language of rights as early as Standard 1 (first grade), and she knew how to use them to negotiate her needs. She did not see "her rights" as something external to her most intimate relationships. In fact, she used her confidence born of successful schoolgirlhood to navigate her relationships with her stepmothers and her own father. Maria's own experience negotiating for herself reinforced her admonishment that Felista directly (and respectfully) approach her father with a proposition: she would trade her "good work" in school (good grades, higher than the boys) for a "present" (plastic sheeting for her mother's house). For many, if not most, of the schoolgirls we interviewed, this advice to breech conventional Maasai rules for respect would come across as nonsensical, even impossible, to realize. Yet Maria knew that the rules for being a good daughter were fundamental to being a good schoolgirl. Only enabled by the persuasive power of good grades, Maria reasoned, would Felista be in a position of relative "power" to make a direct request of her father. According to Maria, if Felista worked hard enough at home and even harder than the boys at school, she might be able to persuade her father to secure her mother's dung house with plastic sheeting. Moreover, she might be able to persuade her father that her time was well spent in school and that her schooling, rather than her "early" marriage, could bring "fruits" to her family. Ultimately, Maria's assertion that "even the government will be involved" on Felista's behalf suggests that Maria, like Aloya and Helen, understood that if the local patriarchy failed to secure a schoolgirl's rights, the state would be the only institution with enough authority to challenge a father's claims and intervene on the behalf of a daughter.

Maria's advice also reveals her internalized understanding of girl-effects logic diffusively disseminated in everyday discourse. As a primary conduit of "development," school structures the knowledge, attitudes, and affective attachments that provide girl-children with the resources (discursive and material) to meet their own needs (or at least the aspirational imagination to do so) as the structures around them do not respond to (or work in opposition to) their needs. By sheer individual will, self-sacrifice, and the intensification of her own gendered labor, ingenuity, and respectful manipulation of structural forms, the girl-child learns to think and act like a schoolgirl and, consequently, a citizen—the generalized subject of neoliberal development (DeJaeghere 2016). Employing a pointedly neoliberal version of responsibility based on self-discipline and self-sanction, Maria instructed Felista on how to negotiate patriarchal authority by merging expectations for proper daughters with successful schoolgirl practices. Maria neither suggested that Felista run away or otherwise actively defy her father's authority nor advised her to seek a collective intervention through the church or a local NGO to mitigate her and her mother's structurally created insecurity. To the contrary, Maria advised Felista in strategies of individual "self-practice" in order to be a *better daughter* and a *better student*. In so doing, Maria suggested that Felista alone could mitigate the risks of girl-childhood and the burdens daughters bear. Felista alone, Maria suggested, could ultimately create security without explicitly resisting gendered and generational norms.

To "fight fire with fire" is to counter the insecurity and uncertainty of girl-childhood with the gendered determination and hard work required for schoolgirlhood by digging deep into the wellspring of gendered obligation, respect, and duty defining daughters. Girl-effects logic presents schooling as the solution to overcoming the kinds of fears that Felista faced, yet schoolgirlhood in this frame failed to account for expectations for daughterly obedience. Maria's advice pivoted on the overlapping realities of girl-childhood and schoolgirlhood rather than any assumptions that these ways of being are fundamentally distinct or opposed. Felista seemed to want or need some other kind of advice from us, something that could help her realize her desire to stay in school without engaging her father or patriarchal authority. Maria, however, seemed to suggest that small shifts in gendered power could only come by maneuvering in-between the rules in order to create new ones.

"Grown Completely": The Girl-Child Becomes a Schoolgirl

Nashipae stood out from the other schoolgirls gathered in the primary school classroom because she was a good head taller than the rest, but more than this, she eagerly made eye contact and introduced herself without waiting to be asked. At my request, as we arranged in every school, the head teacher assembled the thirteen girls we would interview over the course of the following few days for a group meeting. The sparkle in Nashipae's eye was hard to miss as Alice and I introduced ourselves and explained the research. When invited, Nashipae and her classmates asked us questions for more than an hour, and she was a clear "leader"—confident, assertive, and eager to use her English with an American.

As Maasai would say, you could tell very quickly that Nashipae was *kitok* (big).[17] Her "bigness" was in part explained by her age; we learned that she was seventeen years old and in Class 6 (sixth grade). We also learned that her "bigness" seemed to come from the emotionally painful events of her recent history that forced her to come to terms with adult circumstances even more quickly and abruptly than many Maasai children, particularly those from homes in which schooling was prioritized and childhood was subsequently reconfigured and extended. Nashipae did not describe her experience as painful, but she did cry a little as she told her story; all three of us did. Archambault (2009, 291) writes that for Maasai, pain, through corporeal punishment, particularly in childhood, "represents future struggle" as "there is a symbolic connection between pain and adulthood." Moreover, she explains, for Maasai "pain and personhood are . . . intimately interconnected." As one female Maasai primary school teacher tells Archambault, "You cannot gain without lots of struggle. Struggle is power. If you want to be powerful, you need to struggle" (290–91). With this in mind, I submit that perhaps some of Nashipae's confidence might have come through emotional, not (necessarily) physical, "struggle."[18]

Not only did we all three react with tears to the struggles for schooling Nashipae had endured, in the space of the same interview, we also cried from laughing. She, like nearly every girl we interviewed, asserted that school was the only place to learn anything of value and that there is "nothing" to be learned at home, particularly for girls, except household chores. But she also said that at home, a girl can learn Maasai "long ago tale[s]." We asked her to tell us a tale she had learned at home; she agreed, and rendered Alice speechless with laughter over her elaborate rendition of the tale of "the girl who was collecting firewood and was met by a forest creature called Mbiti and taken [to her] home." In Naomi Kipury's (1983, 19) version of the tale, the young girl was collecting berries with her older sisters who tricked her into returning to the forest alone, where she was confronted by *nkukuuni* or *ng'wesi*—"some fearful monster or ogre"—named Mbiti, who offers the girl a choice: "Shall I eat you or make you my child?" The girl chooses to become Mbiti's daughter and goes with her to her home in the forest.[19]

According to Nashipae, the "forest creature" hid the girl in a hole in the ground. She kept her there "until she grew completely." Each day Mbiti pricked the girl's arm with a thorn to see if blood or fat came out; when her pricked skin bled oil, the creature knew she was fat enough to cook and eat. The girl left the hole in the ground and encountered a crow who told her that the creature had been holding her until she was "grown completely" so she could eat her, and that the time had come. For a piece of ugali, the crow agreed to tell her how to escape. The crow told the girl that she should disguise herself by rubbing ash all over her body so she could sneak away without being seen. Meanwhile, Mbiti called all the other creatures in the forest to a big feast.

Nashipae explained that after the girl covered herself in ash and ran away, she encountered three different groups of creatures on the path. Each different group said, "Who are you? It seems that you are not the daughter of Mbiti we [were called] to feed on. You don't look like that girl." Each time the girl replied, as the crow had instructed, "Oh no, I am not her; I am a poor girl just going [on my way]." In each case, the creatures continued on to the feast while the girl, unrecognized, made her escape by running farther away from Mbiti's compound. Meanwhile, Mbiti, realizing that she had no fattened daughter to share with the other creatures, tried to hide herself because she knew that she would be eaten instead. Her hiding place was revealed when a nursing baby ogre pointed to the only part of her not covered by dirt, Mbiti's tail. Once identified, Mbiti was eaten, and the girl escaped in her ash disguise.

Designed to "entertain as much as teach," Kipury (1983, 20) notes that in the taxonomy of folktales in Maa, the tale of Mbiti is categorized as an ogre tale in which "weird" creatures portrayed as greedy, cruel, and misguidedly intelligent interact with humans who are often tricked or haphazardly end up as victims, and the monster always dies in the end. Although it is not clear where the escaped girl was headed or where she ended up, it is clear that the relative unknown was preferable to her than her arranged fate. Nashipae herself made little commentary on the tale itself, except to laugh with Alice until they were gasping for air at the antics of the girl who outsmarted a creature who stole her, called her "daughter," fed and sheltered her, and all the while was intent on eating her. Nashipae's own story of escaping her positioning as "a girl of home" and walking away from her obligations as her father's daughter to become a "daughter of the government" was much more serious to her.

Nashipae's father had one wife and nine children—four girls and five boys.[20] Her sisters were all married; she was the only girl "left at home," while all of her brothers were in various stages of schooling, including one brother at Makerere University in Uganda.[21] Nashipae explained that her "father never wanted to educate girls, only boys," so she knew that it was a matter of time before she would "be grown" and be "married off" like her sisters. She said at home she spent her time herding her family's goats and helping her mother cook, clean, fetch water and firewood, and care for smaller children. She also worked as a "housegirl" (maid and often nanny) for another household, the earnings from which she said were "used to look after [her] whole family." She said that she "never wanted to be married" because her sister "was married by an old man and when he died she was left very young" so she "never wanted to get such problems." Echoing many schoolgirls' explanation for why girls are not taken to school, she indicated that her parents "[did] not know the importance of education and only wanted dowry."²² Nashipae said her parents "usually believe that when a girl gets education she can't go anywhere, only to Class 8 or even Form 4, get pregnant, and just go home." As a rationale for not educating girls, girls' education as a wasted investment still existed alongside the more recent consensus that girls are the best investment.

As it turns out, her father had arranged her marriage as she predicted. She was circumcised in 2003 at age fourteen and informed that her husband had been chosen. Of her father, she said, "He wanted to sell me to an old man so that I refused to go there. I came to school and talked to the headmaster about my problem, that my father was to give to me to somebody, and I didn't want that because I want to learn. The headmaster helped me, and the following day I came to school." When I asked why she thought the head teacher would help her, she explained.

> N: I knew that education was now free. I had it in mind that now if I go asking for help, these people could really help me because they would not have to spend so much money.
> H: How did you know education was free when you yourself were not educated?
> N: When Kibaki became the president, he announced that primary education is free.
> H: Okay. So when you heard that you thought, "This is my chance"?
> N: Yes.
> H: And when you came to the headmaster, what did he say?
> N: He said that he is going to help me. By that time there was another teacher who is now retired. She told me, "You are going to live at my home because [the] headmaster's home is very far from school." So I went to stay with her.

When I followed up with the headmaster, he confirmed her story and filled in some of the details that Nashipae had omitted. The morning after she was informed that she would soon be married, Nashipae left her father's homestead with the goats like she did every day as a girl of the home, but instead of herding them toward greener leaves and water, she walked with them all the way to the primary school.²³ When she reached the school and found the headmaster to explain her story, she had the herd of goats with her in the compound. He told her to take the goats and go back home so she could not also be punished for losing any of the family's herd. He told her to say nothing to anyone but to rise in the morning before dawn and come back to the school. Meanwhile, he would arrange a place for her to board, admit her immediately to the school, and work on getting her the shoes, uniforms, and school supplies she would need. According to him, she complied, and the next day she arrived at the school and has not gone back to family's home since.[24] As Nashipae explained: " [My parents] were very harsh to me [after that]."

Once her parents learned that she was living with a local teacher and attending the school, they came for her. Her father insisted that she would be "removed and give[n] to her husband." Her father's reputation and potential bridewealth were at stake, not to mention the very idea that the state could override his authority when it came to his daughter's future and, by extension, his family's future. But that is precisely what was threatened. Nashipae explained, "the headmaster said that if [my father] continue[s] to say that [he will remove me], he is going to jail. So that pressure came down." The headmaster also indicated that her family followed her and that the father was very angry. I asked about Nashipae's mother, and the head teacher said that she supported Nashipae and wanted her to go to school but "she had no otherwise" but to comply with her husband's decision. In the end, her father gave in to the "pressure" asserted by the headmaster in consultation with the local elders who gathered to discuss the matter and find a solution without actually involving the police. Nashipae's family then disowned her. As she put it: "*Sasa*, they removed me from the list of their kids. I was not among their children. They never, never followed me again as their kid to see if I need food or such things."

"Shall I Eat You or Make You My Child?": Father Fictions and Daughter Obligations

Mbiti, the ogre in the folktale Nashipae shares, presents the girl-protagonist with a false choice: be eaten immediately or live on as the ogre's "daughter." Of course, Mbiti does not tell the girl that she plans to eat her anyway and that her role and status as "daughter" serves only to mark time until she has grown big and fat enough to be eaten. To the ogre, the girl's mature body is divisible; her "fruits" are to be cultivated and shared among the community of creatures invited to feast. It is difficult to miss narrative parallels in this tale and in the basic storyline I heard repeatedly in interviews that some fathers, greedy for cows, are content to raise their daughters until they are "grown" enough to be "eaten" (a common idiom for "using" resources) through arranged marriage to the benefit of everyone, except, as the story goes, the girl. The tensions between educating girls and marrying girls generated social anxieties in which "culture" and "tradition" were reasserted as primary signifiers of immutable patriarchies and the inherent oppression of girls and women. Yet, schoolgirls were not the only ones caught "in-between" systems for securing social legitimacy and fulfilling social obligation in a changing political-economy. Archambault (2011) illuminates the challenges Maasai fathers (and by extension, parents, including mothers-as-wives) face in a world in which all children are expected to be sent to school as a strategy to mitigate crises in pastoral livelihoods, girls'-rights discourses proliferate, particularly among the educated, and yet not all parents are able to accommodate all children. Her analysis of a case in which Esther, a Kenyan Maasai girl who ran away to a rescue center on the eve of her arranged marriage, makes clear that the reductive dichotomies of perpetrator and victim, tradition and development, and patriarchal power and girls' education that structure narratives of girls' education (and particularly narrative of escape and rescue) fail to account for the intimate calculus of costs associated with schooling decisions in the context of generational and gendered hierarchies *and* intergenerational poverty. These dichotomies also fail to account for the complexity of subjectivity within this calculus.

In Esther's case, her father had educated all but eight of his twenty-six children. He explained to Archambault, "[Esther] was not a schoolgirl. . . . She was a girl of the home. . . . We tried to educate all of our children, but it depended on our cows and goats and poverty" (Archambault 2011, 633). Esther's story plays out very similarly to Nashipae's. Like Nashipae's father, Esther's father tried to bring her home and was told by the headmistress that his daughter had become a "school child." Like Nashipae's father, Esther's father's reaction was to disown his daughter by telling the headmistress, "Esther will be your child. . . . You will give her a husband, and she will never set foot in my house again. I don't count her as a child in my family" (Archambault 2011, 633). Both fathers first used Maasai means to claim their rights to make decisions for and about their daughters but eventually relinquished "ownership" of them to the state. In each case, fathers punished willful, "assertive" daughters by explicitly refusing to honor their patriarchal responsibility to arrange good marriages for them and thus officially abrogated their obligation of care. Nashipe's and Esther's state-accorded citizenship rights directly contradicted their fathers' customary rights to them and trumped their obligation as daughters to submit to their fathers' authority.[25] In each case, the refusal to "be a proper Maasai daughter" resulted in a shifting of subjectivity to "a daughter of the government" (Hodgson 1996a, 119), from one patriarchal institution to another.

Felista's and Nashipae's stories reveal the poignantly contingent nature of daughters in patriarchal social arrangements. According to Archambault (2011, 636), "there is no greater gift, as viewed by the Maasai, than having been given a daughter." "Giving out" daughters in marriage secures the girl's (young woman's) future security and happiness and is a key mechanism for "creating powerful linkages to new resources and obligations of mutual and social and economic support." As girl-children, daughters have therefore *always been* conventionally understood as a "means" to development within the pastoral system. As wives, daughters form essential links between families, links that are deepened as the women become mothers and gain social respect as they age and shepherd their own children into adulthood, all the while creating, extending, and sustaining mutual relationships that ensure Maasai modes of development, such as enlarging herds. Yet, despite the care that many parents, particularly fathers as members of local patriarchies, take in the arranging of their daughter's marriages, Maasai girls are customarily not consulted in these decisions taken, on their behalf, among (primarily male) elders. Moreover, as more girls go to school, more "girls of the home" are rejecting the ways in which they have been positioned. In arguing for schoolgirlhood as the very best way to "help" their families, schoolgirls believe that, as educated daughters, they will be even better positioned to "bring development" to their fathers' families, their future husbands' families, and to the community at large.

It is important to note that these narratives suggest a Maasai girl's rights can only be secured by exiting (either by choice or force) one patriarchal institution (home) to another (school/state). Had Nashipae refused her arranged marriage and also refused school, she and her local advocates would have had little recourse. According to the Kenyan government, Nashipae was still a child and a legal minor because she was not yet eighteen years old. According to the UN's Declaration of Human Rights (1948), the Convention on the Rights of the Child (1989), and the Children's Act in Kenya (2001), her status as a child gave her the right to education and the right not to be forced into marriage. According to schoolgirls, "those at home . . . cannot teach you the rights of a girl-child because they don't know"; knowledge of rights, they argued, can only come from school. Nonetheless, even though Nashipae was designated a "girl of the home," she knew "her rights" and how to secure them. Perhaps through development rhetoric disseminated by civil-society networks throughout the county, or through her church, or maybe from age-mates who were in school, she knew that changes ushered by the Kibaki administration had lowered the opportunity costs of rejecting her role as a girl of the home. She explained that the free primary education policy (four years old at the time of our conversation) meant that those from whom she sought support would "not have to spend so much money" to secure her place in school. This specific knowledge emboldened her decision to run away to the school. Because Nashipae was a girl of the home, her decision to run away represented a shameful decision by a delinquent daughter. Yet by pursuing school at all costs, Nashiape believed that she would be a *better* daughter. She explained with a shaky voice that she risked so much to run away from home to school "because I know one day, one time I will become a very big person. I will come to change our family one day. I will change also my life and our culture."

Similarly, according to Maria's logic, Felista could invoke her rights to refuse an arranged marriage as a girl of the school, but to do so she needed to show her father good grades and, moreover, she needed to "work hard to beat the boys' scores." Good performance in primary would make possible the letter of acceptance to secondary school Maria was sure Felista's father "[could] not refuse." Without evidence of success in school, many, if not most, local community members would have seen an arranged marriage for Felista as a credible option for securing her future. As the head teacher who helped his student Helen escape her arranged marriage explained to me, once Helen "prove she love[d] school," and "her marks . . . improved," "everyone," including her father, was "happy." In Esther's case, after several years, "and because [she had] been successful in her studies," her father eventually "recongniz[ed] and appreciate[ed] her as a 'girl of school'" and accepted her back into the family (Archambault 2011, 633). As Esther's father explained, "Had I known she would have been this good of a student, I would have chosen her all along" (636). Although I do not know if Nashipae has been accepted back into her father's good graces, it is plausible that if she continued to do well in school, her success as a schoolgirl could override his anger and disappointment that she ran away, particularly given her plan to "change" her family for the better despite being disowned.

Nashipae understood that as a girl of the home, she had no voice in decisions taken by fathers about daughters. Her only recourse, as she saw it, was to run away. Her self-made path toward schoolgirlhood was enabled, as she explained, by protections enshrined and enacted at the level of the state and within the global consensus ascribed to multilateral conventions. In order to fight fire with fire, she was forced to flip the dutiful daughter script on its head. As a wayward, even "wicked" daughter (Hodgson and McCurdy 2001) who (like Aloya and Esther) challenged her father's authority to decide her future in favor of the authority of the state to secure it, Nashipae used the promise of schoolgirlhood to reconfigure her duty to her family as a daughter. In order to maintain authority, patriarchies are often forced to adapt to changing conditions, and in the process, the extensive edges of patriarchal power can be eroded (Hodgson 1996a). Yet, the girl of the school, the schoolgirl, the daughter of the government, the educated daughter is, not unlike the girl-child at home, also a "means" to development contingent on the decisions and desires of overlapping patriarchal structures. Schoolgirls nonetheless believe that schooling gives them the best possible chance to change their communities (and their "culture") by expanding the spaces for daughters to inhabit, embody, and enact "old" cultural norms in "new" ways.

Conclusion

While support for girls' education has broadened as it has deepened, it is not entirely clear that communities are (or necessarily could be) prepared for concomitant changes in gendered social categories, roles, rights, and responsibilities that often, to varying degrees and effects, accompany changes in institutional access based on sex.[26] Given the imbrications of gender and generation in Maasai communities as in other African contexts, contemporary gender troubles are also inflected by concerns over shifting generational power.[27] Gender and generational dramas of girls' education are one of the primary venues through which the collision of "desire" for development's promise and the actual "decline" not only in economic prospects and possibilities but also in certain kinds of social power, are enacted (Mojola 2014; Stambach 2000; Vavrus 2003). Archambault (2011) argues Maasai fathers love their daughters, want the best for them, and that they, along with their wives, make difficult decisions regarding daughters' well-being as they struggle to succeed as (uneducated) pastoralists in the face of pastoral crises. Yet the ubiquitous narrative of girl effects, at global and local scales alike, relies on the drama in which the victimized girl-child must be rescued from her oppressive father by the modernizing influence of state-sponsored schooling. I suggest that daughters also love their fathers and want to do well by them, despite and within cultural arrangements for father-daughter relations. As a male senior teacher and local elder observed, "Girls learn to be women in school, but they are still girl-children at home." As schoolgirlhood becomes increasingly normalized, schoolgirls struggle to reconcile the tensions between their own and others' expectations for them as dutiful daughters, their fear and rejection of being positioned against their will as "girls of the home," and their ardent desire to be(come)—and remain—schoolgirls.

By choosing to become a schoolgirl, Nashipae deferred the "guarantee" that for Maasai children, "status and power will be bestowed upon them unconditionally with age" (Archambault 2009, 297). Nashipae seemed to know all too well that these status and power upgrades are uneven and incontrovertibly gendered; she opted instead to leverage this "guarantee" against the promises of a different set of "guarantees" made by the logic of girl effects. Once deemed "fully grown" and ready for marriage, she ran away from her home wherein she worked for her family and others as a dutiful daughter, re-dressed herself in a schoolgirl's uniform, and boldly interrupted expectations for a girl of the home and the social obligations and relations (particularly between men) that inhere in this subject-position. Instead of believing she "[had] no otherwise" and complying, she rejected her father's authority and followed her own desires at great risk to herself and her family's reputation. As a Maasai daughter, Nashipae must have known that this break could be permanent and that she would be disowned (and perhaps cursed, although she did not use that word in her narrative to me). In a real sense, when she walked away from her natal home and the social, political, and economic relational obligations between elder men that her marriage arrangement represented, Nashipae was forced to take up a new subjectivity as a person abruptly outside of the system of embedded kinship and male age-set reciprocities that structured her life as her parents' daughter. Disowned and disavowed as a "daughter of the government," she risked as much as she gained when she reinscribed herself as a "girl of school" rather than a "girl of the home."

Although Felista was already a schoolgirl when we met her, she did not portray the same fierce focus and confident conjecture as Nashipae. Bracketing off recourse to differences of temperament, I suggest that Felista's reticence to act boldly with respect to schooling was less an effect of her personality and more an effect of her positioning. As a schoolgirl, Felista could be understood as always and already rescued. Within the global and local discursive economy of girl-effects logic, simply being enrolled in and attending school—being a schoolgirl—marked Felista as already empowered. However, Felista spoke and behaved as a dutiful daughter, unsure of how to negotiate her own needs and desires (and to protect her mother's health and well-being in the process) from a position of disempowerment and real fear that she would lose her tenuous attachment to the protections accorded only to girls who go to school. Maria's seasoned schoolgirl advice that Felista take the matters of her life into her own hands and use her capacity as a dutiful daughter to secure her schoolgirlhood did not seem to register as a possibility to Felista. Although Maria was resolute, and her way of speaking (and being, as a secondary school graduate, employee of an American researcher, and university applicant) offered little room for refusal, Felista's silent response further indicated the precarious position of the schoolgirl when her empowerment (and her rescue) is directly tied to her capacity to self-invent her own reality through "hard work." Unlike Maria or Nashipae, at least at the time of our interview, although supposedly secure inside the institution of education, Felista's fear of her father's authority and her deeply felt sense of obligation as a daughter confounded any empowerment her schoolgirl status purportedly afforded her. Her silence seemed to ask: If she could not speak directly to her father on her own behalf, how could her good grades "speak for her?" A fundamental assumption of fighting fire with fire, in Felista's case, was the possibility of rejecting her father (and therefore her family) to run away and become a better "daughter of the government."

According to girls' education discourse articulated and circulated by transnational development actors at global and local scales, there are two possible subjectivities available to girls living in poverty in the Global South: the vulnerable "girl-child" who is the essentialized and eternal victim of local patriarchy whose designation as "a girl of the home" stalls development, and the self-fashioning, empowered "schoolgirl" who accelerates and multiplies development. As a schoolgirl, her inherent vulnerability as child who is a girl is the condition for her empowerment; her integration into the school as an institution that creates "modern" and "developed" persons ignites her innate girlpower. The symbolic economy in circulation regarding the efficacy of girl's education in conjunction with the actual economy of material poverty and political marginality creates a contradictory nexus for schoolgirls. It provides the means for their reinvention even as it captures them within new categories of control (Hodgson 2001b). Schoolgirlhood explicitly enfolds Maasai girls into the state as citizens with rights. State-afforded recognition gives schoolgirls access to "power" and knowledge that is largely unavailable (at least directly) to girls who don't go to school but proceed expediently to marriage. At the same time, as state-afforded recognition extends certain protections, it also increases new kinds of scrutiny and deepens certain kinds of expectations. The schooled girl will still marry, and her marriage will still be based on deeply embedded relations of blood, friendship, resources, and responsibility. Further, educated daughters' duties extend far beyond obedience to arranged marriage and the benefits of reciprocity for the families she brings together in her role as a wife (and mother); schooled girls are held locally and globally responsible for meeting development goals. Everyone—her father's family, her husband's family, her children, her immediate community, her government, and the world—expects her, as a beneficiary of "education for all," to be an instrument of "economic growth for all."

Felista's and Nashipae's stories (as well as Aloya's and Esther's) suggest that social categories are both delimited *and* dynamic. That schoolgirls are able to find (and create) room to maneuver among shifting subjectivities suggests that their navigational skills have emerged dialectically (DeJaeghere 2016) as a function of their social situatedness. Schoolgirls must construct meanings about themselves and for themselves within dynamic relational networks that are often conflicting, sometimes competing, and over which they have no actual control. A consequence schoolgirls faced in having to position themselves within discourses and embodiments that are internally contradictory and have conflicting expectations was their real fear that they would fail to learn how to use their vulnerability to mitigate their own precarious situations. Nonetheless, the way they saw and articulated themselves disrupted and countered conventional wisdom about them as daughters *and* schoolgirls. The resignification of girlhood as "schoolgirlhood" reduced the cost of their aspirations as daughters by carving out new gendered norms for growing up female. Nashipae, Felista, and their peers reflected and modified girl-effects logic as they studied by paraffin lamp in the dark, smoky chambers of their enkagjii, sang in choral competitions, worried about their mothers and younger siblings, ran away from home, ran to school before dawn to study at daybreak, and daily speculated about how they might meet their own needs. Schoolgirls worked hard to find within themselves the capacity to create and inhabit contingent subject-positions in order to maneuver among contradictory expectations for humble and complete obedience and innovative diligence to be(come) different kinds of girls. In this way, local practice embodies and resists the subject-positions made available in this context.

CHAPTER 4

"We are not enkanyakuai. . . . We are just girls."

Embodying Schoolgirlhood

> The history of a girl is only a history of one who has agreed to a husband.
> —M. Kititi, *Iseuri*, senior elder (quoted in Pratt 2003)

Girl-effects discourse relies on paradoxical representations of female adolescence "in the developing world" as a life stage that is universally disempowering and universally replete with the potential for empowerment catalyzed by investment. Enter the universalized figure of "the 12-year-old girl" (Mensch, Bruce, and Greene 1998, 93). According to the World Bank–funded report *Uncharted Passage: Girls' Adolescence in the Developing World* (Mensch, Bruce, and Greene 1998), this girl is

> one of the potentially most influential figures in the developing world. . . . There are now 50 million of these girls and there will continue to be at least that many every year for the next three decades. . . . In the next few years, this 12-year-old girl will either abandon or continue her schooling, be pushed into marriage and childbearing or develop a sense of proud ownership of her physical self and make independent decisions about her lifetime partner. She will either struggle in poverty or find a socially productive livelihood, submit to a faceless life or thrive as an individual, making her contribution to the world. As her future is reconfigured, so is ours. (93).

Intended to influence development policy, this discourse re-signifies and re-packages the generalized "girl-child" as an "adolescent girl" by specifying her age. Because she is twelve years old, she is positioned by puberty and sexual maturation at a "crossroads" of promise or peril (Switzer 2013). From here, she only has two possible linear and predictable paths toward adulthood that decisively diverge as either positive or pathological. When she "abandon[s] her schooling," she is then "pushed into marriage and childbearing" in which she "will struggle in poverty" and "submit to a faceless life." Caught in this vicious cycle, she cannot make "her contribution to the world." In fact, her existence (and that of her "faceless" children) further burden "the world" rather than better it. However, when she "continue[s] her schooling," she enters a virtuous cycle in which she will "develop a proud sense of ownership of her physical self and make independent decisions about her lifetime partner," "find a socially productive livelihood," "thrive as an individual," and become a legitimate "contribut[ing]" member of "the world." In this persuasive frame, educated adolescent girls move swiftly and definitively from dependence to independence, from being victims of restrictive social norms and abject poverty to being socially autonomous, individualized citizens productively ensconced in "lifetime" partnerships.

During an interview, a head teacher articulated similar local assumptions regarding gendered agency invested in different kinds of girls and different kinds of girlhoods pivoting on participation in school:

> There is big gap between the learned and the unlearned. Some parents seem to hate educated girls because of their attitudes. The old men tend to hate them. Because of the guidance girls are getting in school, they become really tough. . . . [The girl at home] looks after livestock. She doesn't refuse sex. She doesn't refuse anything. But we [in school] are creating a big rift between the educated girl-child and the community. Once she knows her rights, she is tough. She will refuse.

Yet as the cases in the previous chapter suggest, sometimes the girl of the home "knows her rights" and does "refuse" absolute submission to the claims local patriarchies, including sometimes their own fathers, make on their bodies, time, attention, and labor. And sometimes "the educated girl-child" does not feel "tough" enough to challenge, much less "refuse," gendered expectations for dutiful, compliant daughters. Cultural contestations concerning shifting rules for normative girlhoods are constituted and reproduced within an array of historical relationships and practices; girlhood is always socially constructed and mediated. Nonetheless, schoolgirls are not themselves social constructs. Their bodies matter. So do the meanings their developing bodies make in the social worlds they inhabit. As the head teacher's comment suggests and girl-effects discourse rightly asserts, as girls' bodies mature sexually, attention to their embodied potential intensifies.

According to the logic of girl effects, educational participation alchemically transforms the universally contradictory formative conditions of female adolescence—"physical sexuality" and "nonadult vulnerability"—into female empowerment through bodily autonomy (Birdsall 2009, xiii). An educated adolescent girl has a "proud sense of ownership of her physical self," therefore she can "thrive as an individual." This sense of individuated self-autonomy enables her to regulate and manage her body and therefore direct her own life trajectory, thereby bypassing her father, or any "old men," or other "cultural" institutions. Local discourse reflects these assumptions and so scripts schoolgirls as different kinds of girls. As the head teacher asserted, the "educated girl-child," empowered by school knowledge, is "tough" enough to "refuse" rather than submit. Nashipae was an *uneducated* "girl-child" when she refused to submit to patriarchal authority and decided instead to take (and make) her own chances by running away from her father toward the school. Her refusal calls into question this head teacher's observation. At the same time, Nashipae also knew that running to the school was the only way to refuse, which suggests that the very possibility of school offers at least some girls the aspirational, if not the actual, resources to assert themselves.

However, "depoliticized notions of agency and girl power" distort or occlude the fact that schoolgirls are "still bound by the body and sexual difference" (Gonick et al. 2009, 2). As Maasai daughters, schoolgirls' bodies are understood within patriarchal relational networks of affection, care, control, respect, reciprocity, blood, and desire. The reductive binaries of vicious and virtuous cycles fail to account for the intricate cultural politics of gender, sexuality, and generation in the context of the development imperative to educate girls. As we have seen, Maasai schoolgirlhood is a negotiated process full of twists and turns rather than a clear linear progression from girl-child to schoolgirl, from disempowered to empowered, and from victim to victor. Schoolgirlhood is often unevenly experienced as "empowering" and is deeply contingent on girls' situatedness in families, communities and discursive economies of meaning (at all scales), that are continually in flux as sociocultural and political-economic material circumstances change around them and remain largely out of their control. Despite the claims that girls who go to school are effectively and efficiently removed from local structures that define persons and regulate their proper behaviors, schools, and the meaning attached to educational participation, are embedded in local social worlds. The schoolgirls we talked with, therefore, constantly negotiated conflicted and conflicting expectations for female adolescence as a relationally contingent and intimately mediated biosocial process.

In this chapter, I focus on the paradoxes and the possibilities of schoolgirl subjectivity by considering schoolgirlhood as an embodied experience. Educational participation requires new pathways to social maturation, recognition, and accomplishment for girls who go to school. Schoolgirlhood reorganizes and reorients female childhood by sociologically extending girlhood well beyond the onset of puberty and physical sexual maturity and therefore disrupts and reconfigures the archetypal schema for the social production of Maasai female subjectivity. What, then, of the "old" pathways and "old" forms of female personhood? Schoolgirls (and their adolescent bodies) remain intensely embedded in relational structures of interdependency; they sleep, eat, work, worship, and relax with sisters, aunts, cousins, and friends who have similar bodies but have been removed from the category of "adolescent" and married into the categories of "wife" and "mother." Against a still salient cultural ethos in which "the history of a girl is only a history of one who has agreed to a husband" (Pratt 2003), where and when does the schoolgirl, as a relatively "new" kind of person, fit into the cultural female life-course narrative? What are the implications of schoolgirlhood as a culturally salient, if also contingent, way of marking—and making—adolescence as a protracted sociological space for Maasai girls who go to school? As schoolgirls' bodies "develop" and change, how are their bodies seen and socially positioned amid conflicted and conflicting messages about their embodied potential in the service of development?

To explore these questions, I examine the tangle of ideologies at work in the formation and experience of schoolgirlhood through the lens of contradictory accounts of *emuratare oo ntoyie*, girls' circumcision, and the gendered category of *enkanyakuai*. Over the balance of the chapter, I hope to show how social anxieties concerning young female sexuality, implicated in a protracted female adolescence as a new cultural space for the accumulation of knowledge and experience, positions schoolgirlhood as both a break with "old" forms of being and becoming respected social adults and a process for enfolding schoolgirls back into relations of care and control.

Female Adolescence in the Long Shadow of Girls' Circumcision

As noted in chapter 1, before the general decline of male age-set institutions associated with protracted warriorhood, Maasai girlhood was characterized by relative freedom, particularly with respect to *esoto* (dancing) as sexual play with warriors (as boyfriends/lovers) in the *emanyata* (warrior settlement) (Pratt 2003; Talle 1988, 2007). Emurata ended *entitoisho* (girlhood) at late puberty (often, but not always, before the onset of menses) and ushered forth a series of stages, each with its own name and subsequent identity, roles, and expectations that successively legitimized social maturity.[1] Publically and collectively marked by certain clothing, adornment, and shaved heads, a group of girls of relative bodily growth/readiness/age moved through these stages collectively over the course of several weeks to several months.[2] This process rapidly transformed girls' actual bodies as well as their social identities. As initiated people, they exited childhood and became proto-adults endowed with the right to procreative sexual relations within marriage arranged by their parents in collaboration with local patriarchies. For each girl, this process culminated in her physical movement from her father's home to her husband's home as an *esiankiki narikitoni*, "the bride which is being led away," and her ascension to full adulthood as a wife (Mol 1995, 246–47).[3] Ideally, her place as an adult in her husband's homestead was quickly confirmed by motherhood, as the birth of her first child cemented her belonging as a wife in the community of fully realized adults.[4] Before the pressure (and possibility) for all girls to go to school, these stages were communally recognized and celebrated.

In the conventional Maasai schema briefly outlined here, the culturally designated period in which girls physically, emotionally, intellectually, and socially grew up before becoming wives, and all that this shift entails, occurred over the course of weeks or months. Within the conventional schema, in other words, there is no space "in-between" uncircumcised girlhood and wifehood for the accumulation of knowledge and experience. Circumcision definitively ended "growing up" for girls. Sarah, a mother in Loodariak, explained this cultural ideal for the rapid progression toward social and bodily maturity for female people in this way:

> For Maasai, before you are circumcised you are a girl, a baby, and child. You are not supposed to look or act like a woman, a married person. The Maasai used to circumcise girls and then her head was shaved and she graduated from being a girl to being a woman. She is then at another level. She can now believe "I am a grown-up. I am a woman. I can do what other women do." As a grown-up you can be married, you can have sex, all that.

In previous generations, bodily readiness signaled the need for emurata, and the successful completion of emurata signaled bodily sexual maturity and social readiness for marriage. This "graduation" to "another level," from childhood to adulthood, was a collective process for all girls. Although individual girls have no doubt experienced this shift in social subjectivity and embodiment differently, emurata and arranged marriage, as cultural processes, have had relatively stable and coherent collective meanings. Historically there were simply very few other ways for a female person to be(come) a socially recognized adult (Hodgson 2001b).[5]

The schoolgirls we spoke with, all of whom were born in the late 1980s through the late 1990s, had grown up in a "different world" than the one outlined above. None spoke of "initiates" or the ceremonial shaving of girls' heads or the wearing of special black shukas and symbolic ornamentation.[6] The forms of personhood instantiated by the graduated stages outlined above were less visible, unarticulated, and largely not experienced by the schoolgirls we talked with. What does remain of these conventional life-stage markers, however, is girls' initiation, which involves, among other ceremonial processes, genital surgery. While rates of female genital cutting (FGC) in Kenya as a whole are dropping (KNBS/ICFM 2015)[7] as the result of government, civil society, and individual activism to eradicate the practice on the grounds that it that violates girls' human rights, endangers their health, and ends their education,[8] emurata for girls is still very much the norm for the communities scattered around Keekonyokie Central Location, whether they are in school or not.[9]

While Maasai girls' developing bodies have conventionally triggered social rearrangements, contemporary political-economic and sociocultural changes in Maasai life, including the increased pressure for girl's education, have contributed to changes in the institutional practice of emurata for girls. For instance, parents often elect to circumcise their daughters earlier than in the past (as young as age eleven instead of thirteen through sixteen), particularly those girls chosen for school.[10] This decision was and continues to be taken for a few reasons. Some said parents would circumcise a young girl so that by the time she grew physically "big" enough for authorities to pay attention to her as an "adolescent," any intervention to prevent her circumcision would be too late. Others indicated that because schoolgirls are usually not betrothed to a future husband, her parents shoulder the burden of financing the ceremony (instead of her would-be husband in the traditional system). In order to save money, for instance, an eleven-year-old girl would join her fourteen-year-old sister, and her parents would have two circumcised daughters for the price of one.

Relatedly, to save time and stay in step with the academic calendar, emurata for boys and girls tends to happen expeditiously in December so those in school can use the holiday to heal and return to school on time. Moreover, for both boys and girls, while any celebrations happen at home, the procedure itself increasingly occurs at a clinic (despite the fact that genital cutting for any female under age eighteen is illegal in Kenya) rather than in the compound.[11] Everyone also noted that it is still a very strong taboo for a girl to become pregnant before circumcision, so some families elect to circumcise their daughters "early" (prior to signs of "bigness," including the onset of menses) so that if they were to become sexually active (some parents believed going to school increased the possibility of sexual relationships), they would already be circumcised and could avoid stigma, and even exile.

On one hand, these changes in practice from collective celebration to more individualized family and extended-household decisions seemed to confirm that Maasai parents continue to consider girls' circumcision culturally important despite the expense, local Maasai civil-society activism against the practice, and possible state legal sanction. Families invested in the meanings ascribed to girls' circumcision adapted to changing times in order to continue the practice even for their school-going daughters. For those daughters who are not chosen for school, trust in emurata and arranged marriage as the best mechanisms for producing mature female persons remains strongly normative. Girls who are not sent to school cannot consider refusing emurata, and they have little to no recourse for becoming something other than a wife after emurata.

On the other hand, the ad hoc approaches to girls' circumcision seem also to reflect a growing lack of collective coherence concerning the practice, particularly given the pressure on uneducated parents to educate girls, along with changing practices among educated Maasai. For instance, Maasai teachers (men and women) did not plan to circumcise their daughters, although they also expected resistance to this decision among their own families.[12] Mothers expressed ambivalence about the practice, often indicating that emuratare oo ntoyie is something Maasai have always done, explaining, "we found it here." Some mothers questioned and even dismissed girls' circumcision as a cultural requirement. Many imagined that their granddaughters (of their educated and uneducated children) would not be circumcised at all.

"[If I am not circumcised] I will lack nothing that those who are circumcised will get."

Schoolgirls expressed contradictory ideas about girls' circumcision because they received contradictory messages about what circumcision means for girls in the context of school. Janice explained that a Maasai girl becomes a woman "when she is married."[13] And by that logic, because she was not married and is in school (she was thirteen years old and in Class 4), she considered herself a girl. She went on to explain that she was not circumcised but planned to be in December (our interview was in early November) over the school holiday, along with three other girls who lived near her. She looked forward to her circumcision, because, she said, "I want to join that group" and later added, "I don't want to be alone." She looked forward to being "given a lot of oil" to eat so she could "grow huge."[14] She noted her parents would be happy because she would be "grown-up." She expected that her experience would be different in January when she returned to school after emurata because she would "earn a lot of respect and [some people] would head her" in greeting. She imagined that teachers would also respect her, although she did not think their behaviors toward her would change. She did anticipate that along with the positive experiences of increased social respect that she would also encounter "problems" from being seen as "a grown-up": "I will receive a lot of disturbance from boys . . . who try to impregnate [circumcised girls]." She was worried about this pressure from "boys," but her plan was to "avoid them as much as possible" and not to "play [as in sexual play] with them."

While some schoolgirls like Janice looked forward to emurata as a way to gain entrance "in that group" because "children" would be required to publically acknowledge her "graduation" to a new "stage," most schoolgirls insisted that emurata did not change their social experience because schoolgirlhood indefinitely defers adult status and (re)confirms schoolgirls as children. As Resiato, a sixteen-year-old Class 6 student, explained, "There is no difference between a circumcised girl and one who is not circumcised." Eunice, a fifteen-year-old in Class 8 likewise asserted that "circumcision has no meaning. Nothing will tell someone that she is a woman. She is still just heading people [in greeting]." Eunice's sister, Nayian, also in Class 8 and fifteen years old, concurred: "To me [emurata] has no meaning. We are just the same as a girl who is not circumcised. We are still greeting with our heads." Peris, who was not circumcised when we met, was the only schoolgirl who claimed she would refuse emurata by running away because emurata meant marriage, and she preferred school. She insisted, "there is no difference between me and those who are circumcised. . . . [If I am not circumcised] I will lack nothing that those who are circumcised will get." The expression *emurata* itself does not indicate modifications to the physical body but rather signifies a changed person—indeed, a transformed person—who moves from childishness to maturity, an achievement deserving of community respect.[15] Resiato explained that emurata is important for Maasai parents because "they say when a girl is circumcised, she will move from one stage to another, she will earn more respect. That is, when a girl is circumcised she will speak before people."

Yet, relative to "those girls at home" who, after emurata, had no choice but be(come) adults via arranged marriage, and relative to newly circumcised boys who are sanctioned to behave "as men," schoolgirls were neither recognized as adults nor permitted to behave as "women," although they had "graduated" to the next stage. Schoolgirls consistently cited ceremonial greetings as evidence that emurata had "no meaning" and "no importance" in their lives because it did not "change" how they were "seen." As Nayian, explained:

> I think a boy is respected more because when a boy is circumcised, he has changed. When a boy is circumcised he will be a man. . . . He will be just like his father and involved with discussion of men. He will never greet again with his head as he did as a child. He is respected more than a girl. Not girls. Girls are not like boys. [Parents] don't see girls as anyone who can develop the family.

Mariam, a fourteen-year-old student in Class 7 who was initiated when she was twelve, pointed out that "boys like to be called men when they are circumcised." It is not hard to see why. As Nayian explained, when "boys" claimed to be "men," even while they were in school, this association enhanced their relational gendered and generational affiliations; to be recognized as "men" was seen as being in sync with social expectations for circumcised male people born out symbolically in the public respect vividly displayed in traditional greetings.

However, this social legibility and normative shift in subjectivity conventionally attached to passing through emurata creates a paradox for schoolgirls. Rather than ending girlhood and marking a clear exit from childhood and entry into adulthood, as emurata effectively does for girls of the home and all boys, schoolgirls return to school as children. Schoolgirlhood extends childhood for girls as a mechanism for protecting them from arranged marriage, but it also interrupts ascription of social respect attached to emurata. Schoolgirls very much wanted to be "seen" as mature people "who can develop the family," rather than children who are loved but are not necessarily "respected" as capable of participation in "adult" matters. They wanted, in other words, to experience a new sense of social respect attached to emurata, but they rarely did. However, as Janice's comments about unwanted male attention after emurata suggest, they did experience the social effects of changes in their bodies through the overlapping biosocial processes of emurata and adolescence that socially marked them as "grown," sexually mature, and therefore sexually available. Paradoxically, any identification with adult behavior associated with "women" was for schoolgirls immediately sexualized. Mariam explained that after emurata, "girls do not like to be called women. We don't like that name. . . . I don't feel well with that name. . . . I don't want to be called a woman because my mother is also called a woman. Both [of us] cannot be a woman in the same house." Identifying as a "woman" did not ascribe social respect, authority, or legitimacy implicated in the capacity to "speak before others" and "develop the family." Instead, to identify as a "woman" signaled readiness for marriage, the end of schooling, and promised what schoolgirls saw as their disempowerment as (uneducated) wives.

For schoolgirls, the respect and relative social authority said to come with circumcision then marriage, in the absence of education, came at the cost of being in control of one's embodied potential. Nayian noted: "[If she is circumcised and not in school] she is a woman because she is then married; she has moved from her father's home to another homestead; she has her own husband so that she may give birth at any time; she is a wife so she is controlled by her husband and not herself." Schoolgirls refused the idea that they should, could, or would be subject to marriage before they completed their education. For example, Nayian asserted, "[I will] become a woman *only* after I finish my studies," which she imagined happening when she was "36? or 30? or 28." Her marriage, she insisted, would be according to her own timetable and with a man she chose for herself. As a kind of gendered education in the art of living, successful schoolgirls learned to defer their desire to be seen as capable of "develop[ing] the family" to a future self, transformed by educational participation, rather than emurata, as the achievement deserving of community respect. This paradox underscores schoolgirls' contradictory insistence that emurata is meaningless and necessary.

Metian, thirteen years old in Class 6, attended Enkeryian Primary School along with her sisters Eunice and Nayian. Their father has two wives; none of the adults in her household had been educated, but all of the children who were old enough to be in school (seven of eight) were in school. Metian joined the chorus of schoolgirls who insisted that emurata was "of no importance," yet her comments also poignantly underscore the necessity of emurata and the impossibility of refusal when relational belonging is at risk.

> H: So in Maasai culture circumcision is very important but not to you?
> M: Yes.
> H: Why is that?
> M: Because in the Bible, there is a verse that says girls are not to be circumcised, it is only the boys.
> H: Okay, if the Bible prohibits this for girls, why don't you refuse?
> M: Because that is the rule of the Maasai, *so even me I want to be a Maasai.*
> H: You want to be a Maasai?
> M: Yes.
> H: So you don't refuse?
> M: *I can't refuse.*
> H: Why are your parents happy to see you circumcised?
> M: *Because even they are circumcised.*

H: Okay, do you know anyone who is not circumcised, any girl or woman who is not circumcised? Have you ever heard of any girl who refused?

M: In the Bible or on the earth?

H: On the earth.

M: No.

H: No one has refused?

M: In the Maasai?

H: Yes.

M: No. No one.[16]

Metian, like her sisters and every schoolgirl I met, given the choice, likely would not have chosen to undergo the physical surgery involved in girls' initiation because she felt emurata was "meaningless," yet as her comments here suggest, it actually brings significant meaning to bear on how they are seen, understood, and regarded (and how they see, understand, and situate themselves with the larger community). She articulated an existential link between being "being circumcised" and Maasai-ness. As she notes, "even [her parents] are circumcised." Despite her concern that emurata for girls contradicts "the Bible," and despite her everyday experience with emurata's contradictory effects, she expressed tacit consent "because that is the rule of the Maasai" and she "want[s] to be a Maasai." Kenneth, a deputy head teacher, explained community belonging as a relational process that affectively binds people and is integral to "identity":

> [Schoolchildren] want to identify with the community and to be part and parcel with them. Identity is a serious issue. For girls the example is FGM [female genital mutilation]. If they don't do FGM they will be outcasts and not part of the community. Despite the education about it, it comes down to girls thinking: "If I don't do it, I don't belong here, and if I don't belong here, where do I belong?" They say if they don't participate, "no one will talk to us. We have to stay and play with children. We can't handle that. Let's go for this thing and then it's over." So they go for it.

Schoolgirls very much "want[ed] to identify with the community and to be part and parcel with them." They explained that to refuse emurata was to risk too much. One schoolgirl confided, "You will be told many things, like you will feel ashamed if you are the only one who is not circumcised. Others may laugh at you and you may lack a friend." Another schoolgirl echoed Kenneth's comment that schoolgirls want to distinguish themselves from children: "If you are not circumcised you will stay with children and play the games of children." Hope, the head girl for her class, made a reference to the strong curse aimed at girls who get pregnant before circumcision: "According to Maasai if you give birth and you are not circumcised you are not called a woman, you called *entaapi*. You cannot pass through the gate. You are made to pass though the thorn fence followed by a black bull. You don't then belong to them and they hate you completely." And while none of the schoolgirls we talked with told us a story like this (which is not to say that stories like this did not exist among the group of schoolgirls we talked to), Elizabeth explained that "some men are very harsh on their daughters. So even if a girl says no she can be forced. Her hands are tied with string so she can't refuse." Schoolgirls' presumptive agency to "refuse" relational claims on their developing bodies was eroded by the significant threat to their community identity that refusal presented, not to mention the impossibility of going against their parents' wishes. Parents were likewise deeply subject to gendered and generational hierarchies of patriarchal control and care regarding the proper management of schoolgirl bodies. "Despite education about it," and despite their own ambivalent relationship with the practice, refusing emurata felt impossible for most schoolgirls. They wanted to remain "Maasai," even when it meant following cultural dictates they did not necessarily agree with and they did not believe conferred the kind of respect they wanted.

Emurata physically marks schoolgirls' bodies, but it also marks their social bodies. Consequently, the paradoxical condition of emurata for girls who go to school belies bodily autonomy as a simple fact of schoolgirlhood. The experience of emurata traverses bodies; however, schoolgirlhood institutionalizes female adolescence. Schoolgirls are consequently removed from the collective body of "the circumcised" despite the fact that they shared a broadly common historical experience of emuratare oo ntoyie. As I discuss in the next section, collective anxieties around the concept of *enkanyakuai*, a female social category, suggest how schoolgirls' paradoxical social recognition required them to negotiate conflicting messages structured by the rights, roles, and responsibilities conversely conferred by both emurata and schooling.

Misrecognition and Refusal in Conflicting Accounts of Enkanyakuai

I first learned about enkanyakuai (pl. *inkanyakua*) as a Maasai social category and cultural identity reserved exclusively for female people in interviews with schoolgirls. They explained it is the "name" given to a girl who is circumcised, lives at home with her parents, and is not married. For instance, Josephine, a sixteen-year-old student in Class 5 explained, "[After circumcision] at home you will be a woman and to those girls who are not in school, they say you are a woman and married soon, but for schoolgirls, before you are married you are called enkanyakuai." Janice, the schoolgirl who looked forward to circumcision over the December holiday, saw enkanyakuai as a relatively positive "name." She looked forward to being enkanyakuai "because the rest are circumcised and being called that name" and, as noted, she wanted "to join that group." From comments like Josephine's, Janice's, and those of others, I initially understood the term to describe and define the liminal period between a girl's circumcision before marriage when she remains in her father's home and under her parents' authority and care. Often when schoolgirls referred to themselves as enkanyakuai, they used the category as a way of explaining that they were "in-between" *entito* (absolute girlhood) and clearly defined *enkitok* (womanhood/wifehood) because they were circumcised but headed back to school rather than headed toward marriage. Nashipae's comments offer an example of this usage:

> H: They say according to Maasai when a girl is circumcised, she becomes a woman. When does a girl become a woman according to you?
> E: When she gets her own family.
> H: So what do you consider yourself now?
> E: [*laughing*] . . . I am just there in-between. Not a girl, not a woman.
> H: Do you mean *enkanyakuai*?
> E: [*giggling, blushing*]: Yes.

Nashipae agreed to the term *enkanyakuai* when it was applied to her, but she blushed and giggled with embarrassment at the idea. I did not ask her to elaborate on her somewhat hesitant agreement because at that point in the research when the category of enkanyakuai came up in interviews with schoolgirls, it was mentioned in rather neutral terms.

Rose, fifteen years old in Class 5, concurred that enkanyakuai is "neither a girl or a woman" because "if she were a girl she would not be circumcised," and because she is not yet a wife, she is not fully a woman, "enkitok." I noted that Rose had been circumcised, was not married, and lived at home, so I guessed she must be called enkanyakuai. She laughed out loud at this suggestion and explained, still laughing,

> I'm just a schoolgirl. . . . [the difference is] we are called schoolgirls and not enkanyakuai. The ones we were circumcised with, they are called enkanyakuai because they are not in school and have not been married. . . . Maybe your father or mother hates you when you are called enkanyakuai because you have no owner. Schoolgirls are supposed to be called schoolgirls because they are in school. They have been given time to read [study] and continue with their education.

Josephine and other schoolgirls had indicated the opposite, that the girls they were circumcised with and were not in school were called "women" and married soon after (and called "wives"), while schoolgirls returned to school as inkanyakua. Rose's explanation, however, was one of the earliest indications that enkanyakuai was not uniformly understood (or used) among the schoolgirls we talked to.[17] Rose's correction suggested that schoolgirls were operating with conflicting definitions of enkanyakuai. For some, inkanyakua represented an aspirational category, a group who had "graduated" to a new "stage" and could return to school having earned some newfound respect but without the ultimate commitment (and consignment) to adulthood signified by arranged marriage (consensual or not). From this definition of the term I had started to imagine that enkanyakuai could be a powerful, culturally derived way of naming female adolescence as an extended period of "in-betweenness" in which girls who go to school, while still in their parents' care, could physically, intellectually, and socially "grow" in the context of schooling rather than marriage. As inkanyakua, it seemed, schoolgirls could enjoy the social respect said to attach to emurata and continue in school while delaying adult expectations for wives, particularly adult sexual debut, pregnancy, and motherhood.

But the more I asked about enkanyakuai, the more it became clear that, as one elder commented, "enkanyakuai cannot be a good way to talk about girls' education because many will not take it in a positive way." Most schoolgirls and mothers adamantly rejected the name enkanyakuai for schoolgirls, like Gloria, who was sixteen years old and in Class 8:

H: Can a schoolgirl be enkanyakuai?
G: [*laughing*] Yes, some of us they call enkanyakuai. But we are not agreeing that we are enkanyakuai!
H: Why do you not agree to this name?
G: Because we are not enkanyakuai, we are just girls.
H: Okay, why do you hate that name?
G: Aiiii, it's very bad! Even I don't want to hear anybody to call me enkanyakuai!
H: Okay. [*Laughs.*] If I see you there across the compound, and I say hey "*enkanyakuai* come!"
G: [*Interrupts me with horrified laughter.*] I will not come! Even I will not talk with you!
[WE ALL LAUGHED AT THE LOOK OF HORROR ON GLORIA'S FACE.]
H: Why is this name so bad if it is just a girl who has been circumcised and not married who is at home?
G: [*After a pause.*] I think *enkanyakuai* means a person who is just sitting at home without doing any work.

H: Okay.
G: So I hate that name completely! [*Laughs again.*]
H: Because you prefer to be working? Do you work at school?
G: Yes, when am in school, I am working.
H: How long can someone stay enkanyakuai?
G: If she didn't get a husband very fast, she will be a long time.
H: I see. In this area can you find enkanyakuai?
G: A lot.
H: A lot?
G: Yes.
H: And they are doing nothing?
G: Yes.
H: Truly?
G: Yes. They are just sitting, fetching water, and going back at home.

Naisoi, fourteen years old and in Class 6, was also aware that some people referred to her as enkanyakuai because she was circumcised but not married, and like Gloria, she also "hated that name." She was adamant and frustrated:

> I don't like to be called enkanyakuai. If people say it to themselves internally, when it's inside his heart or her heart, I'll not hear and I have no problem because I *am* circumcised and not yet married. But once it is said out loud, I will hear. I hate to be called enkanyakuai. I don't like to be called that name!

For Naisoi, being called enkanyakuai "out loud" was "shameful" "because that name is only for someone who is circumcised and not yet married." She clarified that because "the world has changed" so too have cultural categories of personhood:

> In those days there before [in the past], it could be understandable because when you were called that name [it made sense because] everyone [already] knew [you had been circumcised and awaited marriage]. But right now, the world has changed, and these names are not taken into consideration. And also, I just don't want that name. I just call myself by my own name.

Naisoi did not like the idea that her circumcision status could be known by just anyone, in part because she did not necessarily identify with emurata as a communally acknowledged experience and preferred to see her maturation in individual and private terms rather than as a social and collective process. Moreover, and perhaps more urgently, given her strong refusal, she did not want to be misrecognized and therefore misrepresented by cultural categories (and cultural logics) that she felt where no longer relevant. Naisoi rejected the possibility that persistent meanings from "in those days there before" might actually remain salient and could therefore override her (or any schoolgirl's) claim to schoolgirlhood.

Gloria and Naisoi's similar frustrations and similar refusals echoed the concerns of other schoolgirls and mothers who sought to distinguish and distance schoolgirls from inkanyakua. Both conceded that schoolgirls are called "enkanyakuai," suggesting that those schoolgirls who used this term to describe themselves in neutral or relatively positive terms were in fact participating in a common way of speaking about newly circumcised (school) girls. In the same breath, however, Gloria and Naisoi both made impassioned claims against this signification and the affective relations this signification would suggest. Even though schoolgirls were called inkanyakua they "[were] not agreeing" to what this name, and the process of being socially named this way, implied. They both insisted that they and other schoolgirls refused to be called forward as inkanyakua even though people around them to whom they are intimately connected saw them in this way. Naisoi explicitly recognized herself as a subject of this social world—that is, she understood that the details of her physical and social body fit the cultural definition of enkanyakuai; therefore, she felt she had no way to change how she was seen by others who held "internal" assumptions about her embodied potential. However, she could not abide hearing this name, applied to her, "out loud."

In her quiet refusal to be hailed by ideological structures she felt misnamed and misappropriated her body, mind, and possibilities, Naisoi, like Gloria and other schoolgirls who refused, worked hard to negotiate the relational claims cultural commonsense made on them. It is important to note that Gloria and Naisoi did not reject the social world itself, but rather they adamantly wanted to prevent enkanyakuai, and all that it implied for them, from meaningfully adhering to their social bodies.

Ownership, Female Sexuality, and Embodied Potential

For most of the people we talked with, despite the fact that schoolgirls and inkanyakua were both circumcised, living at home, and not married, these categories of personhood were not and could not be seen as compatible. Jacob, a deputy head teacher who had been teaching for ten years and had grown up in a homestead not too far from his school, explained that the meaning of enkanyakuai "has really changed with the introduction of education. . . . [Schoolgirls] are just regarded as schoolgirls. Enkanyakuai does not got to school." Sarah, the mother from Loodariak mentioned earlier in the chapter, had nine children, five of whom were already married and four of the youngest were in school. She insisted it is "not possible" for a schoolgirl to be called enkanyakuai "because she is under the father in her parents' home," or, as another mother said, "a schoolgirl is still in your hands." The fundamental distinction consistently came down to "ownership"; schoolgirls are in school and, by implication, are still "owned" (controlled and cared for) by their parents. The school itself, as suggested in chapter 3, also "owns" schoolgirls. Along with local patriarchies and parents, schools were endowed with overlapping institutional control and care as an extension of the local community, as well as an extension of the state. Moreover, schoolgirls' adolescence was seen as productive and therefore in need of protection. As students, they were recognized as "doing something" in the present toward the future.

Enkanyakuai, by contrast, as Rose noted earlier, has "no owner," or maybe, as Jacob observed, she has not even been "booked" (betrothed); "Once somebody has been termed as enkanyakuai, you would like to get rid of that name—you know maybe there could be another reason why you're not married. Maybe nobody has ever approached you." Sarah went further to elaborate the problem of "ownership" for enkanyakuai. On one hand, she is "owned" neither by her father nor by her husband; in fact, "no one is controlling her," therefore her sexual "freedom" is ambiguous, as it unfolds within patriarchal social arrangements but appears untethered by them. On the other hand, she owns nothing of her own and does nothing of consequence. Sarah elaborated,

> Enkanyakuai behaves differently [than a girl or a married woman]. [Her behavior] is not of a married lady and not of girl. She does what she wants. She has a lot of freedom. She can have many [male] friends. She is not under the control of anyone. A married woman is controlled by her husband. A girl is under the father. Enkanyakuai just has the behavior of inkanyakua. She is not under anybody . . . not even the father. . . . To me, it is not good to be enkanyakuai. . . . She doesn't own anything in that home. She owns completely nothing and no one is controlling her. She is doing nothing there. Her time is of an idle person who is not controlled by her parents.

In this frame, "ownership," as patriarchal control and care, is a fundamental precondition for legitimate contributions to social life.[18] Because the schoolgirl is properly "owned" (controlled and cared for), she is therefore seen as productive, even though her "in-betweenness" could persist well beyond her schooling years. For example, if a schoolgirl finishes secondary (or college or university), lives independently in her own house earning her own salary, pays her own bills, and is not married, Sarah explained, "that one is not enkanyakuai. She is a person doing her own work. She is different than the one living with her parents, doing nothing, and just staying at home." In this hypothetical example, the schoolgirl is "doing her own work" and lives independently but not autonomously. The "difference" Sarah sees between the grown-up schoolgirl in the example and enkanyakuai seems to pivot on making proper use of embodied potential. As noted, daughters have always been seen structurally as a means to development, conventionally through arranged marriage and these days through education and subsequent wage work (and then, ideally, a good Maasai marriage). What are the "fruits" expected to come from a circumcised girl's/woman's laboring body? Will her time (and her family's investment) be well spent "doing her own work" and earning a salary that can directly contribute to the development of her family and community? Or will she waste her potential "doing nothing," which is to say, bringing home neither "development" as cash income nor traditional reciprocity linkages through arranged marriage?

Implicit in concerns over ownership and embodied potential were social anxieties concerning the regulation and maintenance of new kinds of girlhood for new kinds of girls within and against "older" social meanings and practices regarding circumcised female sexuality. Alan, a young "parent-paid teacher" working part-time in the primary school he had attended, conceded, "It is *possible* to be enkanyakuai and a schoolgirl." "But," he added,

> now, according to the new mentality of school, those girls who are in school—this is now their stage. They are circumcised, but they are learning. Schooling is now their stage. They will not be playing that role of enkanyakuai. . . . Their parents are not looking for any man to marry them. . . . [Enkanyakuai] means any man can come for you because you are not married. There before (in the past) you find those girls who are just there at home, they grow, are circumcised, and just there. In our tradition, a circumcised boy can come and begin relations with them. Maybe it's just a relationship of [sex]. It's not a strong relationship. They are then specifying their husbands. The dad will just come and say, "I give you my girl." For the enkanyakuai who is not in school now, the parents are looking for any man who can marry her.

Benjamin, a Maasai man who had grown up in Narok County but had been teaching in KCL for about twelve years, was not surprised that schoolgirls refused to be called enkanyakuai: "They are only trying to deny the fact of enkanyakuai. They just don't want themselves to be associated with that because enkanyakuai means someone who doesn't have a husband or a person to marry, so they don't want to be associated because they are not ready to get married. They want to pursue education." Mothers also wanted to disassociate their daughters and any schoolgirl from the implication of marriageability because the benefits of education were at stake, for daughters as well as parents. As one mother noted, "The one who has not gone to school first [before marriage] . . . has no visions and knowledge. Those who have gone to school have knowledge and may have visions on what to do. . . . We want them to help us in the future."

During my interview with Benjamin, as we moved on to talk about other things, he paused and said he wanted to return for a moment to the idea of enkanyakuai. He said, "I just want to say that we don't have any other stage in our language or our dialect to describe this lady. We don't have another word to describe a lady after she is circumcised but not married." I suggested that perhaps "schoolgirl" could describe that "stage" and asked how to say "schoolgirl" in Maa, jokingly suggesting "*entito shuleni*" (an admittedly awkward splicing of "girl" and "school"). Benjamin grinned, shaking his head slowly: "No. *Entito* in the Maa language means a girl who has not been circumcised," he said, laughing. "You can't say *entito*." "You see," he added, "there's no way to say it. It is just *enkanyakuai*. That is why I want to bring my argument here."

Over the course of fieldwork, several people explained that there was no way to say "schoolgirl" in Maa, but Ben was the only one to suggest that his language, and by extension his culture, could not easily accommodate "the schoolgirl" as a form of personhood. In this frame, the schoolgirl is difficult to rationalize culturally because she is someone who cannot be: a circumcised child. This insight highlights the gendered cultural ambivalence and social danger inherent to schoolgirls' "in-betweenness" because they carry paradoxical meanings for emurata on to their often visibly developing bodies at home and at school. Their status as circumcised marked them as "fully grown" and available for adult sexual debut, yet their status as children excluded them from access to social respect and adult sexuality reserved for mature people. What is more, their status as students marked their bodies as sites of certain kinds of potential and therefore worthy of certain kinds of care and control. This contradictory convergence of assumptions compounded the experience of adolescence for schoolgirls and formed the ideological milieu in which they worked hard to negotiate their sexual selves by, among other things, passively consenting to emurata and actively refusing to hear themselves called forward as inkanyakua.

Disciplining Schoolgirls' Bodies and Minds

In these discussions, meanings for "enkanyakuai" and "schoolgirl" were contingent on mutually informing social relations. Expectations for schoolgirl discipline and hard work influenced assumptions about inkanyakua as idle and errant. Schoolgirls negotiated their subjectivities within this dialectic, which was itself embedded in their lives. For instance, they were invested in staying in school, although they were all intimately connected to many girls and women who had never been to school or who had left school without finishing. Soinka was one of twenty children in her father's home. Neither her father nor his wives had gone to school. Although the oldest children of his first and second wives had been married, the rest who were old enough were in school. Soinka's mother was her father's third wife, and all of the children in her mother's house, except the second-born, her sister, were in school. She explained, "I was told I was to be married, but at that time I was still young. When the men came looking for a wife, I cried and cried. [My elder sister] said I should be sent to school. The father let her to be married. She had no choice. I was then sent [to school]." In most cases, however, schoolgirls simply said they did not know (or were unwilling to share) the specific reasons why some children in their families were sent to school and some were kept home for marriage. They were very sure, however, that Maasai parents in general were more likely to send boys to school than girls and that girls, more often than boys, dropped out of school before finishing because of a simple fact of adolescence as a gendered biosocial process: "Girls can get pregnant and boys cannot."

Across the interviews the "problem of schoolgirl pregnancy and dropout" was explained as frustration and concern regarding schoolgirls' proper sexual embodiment, social comportment, and individual attitudes. Because they were still "owned" by their parents, schoolgirls were expected to "behave as girls" despite their circumcised status. Mothers and teachers indicated that schoolgirls were counseled at home and at school to be "disciplined" and "avoid [the] distractions" of relationships with boys/men. Schoolgirls also emphasized other schoolgirls' attitudes and behaviors as problematic and seemed to take it as self-evident that it was their responsibility to manage the contradictory meanings their developing bodies made in social life, including mitigating the constant threat of sexual propositions and predations from "boys" (circumcised male peers/age-mates in school) and "men" (circumcised males who were not in school) through self-regulation.

"They have not put in their minds that they are school"

Sarah explained that "boys can continue all through schooling with no problems," but "when girls reach the age of ten and above," the biggest "problem" they face is "pregnancy and dropping out." Agnes, a mother from Enkeriyan, noted that from her perspective, cultural barriers to access were no longer an issue, "because now every home, everybody has sacrificed for their children to come to school." "But," she continued, "girls themselves face that problem of dropping," suggesting that daughters' behavior presented problems for their persistence in school. She explained, "In our house we give girls secure places to sleep. Boys are kept separate. They find their own place to sleep. But when [schoolgirls] leave for school, they don't go to school, they go to rivers to have sex, so they don't get pregnant at home, but elsewhere in the bushes, in the shade because she says 'I am going to school.'" Damaris, another mother in Loodariak, concurred.

> Today most parents they want to see their daughters and sons going to school. They want to see them really progressing, but here is a problem. Our daughters are not seeing that it is a privilege and luck to be in school. So they go play, have bad friends, and as a result of those bad friends they end up getting pregnant. Nowadays the fathers cannot say I have this girl and because she is now a big girl I will ask a friend of mine to marry her. The girls who are being married off today are only those who drop from school, but if you have not dropped from school because of pregnancy you are given that chance to continue.

For mothers, the real "problem" at the heart of "schoolgirl pregnancy and drop out" was that some schoolgirls failed to act responsibly because "they have not put in their minds that they are in school" despite what mothers believed to be social support (and sacrifice) for schoolgirlhood as a new kind of gendered childhood. That schoolgirls were forced to negotiate conflicting (and sometime coercive) claims on their developing bodies (including their own desires) did not seem to register for mothers, much less factor into their perceptions of proper schoolgirl attitudes and comportment.

In this milieu, schoolgirls' bodies matter, but so do their minds; how schoolgirls' chose to receive and act on the contradictory messages was seen as key to their success as schoolgirls. No one mentioned emurata per se as a problem for schoolgirls in relation to sexual debut; instead, they indicated that adult sexual behavior ascribed to circumcised female people was problematic for girls in school precisely because pregnancy ends schooling.[19] Hannah, the mother from Loodariak we met in the introduction who owned "The Hilton," noted that the cultural belief that emurata changes girls was still explicitly communicated. She explained, "When a girl is circumcised, they call her a woman. Then they don't fear men. They can go with any man." Constance, a talkative fifteen-year-old in Class 7 who spoke in English for her entire interview, echoed Hannah's comments: "When a girl is circumcised, she is being told, Wake up! You are now a woman! So, she sees herself as a grown-up." She said this message is communicated to all girls, whether they were in school or not, but it resonated differently with different girls. Naneu, a schoolgirl at Innyonyorri Primary School, observed, "Some girls say those who go to school are foolish and wasting their time. They don't want school." As comments about men who seek out inkanykua because they are circumcised, not married, not in school, and therefore sexually available indicate, still-salient cultural expectations and operative social norms invested in (circumcised) male access to adolescent female bodies remained generally unchallenged. For the girl of the home, there is purportedly no contradiction in the fact that "they can go with any man." For schoolgirls, however, "going with any man" is fraught with social danger. When I noted that all of the schoolgirls we had talked to who were circumcised insisted they were still "girls," Hannah was pleased to hear this: "It is good if they go by that. . . . If they don't want to have sex, then they won't allow themselves to be called women."

For those girls who are already in school when they pass through emurata, according to Constance, some schoolgirls—"the proud ones"—"see themselves as if they have been to a far place, that they have gone to the highest level they can be." She went on to explain that circumcised boys also fell prey to being "too proud," and as a consequence they sometimes dropped out of school. But if they decided to stay, "boys can finish because they cannot get pregnant." Proud schoolgirls, on the other hand, were at risk because they can. She elaborated:

> Girls start to see that they are in that high level. Even when the teacher is in front of them, they don't obey the teacher. They see themselves as just like him. So they don't listen, and they don't learn. They can't perform well. Because of that proudness they don't feel like being in school. She may say, "Now I'm a woman, what need is there to go to school? It's better to be married." They pretend to be a woman, and that's why they drop out of school.

Similarly, one mother observed that under the pretense of "womanhood" ascribed to "graduating" from emurata, schoolgirls complicate how others around them see them and invite attention from men: "Some do change [their behavior] after circumcision. They see themselves as grown up because they are circumcised. You see that girl associating with grown-ups, married women, and other circumcised women. Taking yourself to that level, you are telling other people from outside there that they can approach you." According to the gendered and generational norms for proper female comportment, uncircumcised girls should keep a respectful distance from circumcised people. That is, they should keep themselves in the company of children. All of the mothers and teachers we talked to considered circumcised schoolgirls "children," and as such, they were expected to register social maturity as "discipline" and "focus" trained faithfully on the hard work of school. According to this reasoning, if schoolgirls saw themselves as children, acted like children, and associated themselves exclusively with children, then they would be seen as children despite the mixed cultural messages and social assumptions still attached to their circumcised bodies. The circumcision paradox therefore put schoolgirls in a tricky position. Associating only with children denied their desire to be seen as people "who could develop the family." However, a schoolgirl who chose to "take herself up to the level" of other circumcised people ran the risk of suggesting that her mind was not on school but on "behaving as a woman," which in turn threatened her conditional relationship to school. Successful schoolgirls had to learn to manage "proudness" unleashed by emurata as embodied potential and channel it toward the hard work of school.

"The girl forgets what she wanted, so she accepts"

When asked about the term "adolescence" specifically, schoolgirls consistently defined it as a potent mix of biological and social facts: "the breasts grow," "pubic hair appears," "periods" begin, and "disturbances" in the form of unwanted male attention ensue. Pregnancy as a result of sex (in the absence of birth control, which only came up implicitly as abstinence) was taken by adults and schoolgirls alike as a self-evident fact of physical maturity for girls (circumcised or not). They "learned in school that when you have your periods and you have sex, you get pregnant," and on the whole they struggled to varying degrees with these realities. Although they did not list emurata as a "fact" of adolescence, to return to Janice's comment from earlier in the chapter, they tacitly knew circumcision was an instigator of "a lot of disturbance from boys who try to impregnate [circumcised girls]." Many schoolgirls insisted that "disturbances" from peers in school and "men from the village" (reference to any circumcised male person who was not in school) in the form of sexual propositions and coercions ("cheating") were common. After repeated mention of "disturbances," I asked Alice, if she was ever "disturbed." She laughed at my question, answering, "Yes, every day." She indicated that primary school is "where it begins" and reiterated that in her experience, the pressure was constant, particularly in secondary. These concerns had implications for parents' attitudes about girls' education. Jane, a student in Class 5, said that some parents were hesitant to send daughters to school because "they usually believe that girls can be cheated by boys, then they break from school." As another schoolgirl explained that "once there is a relationship between a girl and a boy, boys cheat girls when they are still young, and they make them pregnant, and then they go home." Schoolgirls tended to characterize parents' concern as less about the fact that boys/men would "cheat" girls and more about the fact that cheating/disturbances meant sex, and sex meant pregnancy, and pregnancy meant the end of schooling.

Schoolgirl "dropout" rates because of pregnancy or otherwise were consistently attributed to schoolgirls' failure to mitigate any distractions, particularly "disturbances" that could lead to sex. Success, everyone agreed, came down to schoolgirl diligence and discipline, because, as Damaris noted,

> there are people who are focused in life, those who aim for a vision, while others have very little focus. We talk to our girls and maybe the parents are talking to them, but they are not focused. One [girl] can remember what the parents have said and another can forget, and they can then drop from school.... [She] fails because she is not disciplined enough. She can have a target but she cannot get to that target because she is not disciplined. She has to have it in her mind."

Schoolgirls acknowledged that "there are those girls who don't read [study] so they repeat one class [grade] two or three times, so the father decides to remove her from school because she is not working hard and marry her off." Naneu noted similarly that girls who are not performing well in school drop out, but rather than be removed by a frustrated father, frustrated girls remove themselves: "Some girls stay in school for long but aren't promoted. They are frustrated when they see that they cannot succeed, so they drop and prefer to be married." She explained that they might not find success in marriage either, "but they say that it's better than wasting time in school." Although there are many reasons some girls "cannot succeed" in school, these possibilities were either ignored or pushed aside in favor of articulating schoolgirls as failing to focus on school.

Schoolgirls wanted to stay focused, like Jennifer, the head girl in her class, who asked us, "How can I stay strong to complete my studies without any disturbances?" She was worried about sexual pressure, and she was also worried about her parents not having school fees. Nashipae, as we learned in chapter 3, had to contend with *starting* school at fourteen. She acknowledged that her body was "big" (and blushed even talking about it). Yet, she asserted: "I will work hard to avoid pregnancy so I can become a doctor." Even though she received unwanted attention at school, "not many of them" bothered her because, she said, "they know I am a Christian.... so they respect me a lot." Moreover, she strongly believed that a schoolgirl's mind was key to avoiding pregnancy: "It [is] not a must to get pregnant because it is something you have not put in your mind. You think, 'I should not get pregnant.' But those who do get pregnant they just . . . no boy will force you to have sex, only you take yourself and agree to have sex with him and you get a baby." I asked, "What if the schoolgirl is poor and hungry and the "old man" brings her food?" Nashipae was resolute: "If it were me, I will tell the man, the food is only for a day or two days. And my life, maybe you will come and infect me with diseases that will never be cured. So I better stay hungry and in peace."

Nashipae's resolve presents schoolgirl "toughness" as a function of a disciplined mind and self-regulated body. The idea that schoolgirls are always involved in consensual sex because girls are the gatekeepers to sex was fairly consistent across the interviews and reinforced the presumptive power of the schoolgirl to "refuse" "pressure" for sex. Damaris's comments bear this out:

> Yes, pressure is there. Or, I can say it's there and it's not there. The girl can decide to say, "No, I don't want any association with boys, as far as they are trying to cheat me to go into sex." But you find them coming together and you know, the girl is given small, small, small money to buy a dress, to buy shoes, to buy something like that and of course by giving those small things the man is cheating the girl. The girl forgets what she wanted, so she accepts. The reason why am saying there is pressure and not pressure is because she can refuse! She can say "I don't want your money, I don't want this." Yes, it's pressure, but the girl can still say, "No, I don't want all these things you are trying to give!"

Damaris used a story of her own daughter to illustrate the voracity of schoolgirl "toughness."

> There is an example of my daughter. She just woke up one morning and told me that "I am going to report this to my father, there is this boy who comes here every night trying to approach me and I didn't want it." I told her, "Don't tell your father because he will quarrel with this boy," but "you must avoid the boy." But the girl said, "I will avoid the boy but I will have to report this to my father." So the girl reported to the father, and the father warned the boy so from that time that boy never came to this girl. The girl has finished high school. She is now in teachers' training college. I think I helped her because after she met the father I said to her, "You have to be very careful now. You have to fulfill your vision because you have reported this to your dad and tomorrow we cannot see you dropping out of school after all this." The daughter said, "I am not going to drop from school. You will see am not going to drop." I told her, "It's good you don't drop because what will your father tell you after you have reported the case of this boy and then tomorrow you drop from school [because of pregnancy]?"

For adults and for many schoolgirls, the problem is not that boys and men "cheat" schoolgirls. A collective silence around the commonplace experience of coercive sexual advances shifted any disciplinary focus away from boys and men and focused blame on schoolgirls who "forget what they wanted," and, as Nashipae argued, they "accept." Damaris's daughter broke this silence to report manipulative and coercive sexual advances to her mother *and* father (thereby breaking with social custom that girls avoid direct communication with fathers), and although the boy was warned, responsibility ultimately fell to the schoolgirl to "be very careful" to preserve her access to school and the promised future schooling. As these message were repeated in homesteads, classrooms, and fellowship halls, schoolgirls internalized the responsibility to manage misappropriations of their bodies by disciplining their minds. Most claimed to be confident in their ability to "refuse." Some schoolgirls in these situations, however, struggled to mitigate their own vulnerability with "tough" resolve.

A well-respected senior teacher who regularly admonished her female students to avoid distractions with boys and stay focused on their educated futures told me of a meeting that the girls at her school arranged to talk with her about how to handle their relationships with "boyfriends." They had each written their concerns anonymously on scraps of paper and collected them in a pile; one girl read them aloud. The teacher took notes at the meeting, which she shared with me during our interview. While all the schoolgirls' comments evinced manipulation and coercion by "boyfriends" (boys and/ or men), some suggest that schoolgirls were also struggling with their own conflicted desires. One wrote, "I have a boyfriend who promises to get me everything except a car." Another wrote, "My boyfriend says he loves me. His kisses touch my heart. He kisses me more than my parents ever have. What can I do?" Another worried, "I have a boyfriend. He gives me love and money. I am addicted to that love and that money. What can I do?"

Other girls struggled with intimidation and fear. One noted, "When I refuse [sex] my boyfriend cries in pain. What can I do?" One girl wrote of being intimidated when she tried to refuse sex, saying, "The pastor tells me he sees me when I am standing with other people. When I refuse him he tells me he will tell my parents [about us]." Finally, one of the statements revealed possible rape: "My boyfriend forced me to have sex, but I haven't told anyone." The teacher explained to me, "The questions they have are questions we have never seen, and we ourselves did not have. When I read these I can laugh at some, but most just make me want to cry." This teacher had assumed because being in school protected girls from sexual debut guaranteed by arranged marriage, that they were also protected from sexual harassment and violence.[20] Another head teacher exclaimed in despair, "Some schoolgirls are like lambs to the wolves!" after he learned that the Class 8 head girl in his school had to drop out for pregnancy. The schoolgirl's mother was a widow, and when the head teacher met with her, the mother begged him not to confront the "boyfriend," who was a young, unmarried teacher at another school. This mother's only option for income was to cut and burn wood to make charcoal. Her family needed the resources her daughter's "boyfriend" offered. She was afraid that confronting him for "defiling" her daughter would scare him away. The head teacher was devastated that his smart, studious pupil would leave school, but he felt like his hands were tied.

Schoolgirls were expected to bear the burdens of girls' and women's work at home (which often intensified post-emurata, as they were seen as "big" enough to carry heavier loads, for example), the hard work of school, and the continuous work of promulgating and preserving schoolgirl adolescence as new commonsense in order to secure their success in school. Yet the collective silence, particularly from mothers, around the sexualized pressures schoolgirls faced was striking. As an effect of this silence, individual schoolgirl desire (to consensually engage in sexual relationships and to refuse coercions) was countered by collective "ownership" over what were seen as schoolgirls' individual decisions. That is, schoolgirls' embodied potential was seen and held relationally and communally because schooling investments entailed sacrifices for all families. As one mother reminded me, "One of the reasons [parents are upset] about a girl dropping is that when the girl starts going to school, we are the people to take over the responsibility of looking after [the livestock]." Beyond their investments of resources and time, parents were emotionally invested in their daughters' success in school because they were not intended to advance the prospects of an individual girl (although parents obviously cared about their children as individuals) but for the advancement of the girl-in-relation-to-others. Damaris seemed to speak for all parents:

> I can imagine a situation where this daughter goes all through primary grades and just drops without going to secondary, going to college, without acquiring a degree. That one, I really feel it, and of course when we are sending these people to school, we just don't want standard up to eight and then drop. Our intention is for this person to go and finish a university and get a good job, and by getting a good job you come and help the people so that's our intentions, so if you see somebody dropping in the middle we really feel bad.

As a continuation on a theme inherent to girl-effects logic, in order to "preserve themselves for education," schoolgirls were expected (and expected themselves) *to be the solution* to the problem of schoolgirl pregnancy by disciplining their bodies and minds. Schoolgirlhood offered new opportunities for a measure of control over one's body in ways that girls at home did not have, yet schoolgirls were still beholden to gendered and generational control of their sexual selves. While their in-betweenness gave them room to negotiate some expectations, they could not expect both social respect *and* social protection. Their bodies—or, more accurately, the contradictory meanings attached to them—could easily betray them and threaten their ability to stay in school in ways that boys never faced.

Conclusion

Dorothy Hodgson's (2001b) analysis of the changed meanings of the category and concept, *ormeek* (pl. *irmeek*), in Kisongo Maasai communities in Tanzania illustrates how engagements with development have implications for how people understand themselves and others.[21] Initially used by Maasai in the colonial period as a derogatory term for "those Africans who were educated, spoke Swahili, worked in the government, or were baptized" (251), *ormeek* was eventually used to refer to any Maasai man who prioritized any of these behaviors in his own life. To mainstream Maasai, any man who agreed to marry only one wife and submit to a higher authority (God), who did not know how to properly care for cattle because he was engaged in other work, and who did not distinguish himself among his peers in pastoralist terms was considered "profoundly not Maasai" (252). For the elder men and women Hodgson interviewed, to be named ormeek was a statement of existential fact; the distinction between the inferior masculinity associated with irmeek and the dominant masculinity associated with Maasai men was articulated as a "vast, unbridgeable gap" (253).

However, as Hodgson illustrates, these two social categories, embodied experiences, and gender ideologies were mutually coproduced and contingent. As pastoralism became increasingly less viable, those who had gone to school, worked in the wage economy, and raised their children to do the same were more likely to prosper in a changed and changing world than their uneducated age-mates. Over time, even venerable elders had a hard time delineating ormeek behavior from what had become normative masculine behavior—that is, a mixed means for crafting a "modern" life in the face of the decline of pure pastoralism.[22] Similarly, younger Maasai men and women could not point to irmeek behaviors beyond the superficial (wearing "modern" clothing, for example). By the 1990s, Hodgson argues, ormeek had lost "any fixity of meaning" and had become "a sign without a referent" (255). I would suggest that the sign itself continued to signify meanings that were no longer fixed but no less meaningful. A cultural notion of ormeek continued to exist and inform experience, even as ormeek as a distinct kind of person was hard to recognize. I think a similar process is at work with enkanyakuai and emurata in the schools and surrounding communities in which I spent time. Everyone was sure of the meanings they attached to these concepts, while at the same time, they also knew competing definitions and acknowledged that their own definitions were contradictory. Enkanyakuai and emurata were once stable signifiers, but these days, "because of education," it is hard to be completely sure about their meanings. I am certain that it will not take the full balance of the twenty-first century for these categories to similarly diminish in significance and, soon enough, disappear.

Nonetheless, the majority of schoolgirls who refused to be called "enkanyakuai" were committed in their rejection. As the head teacher suggests in the opening of the chapter, their certainty was enabled by their subject-positions as schoolgirls. It is possible to read their confidence to refuse as a reflection of girl-effects logic at work in positive ways in actual girls' lives. That said, as discussed throughout the book, schoolgirls had internalized the intentional intensification of their own gendered labor to stay in school. Negotiating, managing, and rescripting contradictory social and cultural expectations for their developing bodies, even in the face of persistent sexual harassment, was understood as simply more of the hard work of school.

By valorizing schooling as the singular process that transforms girls into empowered actors, girl-effects logics (at all scales) engages in its own willful refusal to recognize the intense gendered burdens schoolgirls have no choice but to willingly bear in order to realize the promise of education. Moreover, girl-effects logic reduces girls' relational belonging to personal accommodation and/or resistance to norms that marginalize and disempower them. This framework for agency cannot account for everyday circumstances in which schoolgirls move in-between direct resistance and full accommodation of conventional norms (Mahmood 2005).

I suggest the collective refusal to associate schoolgirlhood with enkanyakuai as a social category indicates a "choice [that] concerns insistence, not resistance" (McGranahan 2016, 322). The general refusal of enkanyakuai was less about denigrating inkanyakua in and of themselves (after all, circumcised, unmarried girls-cum-women were schoolgirls' relatives and friends) and more about insisting on the cultural legitimacy of schoolgirlhood as a "new stage" in the life-course narrative for Maasai girls who go to school.

• • •

As I was wrapping up an interview with another head teacher in another school, I commented that I had an interview after his with one of his students, Tatiana, and I wondered if we could use his office to talk. "Yes, of course," he said, and then added offhandedly, "the girl who is coming now is grown. Her body is big. To many, she would make a good wife, but," he paused, "she loves school."

At the time, I did not reply to his comment. It happened quickly; he spoke to me as he was moving toward the door; I was searching in my bag for the audio recorder and wondering if Maria was finished transcribing. I did, however, briefly jot down the scene in my notebook after he left, as I waited for Tatiana to arrive. I noted what seemed like a subtle shift in his tone, the pause at the "but" before his concession, resignation, almost . . . almost, disappointment: "she loves school." I struggled then, and I am not completely sure now, but I want to suggest that the ambivalence I detected in this brief statement encapsulates the complex of desires at play when rather suddenly (by historical standards), physically maturing adolescent girls who would otherwise have been new wives to "old men" are instead rearticulated as children, their womanhood deferred for as long as possible. According to this head teacher, Tatiana was seen "by many" as "grown," not because she was a high-performing student or because she was an articulate leader among her peers but because her "her body is big." Her developed body signified the end of her growing and signaled her readiness for marriage. Her "love" of school was the only social force with the potential to deflect misrecognitions imposed upon her social body.

Schoolgirls' experiences demonstrate how gendered cultural shifts are embodied. All but three of the schoolgirls we talked with were circumcised or soon would be. The schoolgirls who appear in this book therefore carry cultural codes in their flesh; the also carry cultural meanings ascribed to their social bodies. As they work hard to negotiate and navigate conflicting expectations for their bodies in their present and their future, "old men" who constitute local patriarchies, along with their wives, also have to come to terms with changing gendered expectations for sexed (and gendered) bodies. As more Maasai daughters have access to school and more girls-daughters-young-women-wives-mothers come to see themselves, and be seen, differently as a result, the cultural politics of proper feminine comportment, social recognition, and relational belonging also shift. I would argue that parents, and specifically "old men," do not necessarily "hate" educated girls. On the whole, girls cannot be educated unless "old men" agree they can (and should) be. Schoolgirls live in families and communities that enable their schoolgirlhood, and as such these places are sites of encouragement and strength, even empowerment (Goldman and Little 2014).

However, relational investments (economic and emotional) create complex forms of belonging that can disempower as well. Everyone noted at some point when we talked that some Maasai fathers still refused to educate girls. No doubt some, even many, men (and not just "old" men) are frustrated and confounded by changes, however small, in their own structural positions, particularly as they struggle to survive and thrive as challenges to traditional pastoralism (and pastoral institutions) continue to mount. As I came to realize, moreover, the specter of being "married off" by "old men" who may "hate" them haunts all schoolgirls, regardless of their own fathers' potential intentions, in part because the threat of sexual propositions and coercions are omnipresent; to be a girl in school is, to a very real degree (for some more than others), an existential risk. Schoolgirls acquiesced to emurata's physical coding because they felt they could not refuse. Yet they also believed participation strengthened their sense of belonging while, yet again, they recognized that it complicated their social positioning by marking them as circumcised children. Schoolgirls' shared ambivalence and refusal regarding emurata and enkanyakuai evidence an implicit critique of "old" forms of sociality and indicate a kind of rooted agency—"the socially mediated capacity to act" (Ahearn 2001, 118)—that animated schoolgirls' hard work toward the socially risky habitation of "old" social norms and cultural forms infused with new meanings. Paradoxically, participation in emurata positioned schoolgirls to better leverage a locally derived capacity to act on their own needs and desires, including action toward the erosion and eventual eradication of emuratare oo ntoyie and then, by extension, inkanyakua.

Conclusion

Becoming "People Who Use Both Hands"

There is no short cut to empowerment.
—Arjun Appadurai

When Maria first started as my research assistant, she walked about five kilometers from her uncle's home, where she lived, along the shortcut through the thorny brush to my room in the Kilusu compound where we worked each day. One morning, as she sat down for a cup of tea, she mentioned that on the way she met and chatted briefly with one of her age-mates she was circumcised with years before.[1]

Naipanoi, a resident of the Loodariak area, was heading back home with her youngest child after collecting firewood. I did not see Naipanoi that day, but I have seen women carrying large loads. I imagine her bent slightly forward, the hacked branches tied together with a leather strap and then tied to her back with one sash around her waist and another forming a kind of handle that comes up, crosses her forehead, and then attaches on the other side of the load. Her baby would be tied with a colorful cotton wrap to her chest. As an effect of this arrangement, women carrying loads walk looking ahead of themselves, but with their faces angled slightly down, forehead first. In my observation and experience, a woman carrying a load will stop to chat despite the weight, both hands on the straps framing her head, face down, talking to the ground. Maria, in contrast, was carrying only a notebook and small purse for her cell phone, a pen, and her handkerchief.

Maria said that she told Naipanoi that she was walking to meet me for our work together. As they "chewed the news," Naipanoi said to Maria, "in your work, please remember the women like me who are carrying heavy loads in the hot sun instead of papers and books."

Naipanoi's vivid language to describe her position in comparison to Maria's is incisive and profound in its commentary. Despite the fact that the material conditions of their lives had been, and were still, very similar, the things they carried on that day symbolized different current realities and future trajectories. As narratives throughout this book have shown, access to, and experience and persistence in, formal schooling produces gendered and generational identities and social categories that have very real bearing on schoolgirls' everyday lives. Likely, in four months as a research assistant, Maria would earn more than Naipanoi might in twelve making beaded jewelry. Even though they had been circumcised together seven or eight years prior, Maria was still a kind of schoolgirl because she had just graduated from secondary school. She was not yet a woman because "she was still learning" and, moreover, because she was not a wife. As a classificatory student and a wage earner (although in the informal economy), she was seen as someone "doing something" aimed toward an expansive future in which her contributions to national development would be measured by her place in the formal workforce as an employee and taxpayer, her increased tendency to vote or participate in public matters, her expanded consumption capacities and patterns, and by the small size of her healthy, educated family as the result of her "delayed" marriage.

Naipanoi had never been a student. Instead, she had been a woman for years already, when she "graduated" from childhood to adulthood through emurata, was quickly married, and started down the path of wife and mother. According to the discourse of relative development that frames the divergent possibilities instantiated by the bundle of firewood and the baby compared to the notebook and the pen, Naipanoi's future would be seen as finite. Her contributions to gross domestic product were zero, she is assumed to be disconnected from "public" affairs of the state and marginalized within "women's programs" in civil society if at all, and she would be expected to produce more children than she could adequately feed, medically treat, or formally educate, all while subservient to her controlling husband. Her possibilities, if considered at all, would best be given expression by what her children might do or become.

Schoolgirlhood as a normative subjectivity arrived as an analytic directly from the ways in which Maasai school-going girls, and some of the adults in their lives, talked about their own immediate circumstances and their aspirations for the future. By claiming the schoolgirl category as their own, schoolgirls attempted to draw clear, new lines in the Rift Valley's red soil around who they were, who they were not, and who they wanted to be. Maasai schoolgirls very much want to be exceptional, girlpowered girls who create the lives they want for themselves, their families, and their communities despite the compounding odds of gendered, generational, ethnic, socioeconomic, and political-geographic marginality. The unified subject-position they seek—being Maasai and being schoolgirls—has significant implications for access to social, cultural, political, and economic resources, which is to say the complex combination of social meanings and materiality in Maasai communities and beyond.

At the same time, from the narratives presented throughout this book, it is clear that the seeming contradictions embodied by Naipanoi and Maria and the things they carried when they met on the path cannot be resolved by exceptionalizing celebratory rhetoric and targeted policy intervention aimed only at girls. I argue in the following section that poor, non-Western girls' lives have become increasingly visible and coded with importance in transnational development discourse as a function of their perceived value as human capital to global growth. Yet, decisively interrupting the persistent reproduction of structural violence and social exclusion at all scales and across all axes of difference for the just (re)distribution of material and recognitional resources *has always been* vitally necessary. Within the uneven unfolding of modernity, poor girls, particularly poor girls of color and indigenous girls, in the Global North and Global South have always lived particularly precarious lives. As with many of the dire problems facing multiple marginalized peoples today, most of whom are girls and women, persuasive and pervasive shareable declarations that reduce girls to iconography and their lives to virtuous and vicious cycles are insufficient to capture or change the intersectional and interdependent structural oppressions they face on a daily basis. These oppressions are often intensified by neoliberal development aimed narrowly at opening markets, inculcating economic subjectivity, and individualizing risk. How do we attend to Maasai schoolgirls' marginalization as embodied socially located subjects and their invested desire to erode these margins through the gendered hard work of school while also attending to the regulatory power of girl-effects logic? The compelling and complex contours of a still-unfolding Maasai schoolgirlhood discussed throughout this book raise some conceptual (and therefore political) questions about the convergence of power and knowledge shaping current commonsense for girls' empowerment through development investment.

Girls Become Important: The Coalescing of Girls in Development

I have argued that neoliberal postfeminist rationalities for shaping identity and producing subjectivity honed in the Global North travel swiftly and strategically to the Global South through circuits of development-policy discourse, financing, and programmatic interventions aimed at impoverished adolescent girls. As an effect of these transnational circulations, the "particular framings of the problem and the solution ... [that] gain purchase" are always a reflection of institutional power (Cornwall, Harrison, and Whitehead 2008, 3; Dingo 2012) and consequently, institutional (and institutionalized) knowledge. In the marketplace of imperatives, institutional actors have no margin for indicating "doubt" or "uncertainty" about either the problem or the solution, the target or the intervention (Cornwall, Harrison, and Whitehead 2008, 8). This referential self-certainty drives consensus (despite contestation), promotes instrumentalizing complex social formations (despite intentions to do otherwise), and (inadvertently or not) fortifies the discursive and affective conditions for ideological hegemony. Thus in the current "economy of statements" that accompany the political economy of development, girlpower is the ideological currency against which girl-effects logic holds its value as the medium of exchange (Escobar 1995, 55).

In the past five or so years a growing body of feminist scholarship, my own included, has argued that a discernable and powerful regime of truth (Desai 2016) regarding girls in the Global South now produces the "Third World Girl" (Moeller 2014a) as the racialized, neocolonial, exceptional subject of development through a concerted representational regime (Switzer 2013; Bent 2013) that shapes a particular configuration of the future (Khoja-Moolji 2015).[2] I begin to outline here what I see as these ideological formations coalescing into Girls in Development (GID) as a knowledge paradigm for producing adolescent girls as development targets and authorizing interventions on their behalf that is related to but different from the enduring, as well as dynamic and contested, paradigms that have dominated development thinking about women, gender, and development for more than forty years: Women in Development (WID) and Gender and Development (GAD).

WID and GAD Reworked through Neoliberalism: A Brief Genealogy

Feminist scholars, development professionals and activists have debated WID and GAD for decades (Kabeer 1994).[3] Since the 1970s, WID proponents in mainstream development institutions have argued that integrating women into development through schooling, job training, and market participation promotes gender equity between men and women by eroding patriarchal power in local contexts (perceived to be backward, conservative, and oppressive to women) and undermines sexist bias in setting agendas within development institutions in the Global North (Chowdury 1995; Razavi and Miller 1995). Characterized as the "efficiency approach" (Moser 1989), WID advocates promote "funding programmes with gender equality aims on the basis of broader social and economic impact" (Chant and Sweetman 2012, 518). Among WID's enduring achievements has been its ability to persistently emphasize the political implications of the ways in which patriarchal power structures marginalize, exclude, and oppress women (Wilson 2015) and to provide strategic room for the advancement of feminist agendas in otherwise resistant development institutions (Calkin 2015; Razavi 1998; Bergeron 2013).[4] As I will go on to show, elements of WID principles and presuppositions inform and inflect GID discourse.

In the 1980s, GAD emerged as a critique of WID. Critics have argued that WID instrumentalizes women as tools for economic development while reifying as universal Western normative understandings of gender relations among men, women, states, markets, and culture. Gender and development theories, innovated by feminists from the Global South and women-of-color feminists working from grassroots social-justice frameworks in the Global North, attempted to shift the emphasis from the conventional Western, primarily white, liberal feminist strategy of "add women to markets and stir" to examinations of gender as socially constructed within historical, political, and sociocultural processes of capitalist expansion (including imperialism, colonization, development, and globalization) in order to more fully interrogate power relations between men and women (and among women) within the institutions that shape their lives, such as family, kinship, religion, states, and markets. GAD proponents have argued that gender does not function in a vacuum but rather is always complicated by and coproduced among "entanglements of affinity and connection" (Cornwall and Rivas 2015, 402) and intersected and interlocking axes of social location and markers of difference, most prominently race, ethnicity, class, caste, sexuality, religion, disability, and citizenship status (Crenshaw 1989; Wilson 2015).[5] Moreover, GAD theorists understand social location as locally specific as well as transnationally configured. Consequently, GAD theorists have persistently critiqued WID's ideological blinders concerning the development industry's participation in uneven global capitalist expansion via the continuation of imperialist and neocolonial relations between "donor" states, populations, and financial institutions and "recipient" nations and populations.

While these conceptual shifts held promise then and continue to have salience in the development discourse and practice, particularly among activist and social-movement-oriented organizations, GAD has not retooled dominant paradigms of women and gender in development (Marchand and

Parpart 1995). Wilson (2015) argues that as GAD conceptual innovations were taken up in development scholarship and institutional practice in the 1990s, the incisive idea that gender is coproduced by other markers of difference that create complex networks of power relations was neutralized, ironically, by concerted efforts to "mainstream" gender. As "gender" gained "official status" (Cornwall et al. 2008, 4) in dominant development institutions, those same institutions concertedly shifted emphasis away from state-led liberal welfarist approaches to reducing inequality and meeting basic needs toward neoliberal market-centered economic restructuring approaches characterized by structural adjustment policies (Bergeron 2013).[6] In this process of realignment, institutions strategically "emphasized some aspects of the feminist agenda and pushed others out of the frame" (Cornwall, Harrison, and Whitehead 2008, 4). Rather than radically revising the terms of engagement, feminist concepts such as agency and empowerment designed to get to the root of multiple marginality were (and continue to be) appropriated and transformed in the service of the very systems feminist theorists (GAD and WID) challenged and attempted to reconfigure. Neoliberal frameworks use a hollow version GAD's notion of "gender" as a rubric to recuperate WID notions of women as individual rational actors, but under a reconfigured social contract, women are now "empowered" to be perpetually responsive to novel forms of risk resulting from macroeconomic institutional restructuring in the name of development.

As I mention in the introduction and trace throughout the chapters, Sylvia Chant's analytic, the "feminization of responsibility and obligation," provides important insight into the ideological reworking of elements of WID and GAD that have implications for coalescing of GID as knowledge paradigm. Building on Saskia Sassen's (2000, 2001) foundation, the "feminization of survival," which foregrounds the fact that "households and whole communities are increasingly dependent on [women for] their survival" (2000, 506), Chant (2006, 2008) focuses in on responsibility and obligation to articulate the multidimensional nature of women's material and symbolic privation as they shoulder the burdens of ongoing economic crises. Under conditions in which men are reluctant to contribute or incapable of contributing "inputs such as labor and financial contributions to household livelihoods," and women remain subject to "persistent gender inequalities in negotiations over obligations and entitlements in households," poor women across diverse geographic and cultural locations express a "growing weight of responsibility" to "assum[e] greater liability for dealing with poverty" (Chant 2015, n.p.; Chant 2008, 182, 191n6).

According to Chant (2008), the responsibility women feel is "non-negotiable," "binding," and inherently gendered and gendering. "Women have less scope to resist the roles and activities imposed on them structurally (for example through legal contracts or moral norms), or situationally (though the absence of spouses or male assistance) and that duty often becomes 'internalised'" (191n6). As social institutions fail to mitigate poverty and disenfranchisement and millions of dutiful, hardworking women step in to compensate for austerity measures, expectations regarding poor women's essential capacity for self-sacrifice, self-discipline, and other-serving are entrenched. Under neoliberalism, conventional gendered expectations ascribed to women as caregivers, who take responsibility for family as an ethical and moral obligation, are sutured to economic efficiency and rational choice and transformed into "responsibilization" (Kelly 2001, 107). As "responsibilized" actors, poor women are expected to draw on this essentialized gendered obligation to take on the social, emotional, and material costs of mitigating institutionally generated insecurity and risk, which compound already complex crises such as food insecurity, civil conflict and displacement, environmental destruction, and "working poverty" (living on $2 per day or less). As feminists in the Global North and Global South in development institutions worked to disaggregate girls as a discreet target category from "women" and "youth" and move them from the margins to the center of the development agenda, they did so in the context of these complicated politics.

WID→GAD→GID: Corporatizing "The Girl" for Development

Since the 1980s, the World Bank has forwarded a human-capital-investment discourse as a central argument for targeting girls. Former World Bank president Lawrence Summer's (1992, 1993) oft-cited statement that "girls' education is the highest return on investment in the developing world" undergirds early GID concerns about bringing girls forward as specific kinds of development targets. High-profile pronouncements like the UN's 1991–2001 Decade of the Girl Child and the Girl Child Diagnosis (Section L) of the *Beijing Platform for Action* (UN 2001) used repurposed WID and GAD assumptions about women in order to position girls on the development agenda as proto-women-citizen-subjects.[7] This discourse argues that once vulnerable girls are removed from the oppressive structures of local patriarchies and granted access to education and economic participation, they have the potential to be better daughters and grow in to better women, wives, and mothers in the service of economic growth at all scales (Croll 2006; Monkman and Hoffman

2013). Advocates "emphasiz[ed]" girls' "entry into social production" (Croll 2006, 1288) through schooling, job training, and formal economic participation while devaluing their social reproductive roles in household care-labor economies as barriers to educational and subsequent (formal) economic participation. They foregrounded the harm girls experience from "cultural" practices like girl-child wasting, child marriage, and female genital cutting (UN 2001). Consistent with WID's efficiency approach, GAD-inflected justice arguments concerning the protection of girls' substantive and interlocking social, political, and economic rights were sutured to (and largely subsumed under) instrumental causal claims for broad social and economic impact.[8]

As GID gathered force amid crises created by aggressive neoliberal policies, complex contradictions accumulated as GID coalesced as a paradigm. On one hand, it drew "power and legitimacy" from "authentic calls" from the Global South for "education and economic security" for girls and women historically denied access to schooling (Moeller 2014a, 75). On the other hand, the arbiters of mainstream development, such as the World Bank, emerged early as vocal GID advocates, generating and funding research focused on the economic urgency of investment in adolescent girls, particularly girls' education, even though World Bank and International Monetary Fund conditional requirements for development financing had severely undermined education systems, among other social institutions, throughout the Global South (Moeller 2014a). Consequently, poor girls and women were left with the "responsibilized" "choice" to forgo schooling and other "human capital investments" and focus on intergenerational survival.

Nonetheless, by 2000 the UN's Millennium Development Goals (MDGs) codified GID, and particularly girls' education, as a global development priority, and these complex contradictions deepened as GID advocacy increasingly became the purview of corporate-led public–private partnerships. Not coincidentally, during this period, "responsibility became a corporate word" (Moeller 2014a, 76). As transnational corporations (TNCs) continually reach for new markets, they have aggressively marketed themselves as development brokers invested in "doing well by doing good" through corporate social responsibility (CSR) schemes (Calkin 2016; Hayhurst 2011; Moeller 2014a, 76). The trend toward CSR has motivated the "veritable explosion of new development actors from the private sector" engaged in "speeding up" the circulation and consolidation of policy discourse, as well as programmatic intervention through the "density and complexity of international linkages," such as public–private partnerships, and the "global public itself, mobilised by celebrity endorsement" (Biccum 2011, 1333). In the process, TNCs are resignified as "special sources of authority on gender and development" (Calkin

2016, 163), particularly in the field of education (Moeller 2014a). Critique of corporate extractive and exploitive labor practices throughout the 1990s (of Nike Inc. in particular) becomes "almost passé" in the new millennium (Moeller 2014a, 76). As the development industry expands beyond states and multilateral institutions to enthusiastically include corporations, so do markets; more workers and more consumers are enfolded into an expansive capitalism. Rather than alter the fundamentally exploitive character of transnational capital accumulation predicated on free trade and flexible capital, TNCs have taken up the "responsibility" to "empower" adolescent girls in ways that effectively shift responsibilization downstream to girls.

Nike Inc. is only one among an array of transnational corporations attempting to profit from the social capital ascribed to championing girls.[9] Since the arrival of the corporation's CSR wing on the development stage, Nike has aggressively marketed girl-effects logic through its flagship global girlpower brand, the Girl Effect. Co-opting GAD-inflected discourse of gendered empowerment as grassroots social justice through the rhetoric of "movement" building, Nike (ironically) debuted the Girl Effect to a relatively small group of elite powerbrokers at the World Economic Forum in Davos in 2009 and then sought popular support globally among citizens-cum-donors through Web 2.0 platforms. From its trajectory as an ambiguous "rallying point" (Kylander 2011, 2) for transnational corporate executives, heads of state, and everyday citizens to an incorporated formal nonprofit organization fueled by public–private partnerships, the Girl Effect is emblematic of corporatized GID. Under the persuasive marketing cover of "girlpower[ed] development" (Koffman and Gill 2013b, 86), rationalizing GID as "girl effects" has elevated girls' empowerment discourse from a policy stream within mainstream development institutions to a globalizing new commonsense that establishes the legitimacy and authority of the purported predictability of return to investment in poor, racialized adolescent girls and their girlhoods in the Global South.[10] This reasoning is self-replicating; it has become very difficult to consider girls in the Global South (all of whom are impoverished, marginalized, and oppressed by local culture, according to this logic) without thinking about them through visual and textual discourses that repackage, recycle, and recirculate these claims.

Girl-effects logic now extends beyond any single organization to encompass an assemblage of institutional, representational, and ethio-affective social forces coalescing around girls' lives and bodies as ideal sites of development. As high-profile "Girl Champions"[11] like Nicholas Kristof and his wife, Sheryl WuDunn, exuberantly argue in a 2009 special issue of the *New York Times Magazine*, echoing the rhetorical idiom of girl-effects logic, "The world is awakening to a powerful truth: Women and girls aren't the problem; they're the solution." Kristof and WuDunn point to "growing recognition among everyone from the World Bank to the U.S. military's Joint Chiefs of Staff to aid organizations like CARE that focusing on women and girls is the most effective way to fight global poverty and extremism." As they argue in their book, *Half the Sky: Turning Oppression into Opportunity for Women Worldwide*, investment in women and girls as "economic catalysts" can "[transform] bubbly teenage girls from brothel slaves into successful businesswomen" (2009a, xxii). In step with (and co-productive of) this consensus, in the past fifteen years, all major multi- and bilateral development institutions have (re)framed girls as targets for investment and intervention. A large and still growing array of corporations, corporate foundations, private family foundations, large transnational NGOs, small local community-based organizations, advocacy organizations, research nonprofits, and social marketing firms, as well as various partnerships among these private institutions and national governments, are now involved in "girl work" (Greene et al. 2010).[12]

For example, Girl Rising, a transnational business partnership with social aims forged between U.S.-based Intel Corporation and U.S.-based nonprofit 10 × 10, is designed specifically to support girls' education in the Global South. Drawing on the girl-effects playbook, Girl Rising ties justice imagery of girl's empowerment as revolutionary—"one girl with courage is a revolution"—to the celebrity-infused call for a global "movement" to invest in girls' education through its widely distributed eponymously titled film, "Girl Rising," and related merchandise, including a book and a K–12 companion curriculum created by the Pearson Foundation.[13] In search of emerging markets for consumer goods *and* a newly emerging market in girls' empowerment as a signifier of late-modern progress, Girl Rising has recently "franchised" to India. Girl Rising India (GRI) describes itself this way: "Bollywood star power + Girl Rising + private sector support = a nationwide movement to raise the value of the girl, and get more girls in classrooms countrywide!"[14] GRI is formulated, funded, and marketed by the public–private consortium of USAID, Hewlett-Packard, Goldman Sachs, 6Sense (a big-data predictive marketing firm), and Intel Corporation, as well as private individuals and family foundations. "Transnational business initiatives" (Calkin 2016, 159), like Girl Rising (and by extension, GRI), have been integral to the formation of GID. These initiatives tend to operate very similarly through strategic public–private partnerships that extend reach and cultivate legitimacy through provocative, high-production-value corporate branding, often with celebrity spokespersons, effective social-media marketing and "product" circulation, and popular buy-in among everyday citizen who join "the movement," buy products, donate money, and spread the word.[15] For the most part these initiatives employ very similar (if not sometimes the very same, as the repetition of the "movement" rhetoric indicates)[16] visual and textual discursive strategies to communicate a series of coordinated messages that together form the paradigmatic infrastructure of current GID. Many of these structuring claims that provide the meaning-circuitry of GID have also come into play variously throughout this book. Examples: adolescent girls are left out of development; girls' adolescence is a key point of leverage; adolescent girls are victims of local patriarchy; investing in girls is the right thing *and* the smart thing to do; girls have untapped potential; girls have the unique capacity to break cycles of intergenerational poverty; girls' education is the key to empowerment; empowerment always means formal, licit economic participation; girls' education is the key to growth in GDP; girls education is the key to sustainability; investing in girls is the key to every solution; and on it goes.

The trouble with GID as it is currently conceived and communicated is its extractive, neocolonial character. As Chant and Sweetman (2012, 523) aptly assert, "Smart economics seeks to use women and girls to fix the world." Maria Eitel, founding CEO and president of the Nike Foundation (now co-chair) and currently chair of the Girl Effect, and Robert Zoellick, former president of the World Bank (2007–2012), are principle architects of girl-effects logic and partners in its persistence, beginning with the launch of the Adolescent Girls Initiative in 2008. This initiative partnered Nike Inc., Goldman Sachs, Cisco, and Standard Charter with the World Bank and bilateral-aid agencies in four donor states (United States, United Kingdom, Sweden, Denmark) and the City of Milan to "prove the girl effect" by investing in adolescent girls in Liberia, Afghanistan, Nepal, Rwanda, and South Sudan.[17] As Eitel and Zoellick explain, "Taking action" to invest in girls to "stop poverty before it starts" is "simple" when "you" learn to see poor, racialized, non-Western girls as "untapped resources":

> It doesn't mean changing everything. It just takes including girls in what you are already doing. Economic growth and competitiveness. Food security. Climate change. Migration. HIV/AIDS. Population growth. Maternal mortality and reproductive health. Peace and security. You get the idea. If there is an issue you are working on, including girls will deliver better results (Girl Effect, n.d., n.p).

We see in this "simple" framework a singular focus on gender to the exclusion of other markers of marginality and no attention to the intersecting structural institutions involved in any one of these complex crises. In fact, so this reasoning goes, "you" do not need to account for "everything"; all "you" have to do is "include" "girls." The rhetorical address positions citizen-consumers, corporate-citizens, and development experts in the Global North as the "you" with the capacity to act by "including girls" to "deliver better results."

Investing in girls also "delivers better results" for business as well. According to the Global Business Coalition for Education (GBCE), a broker of strategic corporate investment marshaled to "empower, mentor and protect 6 million girls across the world" through public-private partnerships,[18] "it is in a company's direct best interest to identify how it can support girls' education in the short-term and long-term" (Miranda 2015, 10).[19] In the short-term, investing in girls' education provides direct "pre-commercialization access to consumers in developing markets and marginalized communities" that gives "firms the opportunity to gather market intelligence, learn first-hand about consumer habits and practices, and build corporate reputation among future customers and consumers" as well as future employees (11). In the long-term,

> as developed markets become increasingly competitive, and market growth rates slow, the world's poorest economies and marginalized communities become the last frontiers of market growth for many multinational corporations. By increasing access to quality education for girls, businesses will be fueling economic prosperity in those markets and helping to create better-educated, healthier communities, which in turn will increase local purchasing power. Educated girls will become skilled workers, innovators, consumers, savers, and taxpayers—all of which will result in increased future financial returns for corporations. (11)

Transnational business initiatives and public–private partnerships effectively instrumentalize girls' lives as "simple" solutions to historically and structurally produced global problems such as poverty and marginalization, and perhaps most perniciously, they are positioned as the "final frontier" in expansion of markets. Entrenched geopolitical asymmetries of power connecting historical imperialism to the contemporary globalization of "flexible" forms of market fundamentalism and Western political liberalism are not only occluded in this discourse they are re- and pre-packaged as corporate social justice. That is, "justice" for corporations in terms of creating new markets, consumers, and workers, along with "justice" for poor, marginalized communities as exploitable human capital investments.

Empirically, today's girls are already positioned to take on the burdens of a *different* "girl effect": several generations of unevenly distributed economic growth as the continued "ripple effect" of austerity policies and capital expansion over the past thirty years have contributed to widespread crises like devastation from climate change, migration, HIV/AIDS, and endemic food insecurity—precisely the complex institutionally generated problems that GID advocates claim investing in girls will solve. Girls in Development discourse claims girl effects are good for girls, and I have no doubt that "Girl Champions" want the best for girls. Discursive effects, however, exceed intentions; discourse becomes real, and its myriad implications are materially realized, within the power of institutions. Corporatized GID discourse threatens the fragile liberatory possibilities of centering poor, non-Western, racialized girls' lives as lives that matter by positioning their bodies and the space their girlhoods occupy as cheap "resource[s] for global capital" (Grosser and van der Gaag 2013, 80). Understood *as* capital, adolescent girls' proper "development" into entrepreneurial subjects recapitulates the proper "development" of global capitalism in the form of increased GDP for individual states and predictable aggregate growth for all.[20] Strategically creating "markets in girls' empowerment" in which "empowerment itself becomes a commodity" (Banet-Weiser 2015, 255, 1) mutes calls for girls' rights to substantive equality, relational autonomy, and fundamental *mattering* despite centuries of structural violence, much less in recognition of ongoing structural violence.

"Girlpower" in this discourse is substantive empowerment's "uncanny double" (Fraser 2009, 114). Empowerment is no longer about creating conditions in which girls can come to understand the intersecting forces that structure their lives and work in collective ways to challenge and transform the institutions that sustain their marginalization. Instead, empowerment is limited to the "power" to take responsibility for self and others (Cornwall 2014; Cornwall and Rivas 2015). Likewise, "independence" is less about freedom, and more about the "power" to make choices around self-sacrifice and service to others. Under these conditions, when social institutions and structural systems fall short or fail to support girls and their communities, the discourse of smarter economics produces girl-subjects who will already be trained to draw on stores of gendered obligation and responsibility in order to step in and compensate; in fact, the privatization of social goods relies on this inculcation of identity. Further, when girls fail to realize the dream of economic empowerment in the precise ways GID predicts, as responsibilized subjects, they will already know how to place the blame and burden on themselves and not the social institutions that govern their actual options. In both cases, accountability for social success (including survival) is shifted squarely to girls themselves—and not just for everyone they care for, but for distant strangers as well. Ironically, implicit in the promise of protracted adolescence and "growing up in school" is the idea that childhood and adolescence should fundamentally be free from the adult obligations and responsibilities inherent in marriage and motherhood. Maintaining schoolgirlhood through responsibilized girlhood does not guarantee the rights and decision-making power commensurate with what they are expected to give as laborers of love, duty, and obligation. Yet, as we have seen throughout the previous chapters, schoolgirls, their mothers and teachers, and indeed development actors at all scales invest great faith in girlpower to counter or resolve failures of development policy that decades of WID and GAD research and activism have exposed, struggled to destabilize, and also perpetuated.

If we recall Koko, the elderly Maasai woman in Hodgson's research introduced in chapter 1, it is precisely her girlhood rendered through GID as early/arranged/forced marriage, polygyny, violent sexual debut, precocious pregnancy, unbridled fertility, denial of education, patriarchal constraints on freedom and autonomy, and so on that stands in for "Other" girlhoods. Through the lens of GID, Other girls come to matter because schoolgirl success (measured as increased female literacy rates, labor-market participation, political representation, fertility decline, decreased maternal and child mortality rates, arrested HIV infection rates, and so on) stands in for modernity and progress in terms of gender. With its allegiance to corporate-led funding, brand marketing, and agenda setting, current GID frameworks effectively reduce girls to embodied capital and narrow our understanding of their lives to measurable indicators. In the process, schoolgirlhood becomes an *effect* of the ongoing will to improve the Other embedded in Western (neo)liberal (post)feminism that seamlessly covers over the extractive nature of market expansion and perpetuates corporate-led development as the best arbiter of the just distribution of life chances for Other girls and their communities. GID advocates repeatedly and urgently claim that girls can change the world, but as a technique power, GID works to reproduce the world as it is by enfolding responsibilized girls into an imagined global citizenry rather than radically reimaging a more just world for girls and for everyone. The twenty-first-century sequel to the colonial civilizational narrative of empire thus relies on a late-modern twist: GID's Third World Girl is scripted as the one to "save the future of humanity" ("The Girl Effect" video).[21]

Paradox or Promise? Maasai Schoolgirlhood in the Context of GID

This book has told an inevitably partial story about the experiences of a group of Maasai schoolgirls who live in scattered rural communities in one geopolitical location and who reflect, refract, and in some ways resist the ideas that circulate about and around them regarding girls who go to school.

As I have argued, GID as a knowledge paradigm based in girl-effects logics enables possibilities for schoolgirls and it also complicates and sometimes contradicts those possibilities as schoolgirls negotiate the social costs of going to school. At the level of policy creation and circulation, "girls' voices" are often deployed to re-amplify the already-established consensus around possibilities and limitations for girls in the Global South and reinforce the approaches already in place. At the local level, it is possible to read the "hunger" for girls' education as the simple reassertion of girl-effects logic "on the ground." Schoolgirls want to be in and stay in school. They imagine that, as a result of this experience, they will lead the "good life" of educated women. Such a result they, their mothers, and their teachers feel will go far to ameliorate and erode the persistent popular belief that Maasai "hate" education and always have, a notion that contributes to ethnic marginality. Everyone expressed great faith in waged work as the results of education and the positive implications "having your salary" can have for shifting expectations of Maasai women from subservient and "under the husband" to empowered economic actors with increased decision-making power in their homes and in their communities.

"Aspirations," however "are never simply individual (as the language of wants and choices inclines us to think). They are always formed in interaction and in the thick of social life" (Appadurai 2004, 67). Being a "modern girl"—a beneficiary and promulgator of development—has been, and continues to be, tied to educational participation (Thomas 2006a, 50). As I have shown, schoolgirls' bodies and minds become the platform on which the ambivalent condition of being an educated Maasai person is sometimes dramatically, often mundanely, played out. Schools, in Maasai communities as elsewhere, "stand for the possibility of creating new social forms" that offer "new ideas and practical solutions for moving people beyond their past" (Stambach 2001, 9). Everyone talking about girls' education for poor girls and their communities in the Global South has endowed schooling with the power to exceptionalize educated girls, to lift them from their social worlds, and to recreate them as different kinds of people. Yet when it comes to new social forms for girlhood and womanhood, it seems that some changes are easier for communities to navigate than others. This is in part because "old" social forms persist and create friction against "new" variations.

It is also possible, therefore, to read against and around reaffirmations to notice and attend to the ideas, insights, and sometimes-subtle moments in which schoolgirls' stated needs, desires, and observations fall outside of normative GID scripts. When schoolgirls struggle to negotiate the social effects of emurata and enkanyakuai or simultaneously embody schoolgirlhood and girlchildhood, their experiences and articulations defy the borders of girl-effects logic and point to their commitments and aspirations tied not just to market logics of individual success and cultural disavowal. The adults in their lives likewise reaffirmed girl-effects logic but also expressed ambivalence that blurred the confident demarcations around "the educated Maasai woman."

For instance, early in the research I visited Maria at her home. She lived with her paternal uncle and his family, including his wife Agnes, their young son, and his mother (Maria's grandmother), as well as others in a large compound. Maria, Agnes, and I played with Agnes's son and other children in the house that day and chatted about the research. At one point Maria commented, "When elder people call me a girl, I am comfortable with that, but my age-mates? No, I don't want them to call me a girl." Agnes interjected: "Me, I don't like people calling me a woman. I hate that name!" she cried in dismay as she laughed emphatically. "You, you woman!" she yelled using a mockingly male voice, as if a man was ordering her around. "*Aaii*, when you say that word in our mother tongue (*na kitok!*), it just sounds bad!" We all laughed at the look on her face and the resolute tone of her voice. She wanted to use the word "lady" instead but laughed further when I asked if there is a word in Maa for "lady" because the best answer, they decided, was "koko," which is also grandmother. We decided that "koko" wouldn't work, because, as Agnes exclaimed, "me, I am not *old*!" with a look of mischief on her face, reflecting the assumption that a "koko" is someone past her sexual prime. Agnes interjected with playful exaggeration and exasperation, raising her voice some to make her point: "Really, *who are we*?!"

Laughing at her adamance, we decided that we needed a word for a female person who is no longer a girl but not yet a koko, one that reflects and creates social respect; a word that accounts for but encompasses more than "wife" and "mother" without the negative connotations of "woman" as someone who can be summoned like a child by men. I asked: "Do you think this has changed, Agnes? For example, when your mom was coming up, do you think she was confused about who she was? Maria says, 'I am not a girl, I am not a woman, I am in between' and you say 'Who are we?'—do you think your mother had this same problem?" "*Aaii*, no," she declared, and waved her hand as if swatting the thought away like a fly. "Them, they know themselves! But for us, we came to this world when all these things have come. . . . We don't know the real mother tongue. . . . I don't know all of the vocabularies of Maa and even English we don't know it very well, so we are just mixing the languages. . . . For me, I went to school early. We now know school better [than culture]. . . . We lost something [when we went to school]."

As an educated woman, salaried employee, wife, and mother, Agnes has no interest in being called out and disciplined by men like a child. At the same time, she acknowledged that seeing the world through the lens of school knowledge can be disorienting when Maasai frameworks, including language, are still socially vivid. Perhaps Maasai of her parents' generation do "know themselves," but they are also not immune to the disorientation social change brings. As one Maasai teacher said of his elders, who would be Agnes's elders too:

> Today, when [our elders] compare the older days to now, they see that those cultural traditions have lost value. Those of us who went to school are more organized and manage resources better than others. Some are government employees. We have different lifestyles. They are regretting [their decisions] but it's too late. . . . [Yet] they also regret the loss of moranism. They feel the pain and are sad that it's finished and that modern education is imposed. Despite the goodness of the results [of modern education] for the community, there is still serious loss for them . . . of cohesiveness. The traditional society had a feeling of being together—you are ours—but now this communalism is being lost and now it's yours and mine. The poor used to be accommodated. The fabric of life that held us together is wearing out. They partly blame education because [the educated] start to oppose traditions, and they also blame the church.

Development, as an extension of imperialism and capitalist expansion, is always and already a rationality of power that "maps people into certain coordinates of control. The aim is not simply to discipline individuals but to transform the conditions under which they live into a productive, normalized social environment—in short, to create modernity" (Escobar 1995, 156). As Arturo Escobar (1995) argues, "The fact that most women [and girls] in many parts of the Third Word want modernization must be taken seriously, yet the meaning of this modernization must not be taken for granted. Often it means something quite different from what it means in the West and been constructed and reconstructed as part of the development encounter" (189). Unevenly imposed and experienced, neoliberal development policies premised on "it's yours and mine" have gone a long way to empty the dream of modern life of the stuff that makes "modernization" so desirable. Social support from the state is fractured and inconsistent, owing much (including painful irony) to the intergenerational ripple effect of conditions tied to development financing in the past twenty years, compounded by the global market crisis in 2008. Further, the friction between old and new norms that arise from these conditions complicate social support from family and cooperative community approaches in which "you are ours" and vex the realization of social adulthood (Cole 2011; Omolo 2012). For example, formal salaried work was a key aspiration for schoolgirls and their families. Yet despite uneven growth in the overall economy, as the schoolgirls in this book grew into their adolescence and contemplated their adulthood as educated women, the Kenyan public sector contracted, the informal sector mushroomed along with precarity associated with "working poverty" (earning $2 a day or less), the formal sector grew marginally, and wage inequality between out-of-school adolescent girls and boys and adult men and women in formal and informal work, as well as inactivity and unemployment, persisted.[22] Continent wide, only 28 percent of Africa's labor force has stable wage-paying jobs.[23]

These trends suggest that any non-elite Kenyan schoolchild's aspirations for formal-wage employment may be a dream deferred; because the labor market is gendered (and gendering) poor Kenyan girls will come of age and struggle for access to the "modern wage sector." Maasai schoolgirls who dream of becoming pilots, magistrates, presidents, and doctors, particularly if they do not complete secondary school, are more likely to enter the deterritorialized international division of labor that is a predominant feature of neoliberal development. According to Chege and Sifuna (2006),

> Primary school leavers, many of them young women, are likely to be preferred as casual workers in agro-processing factories, such as those for tea and coffee, based on their basic literacy and numeracy skills. In addition, this group of workers would be most suited to work in subordinate positions based on the socialization provided by schools in aspects of punctuality, unquestioning obedience, regular attendance, and the ability to adapt to bureaucratic structures, among other working class attributes. Above all else, they are more likely to accept underpayment. (135)

For Maasai schoolgirls, this deferment is complicated by the persistence of the compounding intersectional challenges of rurality, ethnicity, gender, generational status, and class, not only in overall Kenyan society but also in their local contexts. Perhaps paradoxically, Maasai schoolgirls' firm connection to Maasai identities through language, parental home, and some enduring cooperative, community-based structures of support suggests that unlike girls from communities who have been mainstreamed by development, particularly educational access, since the colonial period, they might initially be insulated from the draw of the coffee and tea plantations and other urbanized export processing zones. But they will, regardless of the employment they seek, be rationalized within the framework of attributes conveyed as commonsense in any capitalist context. Valorization of the individual worker engaged in formal wage work in GID discourse, at all scales, covers over these conditions. Maasai schoolgirls therefore have to contend with navigating individual identity and community belonging at a time when social success in Kenya, as elsewhere, is increasingly individualized, privatized, and incontrovertibly gendered and gendering. Even formal wage earners like the teachers I talked with deliberately supplement their incomes with informal-sector activities. The costs of this work are disproportionately externalized to women and girls, in large part because adult women teach their students, run small shops, and care for and manage livestock on top of their domestic care-labor duties, which are often shared or handed over to daughters or other young female neighbors and kin.

Education as a process of development, like development itself, "is never a totalizing process, but is always a site of mediation and negotiation" (Hodgson 2001b, 276). In these collisions of macrostructural and microstructural forces, "the perpetual production of fluid and fractious social categories" and "innovative modes of . . . personhood" become key strategies for "securing something like a future" (Weiss 2004, 1–9). I have argued that these strategies for social success in the face of institutional insecurity at all scales are gendered and generational. A fundamental presupposition of the girlpower ethos embedded in GID discourse is this same requirement to self-invent and therefore create possibilities for one's future by digging deep into a wellspring of personal creativity, grit, and gravitas ascribed to essentialized expectations for girls (and women) to overcome, circumvent, or otherwise evade historical, structural, gendered, and generational constraints. Successful girlpowered girls are expected to work hard to create themselves as new kinds of persons—and they expect this of themselves—despite still-salient social expectations, and subsequent social harm, that have historically delimited their possibilities. To be a responsibilized daughter is to be implicated in the management and sustainability for systems far beyond one's affections for and obligations to family, community, and nation (DeJaeghere 2014).

As all of the narratives in this book suggest, preserving the legitimacy of schoolgirlhood significantly depends on schoolgirls' internal and external self-practice of the logics of self-determination, individual achievement, alienation from "tradition" and "culture," and self-knowledge outside of kinship norms. As I have shown, schoolgirls do often feel at odds with aspects of their culture that keep them tethered to old cultural norms like emurata. Yet we have also seen schoolgirls use ideas about enkanyakuai and "the girl-child" to forge more indelible parameters for schoolgirlhood, although such a stance relies on the social habitation of circumcised young female bodies in new ways that can be at odds with local gender expectations. I have tried to show, therefore, that current GID discourse at all scales entails risk. The production, performance, and perpetuation of schoolgirlhood as a mode of negotiating historical gendered ideologies about girls-cum-women's roles, rights, and responsibilities in Maasai society reauthorizes and reconstitutes conventional norms—local Maasai norms, as well as transnational norms—for proper feminine behavior. These norms offer a narrow departure from universalized assumptions of girls' gendered capacity for labor and care that ultimately preserve transnational patriarchal claims on girls' time, labor, and desire. Responsibilization discourse generated at the UN *and* in primary-school classrooms shifts accountability from state and local systems of support to individual girls and holds them accountable for taking on institutionally created risk. Within a globalizing politico-cultural ethos in which this regulatory responsibility is deeply internalized, "investments," can "[become] progressively detached from rights and rewards, . . . creating a new and deeper form of female exploitation" (Chant 2006, 208; Hodgson 2011). This is, for me, the negative power of GID as a knowledge paradigm fueled by girl-effects logics.

Nonetheless, I have also argued that this problematic logic wrenches open spaces of possibility that Maasai schoolgirls willingly enter, carrying with them the weight of a dogged faith in their self-disciplined power to meet the demands wagered by GID discourse at all scales. What sense can we make, then, of any openings responsibilized schoolgirlhood creates given the risks it inures? Kenyan idiom emphatically asserts that education is light. What if this light is fire? What might it mean that solutions for gendered exclusion, oppression, and even violence might lie in various strategic intensifications of gendered roles in ways that can foment change?

When the Light Is Fire: Schoolgirlhood as Dialectical Possibility

At the end of each interview with schoolgirls, Maria or Alice and I asked if the interviewee had any questions for us. Some had none; some had questions only for Maria or Alice, or just for me. Eunice, a bright, talkative, fifteen-year-old, Class 5 student at Enkeryian Primary School seemed to relish the conversation and chose to conduct her interview completely in English. I asked her, "Do you have any questions for Maria? She is joining the University of Nairobi in January." I was proud of Maria for graduating from a well-known provincial-level secondary school with marks high enough to gain admission to a four-year university (albeit as a parallel-degree student), as this was an uncommon occurrence for anyone in the area, much less for a girl. I wanted to make sure that the girls we interviewed had the chance to see Maria as a potential role model. Eunice paused thoughtfully before answering. Instead of asking her for advice, as I imagined might happen, Eunice had some advice for Maria. She said, "I have no question. I just want to tell her to work hard, because we are a long way facing the world."

Eunice did not seem shocked or amazed that Maria would be joining the university. Rather, she seemed to take this information in stride, as if these facts confirmed her own expectations for schoolgirl success. Her thoughtful statement reflected her belief stated in a variety of ways throughout her interview, that there is no "distraction" serious enough to deter the responsibilized schoolgirl from taking advantage of schooling to change one's family and community for the better. For instance, she explained that some girls drop out of school because "they just didn't take their minds back to remembering how their family is. . . . They didn't understand the problems in their families like shortage of food, so they just . . . I . . . I don't know why they drop." As her sentence breaks off, all of the intimately complex factors involved in schoolgirl dropout remain unstated, perhaps unknown, and effectively obscured. All that remains is schoolgirl responsibility, which, as discussed in chapter 4, is a blunt instrument against the continuum of gendered violence implicated in the shared understanding that schoolgirls are routinely sexually harassed and worse. These concerns are covered over by schoolgirls' own discourse of responsibility for self and others, obligation to family, community and nation, and the intensification of gendered hard work. Despite the effects on her daily life of myriad institutional failures out of her control, and the regulatory character of responsibilization, for Eunice, like so many of her peers, performing successful schoolgirlhood seemed less oppressive than liberating, even if it carried with it the social weight of the "we" of community and the "long way" of struggle in "facing the world." Managing that weight for many schoolgirls included distancing themselves from those schoolgirls who failed to be responsible, which in turn highlights the impossibility of responsibilized schoolgirlhood for schoolgirls made more vulnerable by relative poverty, patriarchal control, and even consensual sexual desire.

On one hand, this framing of the narrow space schoolgirls inhabit is contradictory, even paradoxical; on the other, the existence of this space, no matter how narrow or how fraught, suggests that schoolgirlhood should be seen as a dialectical site of possibility rather than a straightforward "[sign] of human freedom" (Abu-Lughod 1990, 42). Framed this way, new subjectivities that emerge are not the sum of contradictory parts but dynamic formations that actually tell us "more about forms of power and how people are caught up in them" (42) than evidence of the wholesale efficacy of individuated, autonomous "empowerment" required by GID. Instead, any sense of "empowerment" schoolgirls feel or aspire to feel is and will be embedded in their relational, intersubjective contexts in which new forms of oppression are densely entangled with new found "rights" (Abu-Lughod 2013).[24] Schoolgirlhood maps new "norms for futurity as a cultural capacity" to aspire (Appadurai 2004, 61) and in this way provides Maasai schoolgirls and their advocates and allies a cultural platform from which to imagine and engage their own futures. This platform is necessarily contingent and dialectical. Maasai schoolgirls strongly desire education not for the separation it foments between them and their home cultures, but precisely because of the complex imbrications of Maasai gendered social forms and generational political structures in local schools, and the recursive effects of "new" school knowledge for the future of their communities. A fundamental element in shifting the gendered relations of power within families and communities is less the explicit rejection of conventional gender roles, rights, and responsibilities and more the manipulation of these expectations and assumptions in ways that create possibilities for localized change, even as they can also create new forms of localized exclusion.

Without exception, schoolgirls aspire to be "school people," those who complete at least secondary school and even go on to tertiary study.[25] At the same time, they also want to be "middle people," *iltungana lepolos*, those who "combine some schooling with traditional activities." Middle people are also called *iltungana oviolo inkaik pkira*, or "people who can use both hands" (Sena 1986, 96). They imagine being active members of their community, helping their parents and siblings, and contributing to "development" in Maasailand. And in reality, all of the educated Maasai I met and talked to (teachers and development professionals) actively participated in "traditional activities" in addition to their formal, waged employment. It's not hard to imagine that schoolgirls will be similarly socially ambidextrous. For instance, even if they build "modern houses," drive vehicles, master computer skills, wear blue jeans, and even travel outside of Kenya, they will also buy, sell, and give livestock; attend circumcision celebrations for boys and girls (even if they decline to circumcise their own daughters); contribute to *harambees* to raise schools, build livestock dams, investigate farming, dig boreholes, passionately debate local politics, host weddings, and mourn the dead; they will speak Maa and endeavor to teach it to their children; they will show respect to their elders; adorn themselves with Maasai-made beaded jewelry for special occasions, and laugh until they cry at folktales like "Mbiti." Schoolgirls and their families aspire for them to become people who use both hands in order to cultivate cultural understandings of a gendered future in which all children, and particularly girls, go to school.

• • •

When we had time, David ole Kilusu, local elder and my host in Loodariak, and I sat over tea and discussed the research and life in general. In one of these conversations I said that I thought a byproduct or effect of development might be "confusion—over who people think they are, have been in the past, and want to be in the future." According to my notes, he said: "Is it development, actually, or education?" As I reread these comments now, my answer back to him would be something like: "Isn't it both?" Girls in Development discourse and practice at multiple scales have still-unfolding but no-less-profound implications for Maasai schoolgirls in the case-study communities. They and their families daily negotiate a central paradox of (post)colonialism: the constraints of the condition extend old exclusions and create new ones, while simultaneously opening up new possibilities for individuals and communities (Macamo 2005). Fervent belief in GID as a knowledge paradigm is enmeshed in a deeply held faith in the promise of economic development and modern living, what Fran Vavrus (2003) calls "desire." The desire for development as modern living manifests in the demand for schooling is paradoxically connected with deeply held gendered and generationally derived worldviews that can be at odds with development imperatives, particularly when they are embedded in the precarious economic realities of "decline" (Mukudi 2004; Vavrus 2003).

Schoolgirls do not distinguish between the desire they feel to be educated and the imperative they perceive to be developed. They also see evidence of decline all around them, but this does not dissuade their desire. Instead, it fuels it. Within this often-disconcerting dynamism, new ways of being, like being a schoolgirl, reflect unprecedented opportunities unevenly, dialectically, and contingently experienced. Out of this crucible, schoolgirlhood might be the seedbed from which surprising reconfigurations of gender norms can sprout and trope toward transformative ends within neoliberalism. The central animating questions at the heart of this book offer us pathways for thinking in multivalent (rather than reductive, sloganistic, and mythological) ways about the intimate calculus of girls' education, gender equality, and social change in these particular communities that may resonate beyond them: What does it mean or can it mean to be a Maasai girl and go to school? What opportunities do these subject-positions offer Maasai schoolgirls, and what challenges? Why do identities matter in the discourse of development? My goal has been to be evocative and provocative, to begin to pry open "the schoolgirl" as a one-dimensional social category and blunt instrument for the realization of narrowly conceived development and illuminate the often small but meaningful ways Maasai schoolgirls participate as agents in their own lives. *When the Light Is Fire* therefore aims to preserve radical hope about schoolgirl futures even as it critiques the deeply problematic assumptions embedded in development discourses targeting adolescent girls' bodies, minds, and affective attachments to culture and community. If this book confides a feminist development fable, it is a cautionary one: in our efforts to confront multiple marginalizations produced through historically and structurally unfolding intersections of gender, generation, race, ethnicity, and empire through a compromised and compromising development regime, we must be awake to the risks at stake in contradictions created by the process, alive to the rewards inherent in small ruptures, and always ever-vigilant against the ease with which we, and the girls we cheer for, are seduced by the promise of corporatized development.

Notes

Introduction. "Girls are the most powerful force of change on the planet."

1. All of the names in this book are pseudonyms. Most Kenyan Maasai have a Maasai name and a "Christian" name; readers will note that I have mixed the pseudonyms to reflect this practice. The names of places, schools, and other locations have not been changed.

2. I have been to various areas of Kenya's Maasailand in Narok and Kajiado Counties many times since my first visit in 1999. The data for this book was collected from August 2007 to March 2008, and from May to July 2011. In 2007–08 I lived in Loodariak and traveled around Keekonyokie Central Location (KCL) to each of the nine government-run coeducational primary day-schools in the location at the time: Loodariak Primary School, Innyonyorri Primary School, Oltepesi Primary School, Eremit Primary School, Enkoerroi Primary School, Embolei Primary School, Enkeryian Primary School, Ensonura Primary School, and Olepolos Primary School. In the summer of 2011 I stayed in Ngong and traveled each day to all of the nine schools.

3. As interpreters, they interpreted not only during our interviews with schoolgirls (when needed) but also during interviews with Maasai mothers and any speakers we encountered who did not speak English. They also worked as translators when they transcribed interview data from the digital recorder.

4. A note on language and translation: unless noted as Kiswahili, all non-English words and phrases in this book are Maa, the language of Maasai people. *Matatu* is the Kiswahili word to refer to small vehicles used for public transportation, most typically fifteen-passenger minivans but also pickup trucks.

5. As of 2010 Kajiado District has been renamed Kajiado County in accordance with the new constitution and state reorganization. KCL no longer exists as an administrative unit. As of February 2016, after being gazetted from Kajiado North (established

in 2013), the areas originally within the boundaries of KCL are now known as Kajiado West Constituency. The nine sublocations and their primary schools that formed the case study for this project retained their discreet names, although new administrative boundaries have been drawn as wards (Keekonyokie Ward—Ensonura, Oltepesi, Olepolos, Loodariak, Innyonyorri, Enkeryian, Embolei; and Ewuaso Oo Nkidong'I Ward—Eremit, Enkoerroi) and new schools have been built. In order to preserve the sense of geographic space that constituted KCL and therefore "bounded" these sublocations into a case site at the time of the interviews, I have decided to continue using KCL in the book rather than use several new names to refer to the now multiple administrative sites that are currently still dynamic and contested.

6. Over the course of 2009 Kajiado County and the arid and semiarid lands would go on to experience one of the worst droughts on record.

7. All of the head teachers, and all but one of the deputy head teachers, I met during the 2007–8 data collection were men (most Maasai, two were not). I understand that in the intervening years, at least one of the schools in this study is now headed by a woman (although she is not Maasai).

8. I conducted a total of 127 schoolgirl interviews over the two trips (August 2007 through March 2008, and May through July 2011). I also interviewed over the course of two trips thirty mothers and thirty teachers. Schoolgirl interviews were conducted in a mixture of three languages (Kiswahili, Maa, and English). Interviews with mothers were conducted in Maa. In both cases I worked with my research assistants to interpret for me and our interviewees. All interviews with schoolgirls (except for five) and mothers were digitally recorded, and my research assistants transcribed them into English. I took notes during teacher interviews in 2007–08; in 2011 teacher interviews were digitally recorded. All teacher interviews were conducted in English with no interpretation; I transcribed teacher interviews from 2007 to 2008; a transcription service transcribed the 2011 teacher interviews.

9. Throughout the book I use the terms "Global North" and "Global South" as a way of indicating geopolitical asymmetries among and within regions of the world. It is one phrasing among several, each with their own genealogies: developed world/developing world; first world/third world; the West/the rest; one-thirds world/two-thirds world; center/periphery; donor/highly indebted; postindustrial/industrializing, and so on. At base, Global North and Global South "refer to those, anywhere, who live prosperously and precariously, respectively" (Sheppard and Nagar 2010, 186; see also Mohanty 2003a). I chose this particular phrasing as shorthand for regions of the world targeted for development (the Global South) and the regions doing the targeting (the Global North).

10. A similar construct exists in academic understandings of Maasai, too. Also, as Hodgson (2001b) and others (for example, Hughes 2006) argue, Maasai themselves have capitalized on this image, particularly when it comes to marketing for tourists. This is in evidence when Maasai schoolboys who, short of circumcision, do not practice "warriorhood" in any real sense, dress as warriors, including weaving braids into their own hair, to dance "warrior dances" at safari lodges. They effectively perform

"Maasai-ness" in ways that sitting in desks and reading books would not, according to the stereotypical image of Maasai masculinity. A *rungu* is a Kiswahili word for a club, like a knobkerrie, that can be plain or elaborately beaded; it is iconically associated with Maasai warriors and used as a weapon. There is also a ceremonial *rungu* that Maasai men carry to gesticulate with when they speak in front of groups.

11. This is an altered version of Abosede George's (2014) title of her introduction to *Making Modern Girls: A History of Girlhood, Labor, and Social Development in Colonial Lagos*.

12. While material and ideological investments in youth as the future have historically centered on (middle-class, white) boys and young men, at various historical moments specific categories of girls and young women have also been held up contrarily as social problems (racialized girls, poor girls) to be managed, often punitively by the state, and as beacons of social progress (white girls, middle-class girls) to be encouraged, often exuberantly by the state (and markets). See Harris (2004) and Lesko (2001) among others.

13. See also: *The Modern Girl around the World* (Weinbaum et al. 2008); *Girlhood: A Global History* (Helgren and Vasconcellos 2010); and *Girls: Feminine Adolescence in Popular Culture and Cultural Theory* (Driscoll 2002). Scholars have also documented girlhood in a variety of national contexts and historical periods from the eighteenth through the twentieth centuries. Examples include, in the late eighteenth- through early-nineteenth-century United States: Joan Jacobs Brumberg (1998), Ruth Alexander (1995), Mary Odem (1995), and Marcia Chatelain (2015); in colonial Kenya: Lynn Thomas (2003, 2006a, 2006b), Corrie Decker (2010), and Brett Shadle (2006); in colonial Nigeria: Abosede George (2014); in contemporary Tanzania: Dorothy Hodgson (1996b) and Beth Ann Pratt (2003); in contemporary Sierra Leone: Caroline Bledsoe (1990), Hale (2014); and many others.

14. Neoliberal economic restructuring and neoliberalism as a cultural ethos have had uneven and heterogeneous cultural effects as well as uneven and still unfolding economic results. See Molyneux (2008), Hickel (2014); Mohanty (2003a, 2013); Ong (2006); Cornwall, Harrison, and Whitehead (2008); Harris (2004); Gonick (2006); Hodgson (2011); Peck and Tickell (2002); Kendall and Silver (2014); Ferguson (2006); Wilson (2008); and many others for discussions regarding these dispersed and diverse effects across contexts, time periods, and scales.

15. For examples, see the African American Policy Forum's report, *Black Girls Matter: Pushed Out, Overpoliced and Underprotected* (Crenshaw, Ocen, and Nanda 2014); *Push Out: The Criminalization of Black Girls in Schools* (Morris 2016); *Girlhood Interrupted: The Erasure of Black Girls' Girlhood* (Epstein, Blake, and González 2017); *The Female Offender: Girls, Women and Crime* (Chesney-Lind and Pasko 2013); *Girls, Delinquency and Juvenile Justice* (Chesney-Lind and Sheldon 2014); and *Complicated Lives: Girls, Parents, Drugs and Juvenile Justice* (Lopez 2017). See also examples of historical analyses: Bernstein (2011), Chatelain (2015), and Wright (2016).

16. See Simidele Doeskun's (2015) "For Western Girls Only? Post-Feminism as Transnational Culture" for a compelling critique of the Anglocentrism of the existing

literature on postfeminism, as well as the applicability of the concept for theorizing new femininities in the Global South drawn from her empirical research with affluent, educated young women in Lagos, Nigeria.

17. And as Karishma Desai (2016) persuasively argues, this logic both shapes and anchors investment in girls as a moral imperative.

18. To my knowledge, key components of this public discourse—earlier versions of the Girl Effect website—are no longer available as such, although the Girl Effect YouTube channel archives some of this discourse, and Google searches also render copious textual and visual discourse from the period. The Girl Effect has morphed since its beginning as an affective (and effective) tagline developed to promote the Nike Foundation. See the foundation's first promotional video, released in 2004, "I Dare You," for a first use of the tagline and an early instantiation of girl-effects logic (see Switzer 2013 for an elaboration of this argument). I first encountered the Girl Effect in 2008 after an infusion of $90–100 million from the NoVo Foundation and the debut of the viral videos "The Girl Effect" and "The Clock Is Ticking." With this launch, the tagline was formally "branded" with a consistent color scheme and graphic design as an emerging open-source archive of expertise regarding girls' empowerment in the Global South (https://news.nike.com/news/nike-foundation-launches-new-girleffectorg). This branding also proclaimed the Girl Effect as a "movement." In September 2015 the Girl Effect announced that it had incorporated into an independent nonprofit organization and self-described "social business," though promotional materials made clear it would "always be a movement" (https://www.facebook.com/girleffect/photos/a.140280362375.110434.14159872375/10153653110112376/?type=3&theater). In July 2016 the new CEO Farah Golant launched the "new" Girl Effect to a "new audience" with a new animated video, "Invisible Barriers" (http://www.girleffect.org/what-girls-need/articles/july16/august-launch/girl-effect-uses-invisible-barriers-film-to-launch-new-position/). The current version of the Girl Effect presents a completely different "look" (color scheme and graphic design) and a revised public discourse. An analysis of the Girl Effect as an independent organization is beyond the scope of this book. I can note, however, that the discourse employs less instrumentalizing language, and girls' lives are presented as embedded in cultural contexts and communities that are supportive as well as constraining. These changes are positive and could arguably have come as a result of feminist critiques, including my own. Yet, exceptionalizing adolescent girls' proper physical and entrepreneurial development as key leverage points for managing the proper development of society remains at the heart of the project. An emphasis on changing social norms stops short of historicizing "social norms" in the context of postcolonialism, neoliberal economic restructuring, or development itself as a function of historical processes such as empire. For example, the new discourse explicitly ties "girl power" to "brand power" as a tool for changing exclusionary social norms that disenfranchise girls and keep them from realizing their "potential" (http://www.girleffect.org/what-girls-need/articles/july16/august-launch/ian-burrell-interviews-farah/). Yet, the role of transnational capitalism in the persistence of existing exclusionary norms and the

production of new ones remains invisible. See the newly branded website here: http://www.girleffect.org. See Kathryn Moeller's (2018) multi-sited institutional ethnography of the Nike Foundation and The Girl Effect for a cogent and important analysis of capitalism, feminism, and corporations in development.

19. The Girl Effect (n.d.). Your Move. https://novofoundation.org/wp-content/uploads/2012/07/Girl_Effect_Your_Move.pdf.

20. http://girlrising.com.

21. http://girlrising.com/grow-the-movement/index.html#62milliongirls, last accessed January 4, 2016.

22. http://girlrising.com/blog/category/number-basicmath/, posted October 8, 2012, in advance of the release of the film, last accessed January 4, 2016.

23. See also Decker (2010); George (2014); Bledsoe (1990); Pratt (2003); Vavrus (2002, 2003).

24. Versions of this phrasing saturate girls' empowerment social-action campaigns.

25. See the World Bank's report, "The Girl Effect Dividend" (Chaaban and Cunningham 2011, 2) for this discourse at work, as well as the "stark figures" regarding lost productivity their analysis generates.

26. See also Michelle Murphy's (2012/2013) excellent analysis of these ideological claims for "economic growth as created through girled life" through the "merger" of feminism and finance (4).

27. Although all the mothers prioritized education for children when they discussed what is important to them, not many mothers necessarily had the capacity in their households to realize education as a priority. As a widow, Hannah had more freedom to make decisions regarding household priorities because she does not have to defer to a husband directly even if she must negotiate decisions with her male relatives.

28. See Beth Ann Pratt's (2003) doctoral dissertation, "Childhood, Space and Children 'Out of Place': Versions of Maasai Childhood in Monduli Juu, Tanzania," for an in-depth ethnography of Maasai childhood.

29. The idea of a scavenger methodology comes from queer theory. In *Female Masculinity*, Judith Halberstam (2005, 13) explains: "A queer methodology, in a way, is a scavenger methodology that uses different methods to collect and produce information on subjects who have been deliberately or accidentally excluded from traditional studies of human behavior. The queer methodology attempts to combine methods that are often cast as being at odds with each other, and it refuses the academic compulsion toward disciplinary coherence."

30. For examples of scholarship that fills this gap, see: *Rebel Girls: Youth Activism and Social Change across the Americas* (Taft 2011); *Girlhood and the Politics of Place* (Mitchell and Rentschler 2016); *Girlhood: A Global History* (Helgren and Voscancellos 2010); *Making Modern Girls: A History of Girlhood, Labor, and Social Development in Colonial Lagos* (George 2014); Kirk and Garrow (2003); *Tribute to Jackie Kirk* (2010).

31. For examples, see Floro and Wolf (1990); King and Hill (1993); Malhotra, Pande, and Grown (2003); and Chaaban and Cunningham (2011).

32. See Dunne, Humphreys, and Leach (2006); Parkes and Chege (2010); Parkes

and Heslop (2011, 2013); Parkes et al. (2013); Greene et al. (2013); UNICEF (2004); Barker and Rich (1992); Bloch, Beoku-Betts, and Tabachnick (1998); Mensch and Lloyd (1998); Mensch et al. (2001).

Chapter 1. "Now is not like before. The world has changed."

1. I have purposefully randomized school uniform colors associated with schools in the case-study area.

2. Kiswahili word for "a small kiosk."

3. I heard "hungry for education" many times in conversations, and thus it became part of my idiom.

4. Kiswahili word for "development."

5. These events have been documented and discussed by historians and ethnographers. See Hodgson (2001b), Waller (1988), Jacobs (1965), Koponen (1994), and Merker ([1904] 1910).

6. Hodgson (2001b) argues that what we think of as "development" originating in post–World War II economic policy inaugurated by the Truman Doctrine is more accurately considered an extension of colonialism as the first "development" regime in Africa. See also Quan (2012).

7. Lotte Hughes's *Moving the Maasai: A Colonial Misadventure* (2006) argues that while settlers and local British administrators, particularly the key players in the Moves, were interested in acquiring the "sweet" grazing land that was the northern Maasai territory for themselves, there was significant resistance among a few administrators who were interested in justice, if not for the Maasai in particular, then for Africans in the imperial project broadly writ. She underscores Maasai agency, both in their resistance to colonial "misadventures" and their complicity in them. Hughes chronicles the intricacies of Maasai and British cultural logics as competing and overlapping systems that hinged on a paradoxical British affective desire to protect the "lords of East Africa" and their way of life *and* to control unruly pastoralists. This central paradox of Maasai-Euro relations based in alliance and resistance, and protection and control, endures in the postcolony as the conflicted, contradictory, and limiting dialectic between Maasai (or, static ideas about Maasai) and the Kenyan state continues to have salience in contemporary life.

8. The notion of "agreement" is disputable, particularly in the case of the second Move. Hughes's (2006) evidence suggests that while signatories to the first Move may not have understood the full implications of their agreement, they did not agree under duress. Hughes's evidence strongly supports the prevailing Maasai sentiment today, that the second Move was a duplicitous scheme by some local colonial administrators, a few influential settlers, and one Maasai leader (Olonanna), and that Maasai signatories were forced to comply (see Hughes 2006).

9. Kenya's most famous safari locations: Maasai Mara Game Reserve, Samburu National Reserve, and the Lake Nakuru, Hell's Gate, Nairobi, Amboseli, and Tsavo National Parks.

10. My description here is necessarily brief. For elaborated descriptions and discussions of social structure and norms, see Hughes (2006); Talle (1988); Spencer (1988); Jacobs (1965); Hodgson (2001b).

11. As with girls, this age range has shifted downward to ages 13 through 16 today. My conversations suggest that girls today can be cut as early as age eleven, but systematic research is needed to more definitely document this shift for girls and boys.

12. See Talle (2007) and Pratt (2003) for details on these gatherings, called *esoto*.

13. Emurata for girls in my interviews is translated in English as "circumcision" or "FGM" (female genital mutilation) and appears in direct quotations from interviewees in this way. When I refer to the procedure, I use "circumcision" to reflect this discursive practice, but I want to acknowledge that this phrasing is limiting and reductive as it only refers to the surgical cutting procedure alone. Emurata involves a protracted succession of ritual and ceremonial practices, among them the genital surgery. Many Maasai advocate the eradication of the physical procedure for girls even as they work to preserve the cultural significance attached to emurata as a rite of passage (see also Hodgson 2001b; 2011). In terms of the physical surgical procedure, in 2007 the World Health Organization classified female genital cutting into four broad categories. Type 1 (clitoridectomy): the partial or total removal of the clitoris and/or the clitoral hood. Type 2 (excision): the removal of the labia minora in addition to the clitoris, with or without excision of the labia majora. Type 3 (infibulation): narrowing of the vaginal orifice with the creation of a covering seal by cutting and placing together the labia minora and/or the labia majora, with or without excision of the clitoris. Type 4 (unclassified): all other procedures for nonmedical purposes, such as pricking, piercing, incising, scraping, and cauterization (Population Reference Bureau 2008). Although accounts vary, as noted in the introduction, Maasai have historically practiced excision "to the bone," with the addition of lateral cuts inside the vaginal wall (Mollet, personal communication, 2011). Current practice is somewhere along a continuum, from traditional excision performed by local women in the homestead to removal of the clitoral tip with local anesthesia performed by doctors (often non-Maasai men) in clinics. All of the descriptions I was given by schoolgirls and others included only the removal of the clitoris, or in some cases, "modified emurata," the removal of the tip of the clitoris or the clitoral hood. Some local activists argue that "modified emurata" for girls is easier to negotiate with adherents than its full eradication (see also Hodgson 2011). One source indicates that in Kenya, while 40 percent of older women ages thirty-five to thirty-nine have been cut, only 20 percent of younger women/girls ages fifteen to nineteen have undergone any procedure (Population Reference Bureau 2008). Maasai are not the only group in Kenya to practice female cutting (and not all groups practice male cutting). All female genital cutting procedures on girls under age eighteen are illegal in Kenya, but the practice still persists among Maasai and other ethnicities.

14. Note the linguistic slippage in which the word to describe an adult female person—"woman"—is the same word for "wife."

15. See as examples: Oyĕwùmi (1997); Amadiume (1987); Kanogo (2005); Thomas (2003); Hodgson (2001b); McClintock (1995).

16. Demarcation agreements among missionary societies were not formal; spheres of influence and competition for converts and students were continually negotiated (sometimes violently) between Protestant and Roman Catholics and among Protestant sects (Strayer 1978). In 1848, the Church Missionary Society (CMS) built the first Western-style school for Africans in Kenya, near the coast.

17. The AIM was not the first mission to make contact with Maasai, and not all Maasai Christians were/are AIM adherents. Other protestant missions, including the CMS, the Anglican mission, and the Church of Scotland Mission (CSM), were also active in Maasai areas and often in contention with the AIM for converts (Waller 1999). In 1926, after years of failed schooling, a group of elders circumvented the AIM and approached the CSM to start a school in Ngong, claiming that the AIM had done nothing to promote education (Waller 1999; King 1971). When the CSM leadership sparked the "female circumcision crisis" in 1928, the elders sidestepped the CSM and appealed to the government for a school. The circumcision crisis in part precipitated the Kikuyu Independent School Movement (Anderson 1970). Maasai did not mount a similar movement, and although some educated Maasai men tried to build a Maasai-led school off-mission in the southern reserve, it was not terribly successful; nothing like the Independent School Movement developed in Maasailand (Waller 1999).

18. Molonket ole Sempele (1880–1955) plays a starring role in the AIM missionary record. In the disasters of the 1890s, his father lost his herds to rinderpest and then died, leaving nine wives and a large family (Rigby 1981). Ole Sempele survived by traveling, trading (and thus learning Swahili), and attaching himself to Europeans (and converting to Christianity) he met along the way, specifically John Stauffacher and the AIM. Despite his meager beginnings, he spent the first seventeen years of his life as a celebrated *ol-murran* who was selected by his peers as his local age-set spokesman, and then he was also marked for election as the *olaiguenani kitok*, "great" spokesman, of his entire age-set, *Iltareto* (King 1971; Rigby 1981). Nonetheless, he left this prestigious position and joined the mission. Ole Sempele sold his cattle in 1909 and headed to the United States, where he spent three years at an all-black institute in the South. Upon his return, he continued his work with Stauffacher for more than forty years (Waller 1999). According to Rigby (1981) Ole Sempele did not address missionaries as *bwana* (in Kiswahili, master) and looked them directly in the eye when he spoke. Hughes (2006) details Ole Sempele's attempts to intervene in the second Move in 1911–1913 and Stauffacher's support for Maasai remaining on Laikipia. Although Ole Sempele was a Keekonyokie, the primary section in my case-study area (KCL), his name or legacy never came up.

19. Often, but not always, Maasai/Kikuyu or Maasai/Kamba.

20. Hodgson's evidence from Tanzania suggests use of the term shifted to describing Maasai as *irmeek* beginning in approximately the 1930s. Bishop (2007) found much discussion of irmeek among the Tanzanian Maasai elders she interviewed as

well. I never heard this term in my fieldwork, even when I asked specifically about it. This could be simply a dialect issue, but I suspect it might have more to do with the fact that I did not interview any venerable elders (with the exception of one grandmother, but no grandfathers). See chapter 4 for more discussion of ormeek.

21. Once families (rather than boys or single young men) were established at missions, women were the primary congregants, as males—men, youth, and boys—were often absent with herds, and while Maasai women/wives were among them, many of the women/wives were Kikuyu (Waller 1999).

22. Two central interests largely motivated colonial interventions in Maasailand at this time, including eventual education policy. First, the government was interested in protecting the development of the settler ranching economy by distorting the market in order to restrict Maasai pastoral capacity and directly curtail commodity production (Gorham 1980; Evangelou 1984). According to this logic, policies designed to curtail and control pastoral production included policies to quarantine Maasai stock movement within the confines of the reserve, restrict marketing and slaughter locations, reduce access to water sources, increase stock taxes, and institute mandated destocking. Quarantines were initially enacted in response to a rinderpest outbreak in 1915. The quarantine was imposed in 1916; veterinary assistance was not made readily available, which Gorham (1980) argues indicates that the administration was less inclined to support pastoralism and more inclined to witness its demise. Eventually, education policy became directly entangled with government control over the cattle market when administrators created a school quota system that targeted pastoral labor (boys and young men) and codified fines for households that did not comply. These policies were designed to protect the settler economy to the detriment of the pastoral economy, yet administers claimed these measures—including enforced schooling and punitive measures for noncompliance—were in Maasai best interests.

23. By the end of 1926, enrollment at GMSN was reduced to sixty-one students. The headmaster himself was rarely there, as he was tending his own herds and managing his own subsistence (Gorham 1980). Government Maasai School Kajiado (GMSK) was built in Kajiado Town that same year, which was also the year the prestigious Alliance High School opened in the highlands, still considered the top government school in Kenya and a source of awe and inspiration for the schoolgirls we talked with. The GMSK was closed by 1931 due to lack of enrollment.

24. For example, when the government planned to build the Ngong Veterinary Training School (NVTS) in 1927 in order to train animal husbandry instructors to provide a husbandry curriculum in the reserve schools, it persuaded the local Maasai Native Council to provide experimental herds and three thousand acres of land for the school's new animal husbandry program. Ironically, the Maasai pupils who did persevere in the government schools could not matriculate on to the NVTS, even though Maasai resources enabled the school, because they were not adequately prepared by the shoddy instruction they received at the primary schools in the reserve. The NVTS ended up benefiting the non-Maasai students who came to the reserve for advanced training because the instruction was geared toward dairy farming with

European-derived stock and tailored for highland, water-intensive techniques these graduates could take back to their home communities outside of the arid and semi-arid areas. Maasai students wishing to return to their homes with new knowledge needed to learn enhanced pastoral strategies for dryland, local-stock dairying (Gorham 1980). After skirmishes between Maasai and non-Maasai students and protests about the content of the curriculum, in 1931 NVTS reorganized as "mono-tribal" and focused on recruiting and admitting primarily Maasai students. However, the focus on European-style dairying remained. Not surprisingly, by 1938 there were only three Maasai students at NVTS (Gorman 1980).

25. By the late 1940s, the highlands were burning as Mau Mau, a secret organization of urban radicals and Kikuyu farm laborers on European estates in the highlands, emerged. In 1952 Governor Sir Evelyn Baring declared a state of emergency; the Emergency ended in 1960 (see Berman and Lonsdale [1992] for detailed analysis of Mau Mau, decolonization, and the formation of independent Kenya). The Kikuyu independent schools were closed at the advent of the Emergency on the assumption that they were training grounds for militant political action.

26. Hodgson uses the word for grandmother, *koko*, as a pseudonym.

27. Talle's (1988) study of gender dynamics among Maasai near Kajiado Town in the late 1970s documents young women who did not accept their arranged marriages, sometimes because they preferred schooling and often because they did not prefer the match.

28. A homestead (*enkang*) is a multifamily homestead and livestock corral (also locally referred to as a *boma* in Kiswahili). *Enkangs* are cooperative units for pooling resources, including labor and support. Of the schoolgirls we interviewed, some lived in "modified traditional houses" that have the same floor plan and stick-and-dung-plaster walls but have more windows and higher roofs made of corrugated sheet metals. Others lived in "*mbati* houses," which have poured concrete floors and are framed with timber and covered with corrugated metal sheeting. That I know of, none of the girls in the study lived in what are referred to as "permanent houses." These houses, built of cut stone and plastered together with cement, have pitched, clay-shingled roofs and metal and glass windows. Homestead size is getting smaller: in 2005, the average size was 2.75 families per enkang, whereas in 2008–09 the average size had reduced to 1.93 families per enkang (see Archambault 2013). These house-structure differences can be loosely mapped to socioeconomic differences among the households in the study; my data cannot support strong-enough linkages to disaggregate households by "class."

29. See Pratt (2003, 121–26) for girls' expert knowledge of different types of wood and the process of cutting it: "The knowledge (*eng'eno*) of wood came from quite a long apprenticeship, accompanying mothers, then older girls, until finally a girl knew which wood was good, simply by the touch, smell and sound of it" (126).

30. For example, in the 1962 census, 13 percent of Maasai ages five to nine had at least one year of education, whereas 56 percent of Kikuyu children the same age had at least one year of schooling (Sena 1986, 62).

31. The government's policy of rewarding additional funds to successful self-help efforts widened these disparities that had actually been forming for decades prior to independence (Buchmann 1999).

32. *Ilyankusi* were warriors from 1942 to 1959 (Hughes 2006); during their leadership Maasai girls went to school for the first time. Members of the age-set above them, the *Ilterito*, warriors from 1926 to 1948, also had educated men among them. See Sena (1986, 60, 65) for details.

33. It would be easy enough to identify this man with details about the school he worked for or the university from which he obtained his degree, so I have omitted these details.

34. As stated in the introduction, in 2010 territorial boundaries were drawn and renamed in the process of devolution. These districts were renamed as counties. The spatial area represented by Kajiado County remains the same as Kajiado District, however, within the counties, location groupings have changed, and what was KCL no longer exists as an administrative unit. Today the sublocations involved in this study are parsed out into Kajiado North, West, and Central Constituencies.

35. Gorham is not clear on the ethnic makeup of these students. As in the case of girls, it might be that many of these children were not Maasai. According to Rutten (1992), in 1927 the total population of Kajiado District was 14,799, 86.4 percent of whom were said to be Maasai (non-Maasai, 13.6 percent). By 1979 the total population of the district was 149,005. Of this total, Rutten found that only 62.8 percent were said to be Maasai (non-Maasai 37.2 percent, mostly Kikuyu, but also Kamba, and others—Luo, Luhya, and Somali).

36. This percentage was not disaggregated by sex.

37. Since 1985 the Kenyan education system has been structured on an 8-4-4 model, with eight years of basic education (primary), four years of secondary education, and four years of undergraduate education. Eight years of primary education are divided into standards (lower primary is standards 1–3; middle primary is standards 4–5; and upper primary is standards 6–8); standards are also referred to colloquially as "classes" as in the expression "Class 8" to refer to standard 8. At the end of the primary cycle, all Class 8 students take the Kenya Certificate of Primary Education examination (KCPE). This exam is used to rank and place students into secondary schools. Secondary school lasts four years and is organized in four forms (1–4). At the end of Form 4, students take the Kenya Certificate of Secondary Education examination (KCSE) which is used for admission into four-year universities, two year colleges, and other technical and vocational training institutions.

38. For example, the World Bank allocated 3.7 billion Ksh, Britain's Department for International Development (DfID) allocated 1.6 billion Ksh, the Organization of the Petroleum Exporting Countries (OPEC) allocated 1.2 billion Ksh, the Swedish International Development Agency (SIDA) allocated 430 million Ksh, and UNICEF allocated 250 million Ksh.

39. As of this writing, 1,020 Ksh converts to slightly less than US$10.

40. Mara and Turkana in Rift Valley Province; Marsabit and Samburu in Eastern

Province; Wajir and Mandera in Northeastern Province; Tana River in Coast Province.

41. For 2001, 2002, and 2003, Sifuna reports that 2001 was the worst year for dropouts: 650 girls left school. In 2003, more than 500 girls and more than 200 boys dropped out of school.

42. Education in ASALs has been an ostensible postcolonial priority since the *Ominde Report* (Republic of Kenya 1964/1965, 58), although it has "traditionally been a low priority in public resource allocation and programs."

43. *Boma* is Kiswahili for "homestead," which is *enkang* in Maa.

Chapter 2. "I see that when I am in school, I will have a good life."

1. *Shuka* means "blanket" in Kiswahili and is used to refer the cotton wraps that women wear, as well as the iconic red tartan wraps (which are heavier, like blankets) that Maasai men wear.

2. In connection to the history of Christian missionary education in Kenya broadly and the widespread acceptance of Christianity in Maasailand today, the politics of gendered respectability Abraham gestures toward in his comment are notable. However, my data do not support making stronger links among Maasai Christianity in the case-study communities, education for girls, and new or reconfigured forms of gendered respectability attached to "educated" female behavior and sexuality.

3. I do not know if the schoolgirls involved contributed to the writing of these lyrics. Early in our work together, Maria wrote a prose poem "praising" girls' education and critiquing harsh treatment of "the girl-child" that is also very similar to the rhetorical idiom in this song. A study of schoolgirl choral performances would be a fascinating entry into understanding how girls' education is scripted in rural Maasai areas.

4. Boys participate in these performances as well and they are likewise students.

5. http://cherieblair.org/features-videos/2009/01/the-girl-effect-davos.html, last accessed April 17, 2015.

6. Then Minister for Education, Professor George Saitoti (now deceased) opens his foreword by acknowledging that the Government of Kenya "ascribes to the aspirations" of and is signatory to these agreements.

7. The GPE lists the following initiatives "aimed at improving access": expansion of boarding facilities for girls; introduction of mobile schools and feeder schools for standards 1–4 in the Arid and Semi-Arid Lands (ASALs); affirmative action in bursary allocation for secondary and tertiary admission; appointment of qualified female education managers; gender-balanced intake of pre-service teacher trainees; "gender responsive" and "gender parity-based" deployment of teachers and managers; re-admission of girls who become pregnant in school; engendering the curriculum; gender-issue capacity building for school managers, teachers, and quality assurance officers; gender "sensitization and advocacy"; mainstreaming HIV and AIDS education in primary and secondary curriculum (Republic of Kenya 2007, 5).

8. Kiswahili for tea and rolled, slightly sweetened fried dough, respectively.

9. Particularly "guidance and counseling" teachers, a state function in Kenya designed, in large part, to promote and support girls' education through counseling and provision of menstrual supplies, to reduce "schoolgirl pregnancy," and to keep girls in school.

10. See also Goldman and Little (2014) for their study of women's empowerment in rural Tanzanian Maasai communities and the conclusion for some discussion of this study.

11. Josephine is referring here to lost livestock while herding.

12. Kiswhahili for "open-air market."

13. *Mbati* is a Kiswahili word for the corrugated metal often used as a low-cost building material for houses and other structures.

14. Brazil, China, Democratic Republic of Congo, Egypt, Ethiopia, India, Indonesia, Kenya, Liberia, Mexico, Nigeria, Pakistan, Philippines, and Rwanda: see *I Know, I Want, I Dream: Girls' Insights for Building a Better World (Warner et al. 2013).*

15. It is important to note that schoolchildren—girls and boys—are prohibited from wearing Maasai jewelry of any kind (boys are prohibited from piercing their ears in school and girls cannot shave their heads bald) with the exception of choral practice and performance.

Chapter 3. "The medicine for fire is fire."

1. I borrow this phrasing from Archambault (2011) because it encapsulates the dichotomy. In my interviews the phrasing was more likely to be "schoolgirl" relative to "those girls at home."

2. With the exception of two schoolgirls at two different schools, all the schoolgirls we interviewed elected to have their interviews recorded and seemed to delight in the process. In the case of the two girls who declined to be recorded, my assistant and I made quick notes immediately following the interview. Interviews with mothers were also audio recorded digitally. Teachers seemed distracted by the recorder. I found interviews with teachers went more smoothly if I took notes while we talked. All teacher interviews were in English and therefore neither of my assistants was involved with the teacher interviews.

3. As noted in earlier chapters the Maa word for this rite for males and females is *emurata*, translated in English as "circumcision" (for boys and girls) and also "FGM" (female genital mutilation) for girls only. See chapter 1, note 13, for a detailed discussion of the practice.

4. Schoolgirls mostly referred to their fathers (uncles and grandfathers) as the decision makers concerning schooling and marriage arrangements in their families, although they also referred to "parents" implicitly implicating their mothers as decision-makers as well. Teachers likewise spoke generally of "fathers" or made reference to specific fathers, as in the case of Helen. Mothers spoke of themselves as "parents" and thus included themselves along with their husbands as decision mak-

ers, although mothers also indicated that they defer to their husbands. As Hodgson (2001a, 2005) and Talle (1988) have shown, Maasai mothers have roles to play in marriage arrangements for daughters, sometimes even in utero.

5. I asked repeatedly if there is a word or phrase in Maa that refers to a "schoolgirl" and was told there is no word for this category. However, the written source of record for Maasai vocabulary and grammar, Frans Mol's *Maasai Language and Culture Dictionary* (1996, 271), lists *e-naitengeni* (p. *i-naaitengeni*) and *enkaitengeni* as words that mean "pupil, disciple, school-girl." Mol's work relies primarily on Purko Maasai informants, whereas most of my informants are Keekonyokie Maasai, so perhaps this discrepancy is an issue of dialect; see also chapter 4 for a discussion of the implications of this linguistic/discursive fact for the production of social "facts" about schoolgirls.

6. This word is used throughout the anthropological literature on Maasai society, but it was never used by any of my informants in Kajiado. This is likely because I interviewed girls in school—schoolgirls—for whom the category of "initiate" is anathema because it is synonymous with "soon-to-be-married."

7. See Talle (1988, 92) for some detail on the role and nature of the curse in Maasai social organization.

8. See Talle (1988) for an account of property and ownership of people and livestock among Kenyan Maasai in Kajiado in the late 1970s and early 1980s. She notes, for example, that "even if the term *aitore* (to control, to rule, or to have authority) is applied by the Maasai both when referring to the control of livestock and the control of women (and children), it would be wrong to deduce that women generally are property in the same way as livestock" (75). She argues that changing economic conditions, girls' increased participation in schooling, and changing approaches to arranged marriage had negative implications for women's (and therefore girls') autonomy and decision-making power as wives.

9. *Enkangiti* is the Maa word for "small house" and refers to a stick, mud, and dung-plaster structure that typically houses a woman, her children, and baby goats. When in disrepair, the dung-plaster roof will leak. In this case, Felista's mother cannot repair her own roof. Because Felista is a schoolgirl, she would not have the necessary knowledge to repair the plaster herself. Building and maintaining enkangiti is absolutely women's work. Many enkangiti belonging to several members of an extended family surrounded by a thorn fence to constitute an *enkang*, or "homestead." Men are responsible for the building and maintenance of the thorn fencing that surrounds and protects people and animals alike.

10. Given girls' domestic labor requirements, it is often only later in the evening that girls can find time (and many do not) to study. Light at night in rural Maasailand, like many rural regions of Kenya and Africa, comes from homemade or locally fabricated lamps, usually constructed from empty aerosol cans, that burn liquid paraffin. The light from a paraffin lamp is adequate for moving around (cooking, cleaning, talking, taking tea, and so on) after dark, but it is far inferior to an electric bulb for studying.

11. Kiswahili word for a stiffly boiled maize porridge that is a food staple all over Kenya.

12. "In your mother's house" (*enkaji nabo*, of one or the same house) indicates the practice in which children in polygynous families are distinguished by the name of their mother (Talle 1988, 79).

13. Maria and Alice explained this separation between fathers and daughters happens "very young," as early as six years old (see Archambault 2009).

14. In KCL it seemed that this practice was unevenly on the wane. When it came up in interviews, mothers and teachers explained that all families who could afford to build an enkangiti designated for girls and those who could not afford to build a structure found ways to accommodate girls, especially schoolgirls. Some also conceded that having to find a place to sleep presents some risk for girls.

15. Likewise, around twelve years old, boys will no longer sleep in the same house as their mothers and will display affection only on special occasions (see Archambault 2009).

16. Warrington and Kiragu (2012) conducted interviews with twenty-four schoolgirls in Class 5 attending four schools in Kajiado County. Using Amartya Sen's capability theory as a framework, they found three levels of "unfreedoms" or "capability deprivations": environmental and infrastructural (examples include drought conditions, increased time spent collecting water and firewood, migrating with livestock, herding responsibilities, no water to handle menstruation, and food insecurity); economic (examples include no money for school fees, no paraffin for light to study, and food insecurity); and individual/gender related (examples include female genital modification procedures, early/forced marriage, sexual harassment in school/out of school, and gendered domestic labor).

17. According to Archambault (2009, 288), Maasai parents' perceptions of children's growth is "non-linear and contingent on social and interpretive circumstances." She goes on: "Maasai use the terms 'big' (*kitok*) and 'small' (*kinyi*) to refer not to chronological age or predetermined stages of growth but rather to children's capabilities or maturity in different contexts. Children become 'big' in a particular domain when they are mature and capable enough to accomplish the respective task." The girls we interviewed would often say, for example, in answer to the question, "Why is it better to wait until after you finish university to get married?": "Because I will be big."

18. Further research into the emotional dimensions of "pain" mapping from its physical necessity in Maasai worldviews is necessary to make this case any more strongly.

19. In Kipury's version of the folktake, Mbiti is gendered female by the use of feminine pronouns, she and her. In Nashipae's version Mbiti's gender is unclear.

20. Maasai are historically polygynous, and polygyny is still widely practiced, although not at previous rates, when a wealthy man may have five or more wives; today the average is probably closer to two or three. Monogamy and serial monogamy are increasingly popular, particularly among educated and Christian people. Given that Nashipae's parents are not educated and her father is not a young man, it is notable

that he has one wife. That he is allegedly interested in "dowry" (she means bridewealth) could indicate that he is a poor man, which might speak to his inability to secure more wives and his interest in marrying off his daughters while educating his sons. See Talle (1988) for discussions of male poverty and marriage among Maasai.

21. Nashipae noted that this brother did not know her situation because she had no contact with him, as he had been supported through primary, secondary, and university by "a white man."

22. The use of the word "dowry" is interesting here. Nashipae narrated her story in English, almost entirely without translation (except for the Mbiti tale). What she means to refer to is bridewealth, which refers to the goods given to the bride's family over time as a condition of the marriage arrangement. Dowry, on the other hand, is the goods the bride brings with her to her husband's home. It is not clear to me how this word may have come to be a part of her vocabulary.

23. A distance of easily twenty-five kilometers.

24. Nashipae entered Class 1 (first grade) at age fourteen; she was seventeen at the time of the interview. She passed through five classes (grades) in three years because the school officials allowed her to skip large sections of the syllabus in order to catchup to the proper standard (class) for her age. While this is a common practice, it is also as common to see very over-age children in standards at all levels in primary and secondary. Over-age entry and grade repetition has particular implications for schoolgirls because female puberty has specific implications for girls' social and physical bodies. See chapter 4 for a discussion.

25. Rescued girls can be "cared for" by a combination of government and external donor support. That is, they are housed, fed, and provided with the material support to persist in school. What rescue centers cannot provide is the social and cultural support associated with social maturation, including Maasai marriage—selecting and/or approving the selection of a husband and therefore approving of his family within wider clan and lineage relations, receiving her bridewealth, and maintaining the social relations this entails. Educated elders associated with the local Maasai NGO that facilitated my research were very concerned by the lack of long-term accountability to the rescued girl for precisely these social relationships and worked hard to intervene in arranged marriages in ways that reconciled the girl with her parents rather than removing her to rescue centers.

26. In a survey conducted in 2005 in a rural Maasai community near the case-study area, Archambault (2007, 2011) found that two-thirds (66 percent) of children ages six to fifteen had attended school for one year or longer. Only 47 percent of children ages sixteen to twenty-five had attended school for one year or longer. In a cohort of children ages six to ten, more girls than boys had attended school for one year or longer (64 percent of girls, 60 percent of boys). Among women age forty-six and older, only 9 percent had ever attended one or more years of schooling.

27. See, for a few of many examples, Thomas (2003) and Stambach (2000).

Chapter 4. "We are not enkanyakuai. . . . We are just girls."

1. Between emurata and marriage, Mol delineates initiate (*esipolioi*, pl. *isipolio*), novice (*enkaibartani*, pl. *inkaibartak*), and young lady (s. *embartoni*, pl. *imbarnot*). These words/social categories/forms of personhood did not come up in my conversations.

2. There is no official or mandated amount of time set aside for healing and preparation, as the marriage is typically already arranged, but this will vary by circumstance and cultural practice. Talle (1988) found that the period among Maasai near Isynia in Kajiado district was two to four months in the late 1970s and early 1980s. For Samburu, this period can be as short as twenty-four to forty-eight hours after excision (Lesorogol 2008); in those cases, healing happens in the woman's married home.

3. See Talle (1988) for a detailed description of each of these stages, including "traditional" marriage ceremony and bridewealth and marriage negotiation processes. The "traditional" approach involves extensive interactions between the suitor's family and the girl's family (involving men and women on both sides) in which several ritualized installments over a protracted period create relationships between the families. This is in contrast to a more "recent" trend (emerging at the time of her research in the early 1980s) in which the father will "sell the girl" (*amir e ntito*) (135). According to Talle, in this approach, the girl's father alone is responsible for financing everything for the girl's circumcision, and because of this he comes to see his daughter as his "property." The marriage arrangement with her suitor then becomes a one-time exchange: the daughter for cattle and sometimes cash. In these marriages, it is very hard, if not impossible for a "wife" to return to her natal home as a "daughter" because her family cannot afford to repay the one-time bridewealth payment.

4. In Maasai epistemology, adulthood, and indeed personhood, for both men and women must be conferred definitively through parenthood. Men and women are renamed when the first child is born and addressed as "mother of" or "father of" the first-born (for example, Sereti's parents are referred to as Mama Sereti and Baba Sereti). For Maasai, when someone dies, the living can no longer speak the name of the dead. The existence of children ensures that Mama Sereti and Baba Sereti can live on in the stories of their family and friends.

5. See Talle (1988) for some examples.

6. Payne and Ole-Kotikash (2008) also use the word *enkabartani* to refer to a new initiate, or a young, circumcised girl who is not yet married; but the schoolgirls I asked about this phrase claimed not to know it, though almost all had heard the term *enkanyakuai* even if not all could define it in detail.

7. Kenya is considered a Group 2 Country, where FGC prevalence is intermediate, and only certain ethnic groups practice FGC at varying rates (UNICEF 2005). The estimated prevalence of FGC in girls and women (ages fifteen to forty-nine) is 21.1 percent (Shell-Duncan, Naik, and Feldman-Jacobs 2016). This has been reduced from 37.6 percent in 1998 and 32.2 percent in 2003 (KNBS/ IFCM 2010; see also Achia 2014).

8. See just two examples of local activism to promote pastoralist girls' education (Maasai, Samburu, and others) and eradicate FGC in the process (Kakenya's Dream Academy 2015; Pastoralist Child Foundation 2015).

9. Massailand is concentrated in Rift Valley Province. Based on data from the 2014 Kenya Demographic Health Survey (DHS), Shell-Duncan, Naik, and Feldman-Jacobs (2016) estimate a 26 percent to 50 percent prevalence rate in the province, matched by the same rate in Eastern Province. North Eastern Province shows the highest rates (98 percent), with Coast and Central showing 10 percent to 25 percent.

10. According Shell-Duncan, Naik, and Feldman-Jacobs (2016), based on 2014 DHS data, older women (ages forty to forty-four) report that they had been cut around age fifteen. The younger generation (ages fifteen to nineteen) was cut on average around age ten. Age at cutting tends to vary across different ethnic groups and is, on average, between ages nine and sixteen in Kenya.

11. The influence of rights discourse and civic education taught in school could be seen when the idea of an age of majority and legal adult status, which is eighteen in Kenya, came up in interviews with some schoolgirls who argued emurata did not make them women but they would be "adults" when they turned 18.

12. Shell-Duncan, Naik, and Feldman-Jacobs (2016) indicate that nearly 80 percent of already-circumcised girls and women ages fifteen through forty-nine are open to stopping FGC; a very slim margin (well under 5 percent) are "unsure." The same report indicates a very small percentage of Kenyan women ages to fifteen through forty-nine in the richest quintile (less than 10 percent) support the continuation of FGC, whereas 20 percent of women in the same age bracket living in the poorest quintile do support the continuation. Girls living in the poor households in rural communities are more likely to undergo FGC (KNBS/IFCM 2010).

13. I should also note that while schoolgirls were relatively unanimous in their assertion that a girl becomes a woman when she becomes a wife with "her own husband and house," and wives could never be schoolgirls (once married, a girl-cum-wife cannot go to school), there were several contradictory responses to this question. For instance, some said girls become women when they become mothers, although everyone agreed that if a schoolgirl gives birth and comes back to school, she is not enkitok, a "woman," because she is certainly not a wife. Others indicated that if the girl is "young" and she becomes a wife through arranged marriage even though she is officially enkitok, to them she is still a girl. Some, of course, said that girls become women when they are circumcised, but none of the circumcised schoolgirls saw or called themselves women. Some noted that a girl becomes a woman when she turns eighteen, though they also said that if she is still in school at eighteen, she cannot be a woman.

14. See Talle (1988) for detailed descriptions of emurata for girls as well as their movement through the "stages" Mol outlines. See Hodgson (2001b) for an alternative female circumcision narrative.

15. David ole Kilusu, personal communication, December 2007.

16. All emphasis, with italics, added.

17. Frans Mol's *Maasai Language and Culture Dictionary*, the dictionary of record for the Maa language, defines *enkanyakuai* differently than the variations I heard in the interviews. Mol (1996) lists this term as "the returned one"—"it refers to a woman or a wife who returns to her husband's settlement after having run away from it. The noun is derived from the irregular verb *a-itu*: to return here, of which the pst.t. is *a-nyak-ua*" (27). This definition did not come up at all in interviews with schoolgirls. Mothers did not mention this definition directly either, though when I asked about it specifically they would agree that this can also be a meaning. Some mothers added that enkanyakuai can also be a wife who permanently leaves her married home and "returns" to her father's home. "Divorce" as a permanent separation is possible in Maasai society and seems to be related to one of multiple meanings for enkanyakuai in which a wife leaves her husband's home because of an irreconcilable dispute and returns to her father's home. She might live with her parents for the rest of her life if she cannot be reunited with her husband, despite intervention and counsel.

18. It is beyond the scope of my data to make this claim more strongly, but conversations during fieldwork suggested that men are also implicated in this frame. It would also be socially unacceptable for a circumcised man who has not gone to school to delay marriage and fatherhood for too long. I would provisionally suggest that educated men, like educated women, have more flexibility with this timeline.

19. This is overwhelmingly the case. However, at the time of the interviews, and even more so today, some few families elect to send their daughter back to school (typically she transfers to another school) after she delivers rather than arranging her marriage. The schoolgirl's mother agrees to care for her grandchild. The Children's Act of 2003 makes it illegal for a school to deny a schoolgirl's reentry after she leaves school for pregnancy.

20. "All violence is gendered" within "wider social relations" that "have a powerful influence on institutions," such as schools (Dunne, Humphreys, and Leach 2006, 80). Schoolgirls endure gender violence as sexual harassment and rape in homesteads, community spaces, and school (Chisamya et al. 2012; Greene et al. 2009; Jones et al. 2008; Leach and Mitchell 2006; Maternowska et al. 2009; Parkes and Heslop 2011, 2013; Parkes et al. 2013; UNICEF 2012). In a longitudinal study of violence in schools in Kenya, Ghana, and Mozambique, researchers found 90 percent of the girls in Kenya reported experiencing some form of violence in the previous twelve months, including beating, grabbing, whipping, kneeling, peeping, touching, comments, forced sex, sex for goods, insults, threats, and letters. In Kenya, 10 percent had been raped, and 10 percent exchanged sex for goods (Parkes and Heslop 2011, 2013). According to Goldman and Little (2014), based on a four-year study of Maasai women's involvement in empowerment programs and Goldman's work for more than ten years in the communities in northern Tanzania, "Women rarely named violence as a major problem impacting their communities, or themselves personally. This is not because violence against women is not a problem in these communities, but because it is so prevalent and accepted as a social norm." They note most women "did think beating was permissible in certain circumstances, such as erring with the cattle or

being caught having an extramarital affair. The most common complaint regarding violence was what women referred to as 'beating for no reason,' and that was nearly always associated with excessive alcohol consumption" (767–68).

21. Hodgson (2001b, 253) notes that the feminine form, *emeeki*, was rarely used among older generations to describe the very few women who attended school during the colonial period or those who married irmeek schoolteachers and politicians and "adopted Western-style clothes and Swahili hairstyles." Further, because so many women converted to Christianity relative to far fewer men, Christian women were not called emeeki, whereas conversion marked men as irmeek and therefore "less Maasai."

22. See also Bishop (2007) for a discussion of "ormeek" and its implications in her research.

Conclusion

1. In early September 2007 I interviewed Maria in order to test the protocol and revise it with her help. Her circumcision story comes from that interview. Maria was circumcised "young," around eleven or twelve years old, just after she began menstruation. She was grouped with seven other girls, most of whom were about three years older, and the ceremony was held in December while she was on holiday from school. She was the only schoolgirl in the group. Everyone else was married within months, while she returned to Class 5 (fifth grade). Maria was nineteen when these women met on the path, and Naipanoi was twenty-three and mother to four children. Naipanoi was likely fifteen or sixteen when she was "married off."

2. See also Koffman and Gill 2013a, 2013b; Calkin 2015.

3. Women and Development (WAD) is also a framework that is often discussed as a "necessary detour" from WID to GAD. In the interests of space, I am not detailing WAD here. See Vavrus (2003) and Wilson (2015) for discussion of WAD's place in this genealogy.

4. See Calkin (2015) for a useful analysis of debates regarding feminist complicity and cooptation with neoliberalism concerning WID and GAD. See also Miller and Razavi (1998).

5. In U.S.-based women and gender studies/feminist theory, these concepts are referred to as intersectionality theory. Although articulated as far back as Sojourner Truth's infamous question in 1851—"Ain't I a woman?"—the term intersectionality was coined by critical race theorist and legal scholar Kimberlé Crenshaw in 1989.

6. This package of policy prescriptions as well as an ethio-economic paradigm for (re)structuring social life is often referred to as the "Washington Consensus" (Sheppard and Leitner 2010). In the wake of widespread global protests against the devastating effects of structural adjustment policies as well the fallout from the Asian market crisis in the late 1990s, the Washington Consensus was replaced by what is referred to as (and contested as) the "post-Washington Consensus," a revised package of policy measures that "substituted a discourse of governance and policy re-

duction" for "structural adjustment and privatization" (Sheppard and Leitner 2010, 188). Scholars debate the extent to which "new development economics" break from neoliberal frameworks established during the Washington Consensus because faith in neoclassical assumptions that globalized markets create a rising tide to lift all boats continues to underwrite development policy. See Bergeron's (2013) discussion of gender policy in the context of the "post-Washington Consensus."

7. *The Beijing Platform for Action* (BPfA) is significant as the first (and only) global agenda-setting platform and multilateral agreement to single-out girls as a discreet demographic disaggregated from "women" and "children" in Section L, "The Girl-Child." Although UNICEF began arguing for a cross-sectoral emphasis on girls' development and human rights concerns under the "rubric of 'the girl child'" as early as 1990 (Croll 2006, 1285), girls as a category for development targeting initially found its most widely circulated articulation in the production and dissemination of Section L. The "girl-child" as a subject position, social category, and development target was initially carved out through the confluence of grassroots activism in the Global South and Western feminist activism in the UN/NGO system committed to children's rights, particularly girls' rights. Feminist activists among childhood experts were frustrated by childhood data that failed to gender-disaggregate data on women that failed to account for generational discrimination and violence marked by age or status vis-à-vis the bio-socio-cultural life course (Price-Cohen 1997; Croll 2006). Some advocates for girls regarded the Convention of the Rights of the Child (CRC) as the "most widely accepted framework for action in favor of the fundamental rights of girls" (CRC/C/38, 49, para. 278; 52, para. 299). Some activists worked to articulate and disseminate the generative overlaps between CRC and the Convention on the Elimination of Discrimination Against Women (CEDAW) (Price-Cohen 1997; WGG 2015). Nonetheless, historical reluctance among mainstream Western women's rights advocates to discursively associate women with children and particularly girls worked against singling girls out for development intervention. For example, although the Vienna Declaration mentions girl-children (Price-Cohen 1997), UNICEF delegates attending the World Human Rights Conference in Vienna in 1993 had encountered explicit resistance to talk of girls' rights in the context of women's rights (WGG 2015). In an effort to "ensure that Beijing would not be dominated by that same attitude toward girls" (WGG March 2015, n.p.), the Working Group on Girls of the NGO Committee of UNICEF (WGG) was established in 1993/1994 to facilitate the development of an advocacy network among national and international NGOs on the behalf of girls to convince leaders in state and non-state development institutions involved with the conference (including key leaders of the women's movement in the Global North) that a focus on girls was key to women's rights and access to development (WGG 2015). Out of this intentional networking process, UN Member States Delegates and NGOs came together "to make the plight of girls visible" (WGG 2015, n.p.) to governments and intergovernmental agencies by explicitly inserting girls into the action platform (WGG March 2015, n.p.). The WGG's initial approach to simply "insert the word 'girls' after 'women,'" was considered "too conservative" (WGG 2015,

n.p.). African activists were convinced that girls needed a specific, separate section in the document and argued as much in regional meetings in Africa to review the platform document as well as in WGG networking sessions in New York. After the U.S. and European member delegations declined to bring Section L to the floor of the Commission on the Status of Women (CSW) at the UN General Assembly for consideration for the BPfA, "the Group of 77," the delegation representing developing countries and China, agreed, but missed the deadline. Section L "went to Beijing in brackets," meaning it would be considered for insertion into the BPfA at the CSW after the conference (WGG 2015, n.p.). The WGG formed The International Network for Girls (INfG) in order to extend their networking, advocacy, and lobbying efforts. This massive coordinated Global North-South collaboration resulted in significant language regarding girls' needs inserted strategically in the Declaration and the Platform. The INfG is now defunct; the Working Group on Girls of the NGO Committee of UNICEF is now an independent NGO called, simply, The Working Group on Girls, which has been a key player in the creation of October 11 as the International Day of the Girl and annually collaborates with other girl-serving NGOs to integrate and involve "girl-delegates" in the CSW.

8. In their discourse analysis of three hundred girls' education policy documents, Monkman and Hoffman (2013) find that this is still the case with contemporary girls' education discourse. They document a consistent one-two-punch pattern of "justice" and "utility" arguments for girls' education. "Justice arguments," bolstered with reference to global agreements like BPfA, CRC, EFA, and the MDGs, call for girls' inclusion in schooling, equality with boys, and human rights as self-evident—these arguments "are presented as unarguable statements of fact," and these facts "just [are]" (Monkman and Hoffman 2013, 71). Justice arguments tend to be paired with an array of "utility arguments" which include: "assertions that educating girls will reduce poverty, make development sustainable, foster democracy, promote peace, improve public health, and improve general well-being" (71) as well as strengthen women's roles as future mothers, enable girls to better care for others now and in the future, and ensure girls' employment opportunities. Girls' education discourse makes the causal links between girls' education and a range of laudable and urgent outcomes "sound simple, direct and unchallengable" (71). The iterative, self-referential, and opaque nature of the girls' education policy discourse "makes it nearly impossible to contest or engage with this policy logic" (76). The authors conclude that the discourse actually impedes the possibility of substantive gendered social change from educating girls because the "policy discursively narrows the scope of relevant issues and simplifies complex social, cultural, political, and economic phenomena, thereby encouraging initiatives that are, in many cases, not designed to address the actual causes of gender inequities identified" (79).

9. Moeller (2014a) notes that corporations and corporate foundations include but are not limited to: Becton Dickinson, Chevron, Cisco Systems, Exxon Mobile, Gap Inc., General Electric, Gucci, Intel Corporation, J.P. Morgan Chase, Johnson and Johnson, Mobile Corporation, Nike Inc., Standard Charter Bank, and Starbucks

Corporation. See also Boyd's (2016) appendix for a table, "Survey of the Trend," noting an array of organizational forms and foci.

10. See Hayhurst (2011, 532) for her original articulation of the "girl(ing) of development" that Koffman and Gill (2013b) build upon.

11. For example, in a downloadable document created by the Girl Effect called "Your Move," directed toward funders, policymakers, corporations, and NGOs, thirty-five individuals are listed (from President Barack Obama to Mark Parker, Nike Inc.'s chief executive officer, to actor Ashley Judd along with "400,000 members of the public") who "put girls at the center of [their] vision and witness[ed] change" (n.p.).

12. Greene et al. (2010) mapped the scope and range of "girl work" in the Global South by surveying eleven institutions divided into four types: bi- and multilateral and private donors (such as the Nike Foundation, USAID, and UNICEF); advocacy organizations (such as the Association for Women's Rights in International Development); program implementers and international nongovernmental organizations (INGOS such as CARE, Plan International); research organizations (such as Guttmacher Institute and the Population Council). In this analysis, "girl work" falls into four broad areas: health, education, general empowerment, and economic empowerment. Specific health focus issues are: sexual and reproductive health, HIV and AIDS, primary health, safe motherhood, nutrition, youth friendly services, and others. General empowerment focus issues are: child marriage, life skills, reducing chore burden, property and land rights, civic rights (for example, voter identity cards), protection from violence, and others. Education focus issues include: primary education, secondary education, tertiary education and beyond, educational scholarships, infrastructure (for example, building schools and latrines), and others (Green et al. 2010, 6–17). Despite the range of "girl work" indicated here, the "multiplier effect" of girls' labor (and investment in their ability to work) dominate the discourse.

13. See Karishma Desai's excellent (2016) analysis of the precarious role of "empathy" in this curriculum.

14. http://girlrising.com/engage-india (last accessed January 4, 2016).

15. According to policy brief prepared for the Global Business Coalition for Education, of which Intel Corporation is a founding member, "Girl Rising" is one of the top 100 grossing documentary films in the United States, mobilizing more than $5.3 million to support itself and its NGO partners. In the process, Intel gained brand prestige by using its corporate social media platform (Twitter, Facebook, and online communities) to garner support; in 2013 the corporation's Twitter following grew by 3,900 percent, from ten thousand followers to more than four hundred thousand (Tikolo 2014).

16. Kristof and WuDunn call their campaign the "Half the Sky Movement." See http://www.halftheskymovement.org.

17. https://news.nike.com/news/adolescent-girls-initiative-launched.

18. http://gbc-education.org/task-forces-2 (last accessed December 10, 2015).

19. The Global Business Coalition for Education was founded by "companies that provided significant resources, thought leadership and efforts to establish the [GBCE]

in 2012." These companies include Accenture, Grupo Carso, Chevron Corporation, Dangote Industries, Discovery Communications Inc., Econet Wireless Group, Gucci, Hess Corporation, Intel Corporation, Lenovo Group Limited, McKinsey and Company, Pearson plc, Reed Smith LLP, Tata Sons Limited, and Western Union, among others (see http://gbc-education.org/our-members/companies for current list).

20. For example, the United Nations Population Fund promotes its 2016 report, State of the World's Population, with a campaign called "We are 10." This campaign explicitly draws on the "two paths" imagery (including the notion of a "virtuous cycle" resulting from investment) discussed in chapter 4, but shifts the focus from the twelve-year-old girl to the ten-year-old girl. The discourse also connects the ten-year-old girl's proper development to the proper development of "developing countries." The website states, for example: "How will investments in 10 year old girls play out in the real world? What do girls and countries stand to gain or lose? Imagine a girl, who like her country, is at a pivotal point in her life and development, and consider the different paths her future might take over the next 15 years." See http://www.unfpa.org/swop (accessed August 17, 2017).

21. https://www.youtube.com/watch?v=WIvmE4_KMNw (accessed October 12, 2014).

22. Munga and Onsomu's (2014) analysis of 2009 Kenyan census data indicate that of the total population of youth ages fifteen to twenty-four, 48.6 percent (3.8 million people) were "employed"; 84 percent of these 3.8 million people (3.2 million people) were actually informally employed in precarious positions, placing them in the category of working poverty (living on less than US$2 per day (ILO 2015). Informal work is characterized by job insecurity, low wages, poor terms and conditions of employment, weak safety and health standards, no institutional social protection benefits, and low tenure (Omolo 2012). About 90 percent of these young people have primary school education (Munga and Onsomu 2014, n.p.). Adolescent girls and young women ages fifteen to twenty-four have a 21.1 percent greater chance of being inactive and 26 percent less chance of being employed than adolescent boys and young men in the same age group (compared to 17.1 percent less chances for the adult population) (Escudero and Murelo 2013). Munga and Onsomu's (2014) analysis also reports that 62 percent of youth ages fifteen to thirty-four have some degree of primary education (not necessarily completion); only 34 percent have secondary education, and only 1 percent have university education (n.p.).

23. http://www.mckinsey.com/insights/africa/africa_at_work.

24. Based on their four-year study of women's involvement in "empowerment-based" development interventions in Maasai communities in northern Tanzania, Goldman and Little (2014) showed mixed results for some indicators but found overall that participation in NGO programming run primarily by local educated Maasai women (including adult education and rights-based literacy programs) increased uneducated women's sense of "power" and well-being, particularly concerning their confidence in asserting themselves regarding household decisions about their children's basic needs like healthcare and schooling, including girls' schooling.

The authors contend that "empowerment is necessarily a relational and iterative process. One that involves changing (and sometimes reinforced) subject positions in terms of what it means to be a Maasai woman (strong, capable, respectful, but also with a new set of rights); new concepts of rights for men and women, and new spaces to voice and act out these rights in ways that can lead to changes societally" (Goldman and Little 2014, 773). The experiences I track in these chapters are more fraught than a straightforward invocation of "new" "rights" would suggest because they also indicate "new" forms of oppression entangled with "empowerment."

25. "Schooled Maasai" can be referred to with these expressions: ilashumpa orook ("black Europeans"), iloompala ("bookmen"), ilmusheni ("mission adherents" for those affiliated with a church), ilkaranini ("clerks") or ilmalimuni ("teachers") (Sena 1986, 95). Those who participate almost entirely in traditional pastoralism can be generally referred to with these expressions: iltungana liatua nkishu ("people within cattle"), iltungana liang ("homepeople"), loolkarash ("sheet-clad people"), or iltungana leitu eisuma ("non-literate people") (96). Although Sena's ethnographic work in what is now Narok County occurred more than thirty years ago, these categories are still salient for speaking of broad social categories vis-à-vis schooling (Sena 1986; personal communication, 2015).

Works Cited

Aapola, Sinikka, Marnina Gonick, and Anita Harris. 2005. *Young Femininity: Girlhood, Power and Social Change*. New York: Palgrave Macmillan.

Abu-Lughod, Lila. 1990. "The Romance of Resistance: Tracing Transformations of Power through Bedouin Women." *American Ethnologist* 17 (1):41–55.

———. 2013. *Do Muslim Women Need Saving?* Cambridge, Mass.: Harvard University Press.

Achia, Thomas N. O. 2014. "Spatial Modelling and Mapping of Female Genital Mutilation in Kenya." *BMC Public Health* 14:276.

Acosta-Belen, Edna, and Christine E. Bose. 1990. "From Structural Subordination to Empowerment: Women and Development in Third World Contexts." *Gender and Society* 4 (3):299–320.

Ahearn, Laura M. 2001. "Language and Agency." *Annual Review of Anthropology* 30:109–37.

Ainsworth, Martha, and Deon Filmer. 2006. "Inequalities in Children's Schooling: AIDS, Orphanhood, Poverty, and Gender." *World Development* 34 (6):1099–128.

Alexander, Ruth M. 1995. *The "Girl Problem": Female Sexual Delinquency in New York, 1900–1930*. Ithaca, N.Y.: Cornell University Press.

Al-Samarrai, Samer, and Paul Bennell. 2003. *Where Has All the Education Gone in Africa? Employment Outcomes among Secondary School and University Leavers*. Brighton: Institute of Development Studies at the University of Sussex.

Amadiume, Ifi. 1987. *Male Daughters, Female Husbands: Gender and Sex in African Society*. London: Zed.

Anderson, John. 1970. *The Struggle for the School: The Interaction of Missionary, Colonial Government and Nationalist Enterprise in the Development of Formal Education in Kenya*. London: Longman.

Appadurai, Arjun. 2004. "The Capacity to Aspire: Culture and the Terms of Recognition." In *Culture and Public Action*, edited by Vijayendra Rao and Michael Walton, 59–84. Stanford, Calif.: Stanford University Press.

Appleton, Simon, Arne Bigsten, and Damiano Kulundu Manda (1999). "Educational Expansion and Economic Decline: Returns to Education in Kenya 1978–1995." *CSAE Working Paper 99.6*. Oxford: Centre for the Study of African Economies, Oxford University.

Archambault, Caroline S. 2007. "'School Is the Song of the Day': Education and Social Change in Maasai Society." PhD diss., Brown University.

———. 2009. "Pain with Punishment and the Negotiation of Childhood: An Ethnographic Analysis of Children's Rights Processes in Maasailand." *Africa* 79 (2):282–302.

———. 2011. "Ethnographic Empathy and the Social Context of Rights: 'Rescuing' Maasai Girls from Early Marriage." *American Anthropologist* 113 (4):632–43.

———. 2013. "Pastoral Rangeland Privatization and Women's Well-Being: A Gendered Analysis of Tenure Transformations among the Maasai of Southern Kenya." Paper presented at the Annual World Bank Conference on Land and Poverty, The World Bank, Washington D.C., April 8–11.

———. 2015. "Gendered Perspectives on Rangeland Privatization among the Maasai of Southern Kenya." In *Global Trends in Land Tenure Reform*, edited by Caroline S. Archambault and Anneleis Zoomers, 201–17. London: Routledge.

———. 2016. "'The Pen Is the Spear of Today': (Re)producing Gender in the Maasai School Setting." *Gender and Education* 29 (6):731–47.

Ariès, Phillippe. 1978. "Centuries of Childhood." In *Toward a New Sociology of Education*, edited by John Beck, Chris Jenks, Nell Keddie, and Michael F. D. Young, 37–47. New Brunswick, N.J.: Transaction.

Banet-Weiser, Sarah. 2015. "'Confidence You Can Carry!' Girls in Crisis and the Market for Girls' Empowerment Organizations." *Continuum* 29 (2):182–93.

Barker, Gary Knaul, and Susan Rich. 1992. "Influences on Adolescent Sexuality in Nigeria and Kenya: Findings from Recent Focus-Group Discussions." *Studies in Family Planning* 23 (3):199–210.

Beneria, Lourdes, and Savitri Bisnath, eds. 2000. *Gender and Development: Theoretical, Empirical and Practical Approaches*. Vols. 1–2. Cheltenham, U.K.: Elghar.

Bent, Emily. 2013. "A Different Girl Effect: Producing Political Girlhoods in the 'Invest in Girls' Climate." In *Youth Engagement: The Civic-Political Lives of Children and Youth*, Sociological Studies of Children and Youth, vol. 16, edited by Sandi Kawecka Nenga and Jessica K. Taft, 3–20. Bradford, U.K.: Emerald.

Bent, Emily, and Heather Switzer. 2016. "Oppositional Girlhood and the Challenge of Relational Politics." *Gender Issues* 33 (2):122–47.

Bergeron, Suzanne. 2013. "International Development Institutions, Gender, and Economic Life." In *Handbook of Research on Gender and Economic Life*, edited by Deborah M. Figart and Tonia L. Warnecke, 113–32. Cheltenham, U.K.: Elgar.

Berman, Bruce, and John Lonsdale. 1992. *Unhappy Valley: Conflict in Kenya and Africa*. Athens: Ohio University Press.

Bernstein, Robin. 2011. *Racial Innocence: Performing American Childhood from Slavery to Civil Rights*. New York: New York University Press.

Berntsen, John L. 1980. "The Enemy Is Us: Eponymy in the Historiography of the Maasai." *History in Africa* 7:1–21.

Biccum, April. 2011. "Marketing Development: Celebrity Politics and the 'New' Development Advocacy." *Third World Quarterly* 32 (7):1331–46.

Birdsall, Nancy. 2009. "Preface." In *Girls Count: A Global Investment and Action Agenda*, edited by Ruth Levine, Cynthia B. Lloyd, Margaret Greene, and Caren Grown, xiii. Washington, D.C.: Center for Global Development.

Bishop, Elizabeth. 2007. "Schooling and Pastoralists' Livelihoods: A Tanzanian Case Study." PhD. diss., University College London.

Bledsoe, Caroline. 1990. "School Girls and School Fees among the Mende of Sierra Leone." In *Beyond the Second Sex*, edited by Peggy Sanday and Ruth Goodenough, 283–309. Philadelphia: University of Pennsylvania Press.

Blewett, Robert A. 1995. "Property Rights as a Cause of the Tragedy of the Commons: Institutional Change and the Pastoral Maasai of Kenya." *Eastern Economic Journal* 21 (4):477–90.

Bloch, Marianne, Josephine A. Beoku-Betts, and B. Robert Tabachnick, eds. 1998. *Women and Education in Sub-Saharan Africa: Power, Opportunities, and Constraints*. Boulder, Colo.: Rienner.

Bloch, Marianne N., and Beth B. Swadener. 2009. "'Education for All?' Social Inclusions and Exclusions—Introduction and Critical Reflections." *International Journal of Educational Policy, Research, and Practice* 2 (1):n.p.

Bonini, Nathalie. 2006. "The Pencil and the Shepherd's Crook: Ethnography of Maasai Education." *Ethnography and Education* 1 (3):379–92.

Boyd, Ginger Ging-Dwan. 2016. "The Girl Effect: A Neoliberal Instrumentalization of Gender Equality." *Consilience: The Journal of Sustainable Development* 15.

Brock-Utne, Birgit. 2000. *Whose Education for All? The Recolonization of the African Mind*. New York: Falmer.

Brumberg, Joan Jacobs. 1998. *The Body Project: An Intimate History of American Girls*. New York: Random House.

Buchmann, Claudia. 1999. "The State and Schooling in Kenya: Historical Development and Current Challenges." *Africa Today* 46 (1):95–117.

BurnSilver, Shauna. B. 2009. "Pathways of Continuity and Change: Maasai Livelihoods in Amboseli, Kajiado District, Kenya." In *Staying Maasai? Livelihoods, Conservation and Development in East African Rangelands*, edited by Katherine Homewood, Patti Kristjanson, and Pippa Chenevix Trench, 161–207. New York: Springer.

BurnSilver, Shauna, and Esther Mwangi. 2007. "Beyond Group Ranch Subdivision: Collective Action for Livestock Mobility, Ecological Viability, and Livelihoods." CAPRi Working Paper No. 66. International Food Policy Research Institute.

Butler, Judith. 1988. "Performative Acts and Gender Constitution: An Essay in Phenomenology and Feminist Theory." *Theatre Journal* 40 (4):519–31.
Calkin, Sydney. 2015. "Feminism Interrupted? Gender and Development in the Era of 'Smart Economics.'" *Progress in Development Studies* 15 (4):295–307.
——. 2016. "Globalizing 'Girl Power': Corporate Social Responsibility and Transnational Business Initiatives for Gender Equality." *Globalizations* 13 (2):158–72.
Campbell, David J. 1993. "Land as Ours, Land as Mine": Economic, Political and Ecological Marginalization in Kajiado District." In Spear and Waller, *Being Maasai*, 258–72.
Carr-Hill, Roy, and Edwina Peart. 2005. *The Education of Nomadic Peoples in East Africa: Djibouti, Eritrea, Ethiopia, Kenya, Tanzania and Uganda*. Review of Relevant Literature. UNESCO/International Institute for Education Planning/African Development Bank.
Chaaban, Jad, and Wendy Cunningham. 2011. "Measuring the Economic Gain of Investing in Girls: The Girl Effect Dividend." Policy Research Working Paper 5753, Children and Youth Unit, Human Development Unit Development Network, Gender Unit, and Poverty Reduction and Economic Management Network. World Bank. http://dx.doi.org/10.1596/1813-9450-5753.
Chant, Sylvia. 2006. "Re-thinking the 'Feminization of Poverty' in Relation to Aggregate Gender Indices." *Journal of Human Development* 7 (2):201–20.
——. 2008. "The 'Feminisation of Poverty' and the 'Feminisation' of Anti-Poverty Programmes: Room for Revision?" *Journal of Development Studies* 44 (2):165–97.
——. 2015. "The 'Feminization of Poverty': A Reflection 20 Years after Beijing." United Nations Research Institute for Social Development, http://www.unrisd.org/unrisd/website/newsview.nsf/0/8a36603f76fe20efc1257df80055522c?.
Chant, Sylvia, and Caroline Sweetman. 2012. "Fixing Women or Fixing the World? 'Smart Economics,' Efficiency Approaches, and Gender Equality in Development." *Gender and Development* 20 (3):517–29.
Chatelain, Marcia. 2015. *South Side Girls: Growing Up in the Great Migration*. Durham, N.C.: Duke University Press.
Chege, Fatuma. 2006. "Processes of Adopting EFA Goals: The Kenyan Experience." Presentation to the National Graduate Institute for Policy Studies (GRIPS), March 23, 2004. Minato, Japan.
Chege, Fatuma, and Daniel Sifuna. 2006. *Girls' and Women's Education in Kenya: Gender Perspectives and Trends*. Nairobi: UNESCO.
Chesney-Lind, Meda, and Lisa Pasko, eds. 2013. *The Female Offender: Girls, Women and Crime*. 3rd ed. Los Angeles, Calif.: Sage.
Chesney-Lind, Meda, and Randall G. Shelden. 2014. *Girls, Delinquency, and Juvenile Justice*. 4th ed. Maldon, Mass.: Wiley.
Chisamya, Grace, Joan DeJaeghere, Nancy Kendall, and Marufa Aziz Kahn. 2012. "Gender and Education for All: Progress and Problems in Achieving Gender Equity." *International Journal of Educational Development* 32 (6):743–55.
Chowdhry, Geeta. 1995. "Engendering Development? Women in Development

(WID) in International Development Regimes." In *Feminism/Postmodernism/Development*, edited by Marianne H. Marchand and Jane L. Parpart, 26–41. London: Routledge.
Coast, Ernestina. 2001. "Colonial Preconceptions and Contemporary Demographic Reality: Maasai of Kenya and Tanzania." Paper presented at the International Union for the Scientific Study of Population Conference, August 20–24, Salvador, Bahia, Brazil.
———. 2002. "Maasai Socioeconomic Conditions: A Cross-Border Comparison." *Human Ecology* 30 (1):79–105.
Cobbett, Mary. 2014. "Beyond 'Victims' and 'Heroines': Constructing 'Girlhood' in International Development." *Progress in Development Studies* 14 (4):309–20.
Coe, Cati. 2005. *Dilemmas of Culture in African Schools: Youth, Nationalism, and the Transformation of Knowledge*. Chicago: University of Chicago Press.
Cole, Jennifer, and Ritty Lukose. 2011. "A Cultural Dialectics of Generational Change: The View from Contemporary Africa." *Review of Research in Education* 35 (1):60–88.
Collins, Patricia Hill. 1993. "Toward a New Vision: Race, Class, and Gender as Categories of Analysis and Connection." *Race, Sex and Class* 1 (1):25–46.
Combahee River Collective. (1977) 1982. "A Black Feminist Statement." In *All the Women Are White, All the Blacks Are Men, But Some of Us Are Brave*, edited by Gloria T. Hull, Patricia Bell Scott, and Barbara Smith, 13–22. New York: Feminist.
Commonwealth Education Fund. 2003. *Kenya Strategic Plan 2002–2005*. Action Aid. UK
Department of International Development (DfID).
Cornwall, Andrea. 2014. "Taking Off International Development's 'Straight-Jacket of Gender.'" *Brown Journal of World Affairs* 21 (1):127–38.
Cornwall, Andrea, Elizabeth Harrison, and Ann Whitehead. 2004. "Introduction: Repositioning Feminisms in Gender and Development." *IDS Bulletin* 34 (5):1–10.
———. 2008. "Gender Myths and Feminist Fables: The Struggle for Interpretive Power in Gender and Development." In *Gender Myths and Feminist Fables: The Struggle for Interpretive Power in Gender and Development*, edited by Andrea Cornwall, Elizabeth Harrison, and Ann Whitehead, 1–19. Malden, Mass.: Blackwell.
Cornwall, Andrea, and Althea-Maria Rivas. 2015. "From 'Gender Equality' and 'Women's Empowerment' to Global Justice: Reclaiming a Transformative Agenda for Gender and Development." *Third World Quarterly*. 36 (2):396–415.
Crenshaw, Kimberlé. 1989. "Demarginalizing the Intersection of Race and Sex: A Black Feminist Critique of Antidiscrimination Doctrine, Feminist Theory, and Antiracist Politics." *University of Chicago Legal Forum* 140:139–67.
Crenshaw, Kimberlé, Priscilla Ocen, and Jyoti Nanda. 2014. *Black Girls Matter: Pushed Out, Overpoliced and Underprotected*. New York: African American Policy Forum and Center for Intersectionality and Policy Studies.
Croll, Elisabeth. 2006. "From the Girl Child to Girl's Rights." *Third World Quarterly* 27 (7):1285–97.

CRC (Convention on the Rights of the Child). 1995. "Report Adopted by the Committee at Its 209th Meeting." Geneva, Switzerland, January 9–27.

Davison, Jean, and Martin Kanyuka. 1992. "Girls' Participation in Basic Education in Southern Malawi." *Comparative Education Review* 36 (4):446–66.

Decker, Corrie. 2010 "Reading, Writing, and Respectability: How Schoolgirls Developed Modern Literacies in Colonial Zanzibar." *International Journal of African Historical Studies* 43 (1):89–114.

DeJaeghere, Joan. 2014. "Encountering Friction between Liberal and Neoliberal Discourses of Citizenship: A Non-Governmental Organization's Entrepreneurship Education in Tanzania." *Education, Citizenship and Social Justice* 9 (3):226–38.

———. 2016. "Girls' Educational Aspirations and Agency: The Critical Role of Imagining Alternative Futures through Schooling in a Low-Resourced Tanzanian Communities." *Critical Studies in Education* [online May 31]:1–19. DOI 10.1080/17508487.2016.1188835.

DeJaeghere, Joan, and Frances Vavrus. 2011. "Educational Formations: Gendered Experiences of Schooling in Local Contexts." *Feminist Formations* 23 (3):vii–xvi.

Desai, Karishma. 2016. "Teaching the Third World Girl: 'Girl Rising' as a Precarious Curriculum of Empathy." *Curriculum Inquiry* 46 (3):248–64.

Dingo, Rebecca. 2012. *Networking Arguments: Rhetoric, Transnational Feminism, and Public Policy Writing*. Pittsburgh, Pa.: University of Pittsburgh Press.

Dosekun, Simidele. 2015. "For Western Girls Only? Post-Feminism as Transnational Culture." *Feminist Media Studies* 15 (6):960–75.

Driscoll, Catherine. 2002. *Girls: Feminine Adolescence in Popular Culture and Cultural Theory*. New York: Columbia University Press.

Dunne, Máiréad, Sara Humphreys, and Fiona Leach. 2006. "Gender Violence in Schools in the Developing World." *Gender and Education* 18 (1):75–98.

Epstein, Rebecca, Jamilia J. Blake, and Thalia González. 2017. *Girlhood Interrupted: The Erasure of Black Girls' Girlhood*. Washington, D.C.: Georgetown Law Center on Poverty and Inequality.

Escobar, Arturo. 1995. *Encountering Development: The Making and Unmaking of the Third World*. Princeton, N.J.: Princeton University Press.

Escudero, Verónica, and Elva López Murelo. 2013. *Understanding the Drivers of the Youth Labor Market in Kenya*. International Labor Organization Research Paper No.8. Geneva: International Labor Organization.

Evangelou, Phylo. 1984. *Livestock Development in Kenya's Maasailand: Pastoralists' Transition to a Market Economy*. Boulder, Colo.: Westview.

Fast Track Initiative. 2006. *Roundtable on Challenges and Opportunities*. Association for Development in Africa Biennale Conference on Education in Africa. Libreville, Gabon, March 27–31, 2007.

Feldman-Jacobs, Charlotte, and Donna Clifton. 2008. *Female Genital Mutilation/Cutting: Data and Trends*, 1–9. Washington, D.C.: Population Reference Bureau.

Fine, Michelle, and Lois Weis. 2005. "Compositional Studies, in Two Parts: Critical Theorizing and Analysis on Social (In)Justice." In *The Sage Handbook of Qualita-*

tive Research, 3rd ed., edited by Norman Denzin and Yvonne S. Lincoln, 65–84. Thousand Oaks, Calif.: Sage.

Ferguson, James. 2006. *Global Shadows: Africa in the Neoliberal World Order.* Durham, N.C.: Duke University Press.

Floro, Maria, and Joyce M. Wolf. 1990. *The Economic and Social Impact of Girls' Primary Education in Developing Countries.* Washington, D.C.: Creative Associates International.

Fraser, Nancy. 1989. *Unruly Practices: Power, Discourse and Gender in Contemporary Social Theory.* Minneapolis, Minnesota: University of Minnesota Press.

———. 2009. "Feminism, Capitalism and the Cunning of History." *New Left Review*, March/April, 97–117.

Fratkin, Elliot. 1998. *Ariaal Pastoralists of Kenya: Surviving Drought and Development in Africa's Arid Lands.* Boston: Allyn and Bacon.

———. 2001. "East African Pastoralism in Transition: Maasai, Boran, and Rendille Cases." *African Studies Review* 44 (3):1–25.

Frye, Margaret. 2012. "Bright Futures in Malawi's New Dawn: Educational Aspirations as Assertions of Identity." *American Journal of Sociology* 117 (6):1565–624.

Fylkesnes, Knut, Rosemary M. Musonda, Moses Sichone, Zacchaeus Ndhlovu, Francis Tembo, and Mwaka Monze. 2001. "Declining HIV Prevalence and Risk Behaviors in Zambia: Evidence from Surveillance and Population-Based Surveys." *AIDS* 15 (7):907–16.

Galaty, John. 1982. "Being Maasai: Being 'People-of-Cattle': Ethnic Shifters in East Africa." *American Ethnologist* 9 (1):1–20.

———. 1992. "'The Land Is Yours': Social and Economic Factors in the Privatization, Sub-division and Sale of Maasai Ranches." *Nomadic Peoples* 30:26–40.

———. 1993. "Maasai Expansion and the New East African Pastoralism." In Spear and Waller, *Being Maasai*, 61–86.

———. 2013. "Land Grabbing in the Eastern African Rangelands." In *Pastoralism and Development in Africa: Dynamic Change at the Margins*, edited by Andy Catley, Jeremy Lind, and Ian Scoones, 143–53. New York: Routledge.

George, Abosede. 2014. *Making Modern Girls: A History of Girlhood, Labor, and Social Development in Colonial Lagos.* Athens: Ohio University Press.

Gill, Rosalind, and Christina Scharff. 2011. *New Femininities: Postfeminism, Neoliberalism, and Subjectivity.* New York: Palgrave Macmillan.

Ginsburg, Mark B. 2000. "Questioning Assumptions and Implications of an Educational/Political Slogan." In Brock-Utne, *Whose Education for All?*, xvii–xxii.

Girl Effect. 2008. http://www.girleffect.org.

Girl Effect. N.d. Smarter Economics: Investing in Girls. http://educategirls.ngo/pdf/GirlEffect_Smarter-Economics-Investing-inGirls.pdf, accessed September 11, 2016. This document was originally available at girleffect.org until September 2016 and can be accessed as of January 10, 2018, at http://www.girleffect.org/media?id=3263.

The Girl Effect Declaration. N.d. https://www.girleffect.org/stories/girl-declaration.

Goldman, Mara J., and Jani S. Little. 2014. "Innovative Grassroots NGOs and the

Complex Processes of Women's Empowerment: An Empirical Investigation from Northern Tanzania." *World Development* 66:762–77.

Gonick, Marnina. 2003. *Between Femininities: Ambivalence, Identity, and the Education of Girls*. Albany: State University of New York Press.

———. 2006. "Between 'Girl Power' and 'Reviving Ophelia': Constituting the Neoliberal Girl Subject." *National Women's Studies Association Journal* 18 (2):1–23.

Gonick, Marnina. 2007. "Girl Number 20 Revisited: Feminist Literacies in New Hard Times." *Gender and Education* 19 (4):433–454.

Gonick, Marnina, Emma Renold, Jessica Ringrose, and Lisa Weems. 2009. "Rethinking Agency and Resistance: What Comes after Girlpower?" *Girlhood Studies* 2 (2):1–9.

Gorham, Alex. 1980. "Education and Social Change in a Pastoral Society: Government Initiatives and Local Responses to Primary School Provision in Kenya Maasailand." PhD diss. Institute of International Education. Stockholm: University of Stockholm.

Greene, Margaret, Anjala Kanesathasan, Gwennan Hollingworth, Jennifer Browning, and Eve Goldstein-Siegel. 2010. *On the Map: Charting the Landscape of Girl Work*. Washington, D.C.: International Center for Research on Women.

Greene, Margaret Eleanor, Omar J. Robles, Krista Stout, and Tanja Suvilaakso. 2013. *A Girl's Right to Learn without Fear: Working to End Gender-Based Violence at School*. Woking, U.K.: Plan International.

Grewal, Inderpal. 2005. *Transnational America: Feminisms, Diasporas, Neoliberalisms*. Durham, N.C.: Duke University Press.

Griffin, Christine. 2004. "Good Girls, Bad Girls: Anglocentricism and Diversity in the Constitution of Contemporary Girlhood." In *All About the Girl: Culture, Power and Identity*, edited by Anita Harris. New York: Routledge.

Grosser, Kay, and Nicole van der Gaag. 2013. "Can Girls Save the World?" In *Aid, NGOs and the Realities of Women's Lives: A Perfect Storm*, edited by Tina Wallace and Fenella Porter, 73–87. Warwickshire, U.K.: Practical Action.

Halberstam, Jack. 2005. *Female Masculinity*. Durham, N.C.: Duke University Press.

Hale, Jordene. 2014. *"For a Future Tomorrow": The Figured Worlds of Schoolgirls in Kono, Sierra Leone*. PhD diss. College of Education. University of Massachusetts, Amherst.

Hargreaves, James, and Tania Boler. 2006. *Girl Power: The Impact of Girls' Education on HIV and Sexual Behavior*. Action Aid International.

Harris, Anita. 2004. *Future Girl: Young Women in the Twenty-First Century*. New York: Routledge.

Hayhurst, Lyndsay M. C. 2011. "Corporatizing Sport, Gender and Development: Postcolonial IR Feminisms, Transnational Private Governance and Global Corporate Social Engagement." *Third World Quarterly* 32 (3):531–49.

Helgren, Jennifer, and Colleen Vasconcellos. 2010. *Girlhood: A Global History*. New Brunswick, N.J.: Rutgers University Press.

Hesse, Ced, and Michael Ochieng Odhiambo. 2001. *Reinforcement of Pastoralist*

Civil Society in East Africa: A Programme of Capacity-Building and Participatory Action-Research. Concept Note for the Drylands Program. IIED.

Hickel, Jason. 2014. "The 'Girl Effect': Liberalism, Empowerment, and the Contradictions of Development." *Third World Quarterly* 35 (8):1355–73.

Hodgson, Dorothy L. 1996a. "'My Daughter . . . Belongs to the Government Now': Marriage, Maasai, and the Tanzanian State." *Canadian Journal of African Studies* 30 (1):106–23.

———. 1996b. "Wayward Wives, Misfit Mothers, and Disobedient Daughters: 'Wicked' Women and the Reconfiguration of Gender in Africa." *Canadian Journal of African Studies* 30 (1):1–9.

———. 1999. "Women as Children: Culture, Political Economy and Gender Inequality among Kisongo Maasai." *Nomadic Peoples* 3 (2):115–30.

———, ed. 2001a. *Gendered Modernities: Ethnographic Perspectives*. New York City: Palgrave.

———. 2001b. *Once Intrepid Warriors: Gender, Ethnicity, and the Cultural Politics of Maasai Development*. Bloomington: Indiana University Press.

———. 2005. *The Church of Women: Gendered Encounters between Maasai and Missionaries*. Bloomington: Indiana University Press.

———. 2011. "'These Are Not Our Priorities': Maasai Women, Human Rights and the Problem of Culture." In *Gender and Culture at the Limits of Rights*, edited by Dorothy Hodgson, 139–218. Philadelphia: University of Pennsylvania Press.

Hodgson, Dorothy, and Sheryl A. McCurdy, eds. 2001. *"Wicked" Women and the Reconfiguration of Gender in Africa*. Portsmouth, N.H.: Heinemann.

Homewood, Katherine. 1995. "Development, Demarcation, and Ecological Outcomes in Maasailand." *Africa: Journal of the International African Institute* 65 (3):331–50.

Honwana, Alcinda, and Filip de Boeck, eds. 2005. *Makers and Breakers: Children and Youth in Postcolonial Africa*. Oxford: James Curry.

hooks, bell. 1984. *Feminist Theory from Margin to Center*. 1st ed. Cambridge, Mass.: South End.

Hughes, Lotte. 2006. *Moving the Maasai: A Colonial Misadventure*. New York: Palgrave.

Ikamari, Lawrence. 2005. "The Effect of Education the Timing of Marriage in Kenya." *Demographic Research* 12 (1):1–27.

International Labour Office (ILO). 2015. *Global Employment Trends for Youth: Scaling Up Investments in Decent Jobs for Youth*. Geneva: ILO.

Jacobs, Alan H. 1965. *The Traditional Political Organization of the Pastoral Masai*. D. Phil. Doctoral Thesis, Oxford University.

Jewkes, Rachel K., Jonathan B. Levine, and Loveday A. Penn-Kekana. 2003. "Gender Inequalities, Intimate Partner Violence and HIV Preventive Practices: Findings of a South African Cross-Sectional Study." *Social Science and Medicine* 56 (1):125–34.

Jones, Nicola, Karen Moore, Eliana Villar-Marquez, and Emma Broadbent. 2008. *Painful Lessons: The Politics of Sexual Violence and Bullying at School*. London: Overseas Development Institute.

Kabeer, Naila. 1994. *Reversed Realities: Gender Hierarchies in Development Thought.* London: Verso.

Kakenya's Dream Academy. 2015. http://www.kakenyasdream.org.

Kanani, Rahim. 2011. "The Nike Foundation on Unleashing the 'Girl Effect.'" *Huffington Post*, April 20. Available at http://www.huffingtonpost.com/rahim-kanani/nike-foundation-girl-effect_b_850551.html.

Kanogo, Tabitha. 2005. *African Womanhood in Colonial Kenya, 1990–50.* Oxford: James Currey.

Kantai, Parselelo. 2007. "In the Grip of the Vampire State: Maasai Land Struggles in Kenyan Politics." *Journal of East African Studies* 1 (1):107–22.

Kearney, Mary Celeste. 2009. "Coalescing: The Development of Girls' Studies." *Feminist Formations* 21(1):1–28.

Kelly, Peter. 2001. "The Post-Welfare State and the Government of Youth At-Risk." *Social Justice* 28 (4):96–113.

Kendall, Nancy, and Rachel Silver. 2014. "The Consequences of Global Mass Education: Schooling, Work, and Well-Being in EFA-Era Malawi." In *Globalization and Education: Integration and Contestation across Cultures*, 2nd ed., edited by Nelly Stromquist and Karen Monkman, 247–67. Lanham, Mass.: Rowman and Littlefield.

Kenya Food Security Steering Group (KFSSG). 2009. "The 2008/09 Short-Rains Season Assessment Report." Nairobi: KFSSG.

Kenya Food Security Steering Group/FAO. 2008. "The Impact of Rising Food Prices on Disparate Livelihood Groups in Kenya." Nairobi: KFSSG/FAO.

Kenya National Bureau of Statistics and ICF Macro (KNBS/ICFM). 2010. "Kenya Demographic and Health Survey 2008–2009." Calverton, Md.: KNBS/ICFM.

———. 2015. 2014 KDHS Key Findings. Rockville, Md.: KNBS and ICF International.

Khoja-Moolji, Shenila. 2015. "Girls, Education, and Narratives of Progress: Deconstructing the Discourse on Child Marriage." In *Educating Girls around the Globe: Challenges and Opportunities*, edited by Sandra L. Stacki and Supriya Bailey, 40–58. New York: Routledge.

Kiluva-Ndunda, Mutindi Mumbua. 2001. *Women's Agency and Educational Policy: The Experiences of the Women of Kilome, Kenya.* Albany: State University of New York.

King, Elizabeth M., and M. Anne Hill. 1993. *Women's Education in Developing Countries: Barriers, Benefits, and Policies.* Baltimore, Md.: Johns Hopkins University Press.

King, Kenneth. 1971. "The Kenya Maasai and the Protest Phenomenon, 1900–1960." *Journal of African History* 12 (1):117–37.

———. 1972. "Development and Education in the Narok District of Kenya, the Pastoral Maasai and Their Neighbors." *African Affairs* 71 (285):389–407.

King, Kenneth, and Simon McGrath. 2004. *Knowledge for Development? Comparing British, Japanese, Swedish and World Bank Aid.* London: Zed.

Kipury, Naomi. 1983. *Oral Literature of the Maasai.* Nairobi: East African Educational.

———. 1988. "Change and Gender in Pastoralist Ideology: East African Pastoralists in

Perspective." Paper presented at the African Studies Association Meeting, October 28–31. Chicago, Illinois.

Kirk, Jackie, and Stephanie Garrow. 2003. "'Girls in Policy': Challenges for the Education Sector." *Agenda: Empowering Women for Gender Equity* 56:4–15.

Kirk, Jackie, and Marni Sommer. 2006. "Menstruation and Body Awareness: Linking Girls' Health with Girls' Education." *Royal Tropical Institute (KIT): Special on Gender and Health*, 1–22. Amsterdam, Neth.

Kituyi, Mukisha. 1990. *Becoming Kenyans: Socio-Economic Transformation of the Pastoral Maasai*. Nairobi: Acts Press/African Center for Technology Studies.

Koffman, Ofra, and Rosalind Gill. 2013a. "'I Matter and So Does She': Girl Power, (Post)Feminism and the Girl Effect." In *Youth Cultures in the Age of Global Media*, edited by David Buckingham, Sara Bragg, and Mary Jane Kehily, 242–57. Basingstoke, U.K.: Palgrave Macmillan.

———. 2013b. "The Revolution Will Be Led by a 12-Year-Old Girl: Girl Power and Global Biopolitcs." *Feminist Review* 105:83–102.

Koponen, Juhani. 1994. *Development for Exploitation: German Development Policies in Mainland Tanzania, 1884–1914*. Studia Historica 49. Helsinki: Finnish Historical Society.

Krätli, Saverio. 2001. "Education Provision to Nomadic Pastoralists: A Literature Review." Institute for Development Studies Working Paper 126. Brighton: Institute for Development Studies.

Krätli, Saverio, and Caroline Dyer. 2006. "Education and Development for Nomads: The Issues and the Evidence." In *The Education of Nomadic Peoples: Current Issues, Future Prospects*, edited by Caroline Dyer, 8–35. New York: Berghahn.

Kristjanson, Patti, Ann Waters-Bayer, Nancy Johnson, Anna Tipilda, Jemimah Njuki, Isabell Baltenweck, Delia Grace, and Susan MacMillan. 2010. "Livestock and Women's Livelihoods: A Review of the Recent Evidence." International Livestock Research Institute Decision Paper No. 20. Nairobi: ILRI.

Kristof, Nicholas, and Sheryl WuDunn. 2009a. *Half the Sky: Turning Oppression into Opportunity for Women Worldwide*. New York: Vintage.

———. 2009b. "The Women's Crusade." *New York Times Magazine*, August 17. http://www.nytimes.com/2009/08/23/magazine/23Women-t.html.

Kylander, Nathalie. 2011. "The Girl Effect Brand: Using Brand Democracy to Strengthen Brand Affinity." Hauser Center for Nonprofits, Harvard University.

Leach, Fiona. 2006. "Researching Gender Violence in Schools: Methodological and Ethical Considerations." *World Development* 34 (6):1129–47.

Leach, Fiona, and Claudia Mitchell, eds. 2006. *Combating Gender Violence in and around Schools*. Stoke-on-Trent, U.K.: Trentham.

Leggett, Ian. 2005. *Learning to Improve Education Policy for Pastoralists in Kenya*. London: Oxfam.

Lesko, Nancy. 2001. *Act Your Age! A Cultural Construction of Adolescence*. New York: Routledge Falmer.

Lesorogol, Carolyn K. 2008. "Setting Themselves Apart: Education, Capabilities, and Sexuality among Samburu Women in Kenya." *Anthropological Quarterly* 81 (3):551–77.

Levine, Ruth, Cynthia B. Lloyd, Margaret Greene, and Caren Grown. 2008. *Girls Count: A Global Investment and Action Agenda*. Washington, D.C.: Center for Global Development.

Lloyd, Cynthia B., Barbara S. Mensch, and Wesley H. Clark. 2000. "The Effects of Primary School Quality on School Dropout among Kenyan Girls and Boys." *Comparative Education Review* 44 (2):113–47.

Lonsdale, John. 1990. "Mau Maus of the Mind: Making Mau Mau and Remaking Kenya." *Journal of African History* 31 (3):393–421.

———. 1992. *Unhappy Valley: Conflict in Kenya and Africa*. London: James Curry.

Lonsdale, John, and Bruce Berman. 1979. "Coping with the Contradictions: The Development of the Colonial State in Kenya, 1895–1914." *Journal of African History* 20 (4):487–505.

Lopez, Vera. 2017. *Complicated Lives: Girls, Parents, Drugs, and Juvenile Justice*. New Brunswick, N.J.: Rutgers University Press.

Lugonés, María. 2007. "Heterosexualism and the Colonial/Modern Gender System." *Hypatia* 22 (1):186–209.

Macamo, Elísio Salvado. 2005. "Negotiating Modernity: From Colonization to Globalization." Introduction, *Negotiating Modernity: Africa's Ambivalent Experience*, edited by Elísio Salvado Macamo, 1–19. Dakar, Senegal: CODESRIA Books.

Madhok, Sumi, Anne Phillips, and Kalpana Wilson. 2013. *Gender, Agency and Coercion*. New York: Palgrave McMillian.

Mahmood, Saba. 2005. *Politics of Piety: The Islamic Revival and the Feminist Subject*. Princeton, N.J.: Princeton University Press.

Malhotra, Anju, Rohini Pande, and Caren Grown. 2003. *Impact of Investments in Female Education on Gender Equality*. Washington, D.C.: International Center for Research on Women.

Manda, Damiano Kulundu, Germano Mwabu, and Mwangi S, Kimenyi. 2002. *Human Capital Externalities and Returns to Education in Kenya*. Discussion Paper No. 13. Nairobi: Kenya Institute for Public Policy Research and Analysis.

Marchand, Marianne H., and Jane L. Parpart.1995. "Exploding the Canon: An Introduction/Conclusion." In *Feminism/Postmodernism/Development*, edited by Marianne H. Marchand and Jane L. Parpart, 1–22. London: Routledge.

———. 2000. "Reconceptualizing 'Gender and Development' in an Era of Globalization." In *Poverty in World Politics*, edited by Sarah Owen Vandersluis and Paris Yeros, 119–47. New York: St. Martin's.

Marphatia, Akanksha A., and Rachel Moussié. 2013. "A Question of Gender Justice: Exploring the Linkages between Women's Unpaid Care Work, Education, and Gender Equality." *International Journal of Educational Development* 33 (6):585–94.

Matampash, Kenny. 1993. "The Maasai of Kenya." In *Indigenous Views of Land and the Environment*, edited by Shelton H. Davis, 31–45. Washington: World Bank Discussion Papers.

Maternowska, Catherine, Fátima Estrada, Lourdes Campero, Christina Herrera, Claire D. Brindis, and Meredith Miller Vostrejs. 2009. "Gender, Culture and Reproductive Decision-Making among Recent Mexican Migrants in California." *Culture, Health, and Sexuality* 12(1):29–43.

McClintock, Anne. 1995. *Imperial Leather: Race, Gender, and Sexuality in the Colonial Contest*. New York: Routledge.

McGranahan, Carole. 2016. "Theorizing Refusal: An Introduction." *Cultural Anthropology* 31 (3):319–25.

McRobbie A. 2008. *The Aftermath of Feminism: Gender, Culture and Social Change*. Los Angeles: Sage.

———. 2011. "Preface." In Gill and Scharff, *New Femininities*, xi–xv.

Meena, Ruth, ed. 1992. *Gender in Southern Africa: Conceptual and Theoretical Issues*. Harare, Zimbabwe: SAPES.

Mensch, Barbara, Judith Bruce, and Margaret E. Greene. 1998. *The Uncharted Passage: Girls' Adolescence in the Developing World*. New York: Population Council.

Mensch, Barbara, Wesley H. Clark, Cynthia B. Lloyd, and Annabel S. Erulkar. 2001. "Premarital Sex, Schoolgirl Pregnancy, and School Quality in Rural Kenya." *Studies in Family Planning* 32 (4):285–301.

Mensch, Barbara S., and Cynthia B. Lloyd. 1998. "Gender Differences in the Schooling Experiences of Adolescents in Low-Income Countries: The Case of Kenya." *Studies in Family Planning* 29 (2):167–84.

Merker, Moritz. (1904) 1910. *Die Masai: Ethnographische monographie eines ostafrikanischen Semitenvolkes*. Berlin: Dietrich Reimer.

Mitchell, Claudia, and Carrie Rentschler, eds. 2016. *Girlhood and the Politics of Place*. New York: Berghahn.

Miller, Carol, and Shahra Razavi, eds.1998. *Missionaries and Mandarins: Feminist Engagement with Development Institutions*. London: Intermediate Technology Publications/United Nations Research Institute for Social Development.

Miranda, Alisha. 2015. *The Journey of a Girl: Opportunities for Business Investment in Girls' Education*. Working Paper. New York: Global Business Coalition for Education.

Moeller, Kathryn. 2013. "Proving 'The Girl Effect': Corporate Knowledge Production and Educational Intervention." *International Journal of Educational Development* 33 (6):612–21.

———. 2014a. "'The Girl Effect': U.S. Transnational Corporate Investment in Girls' Education." In *Globalization and Education: Integration and Contestation across Cultures*, 2nd ed., edited by Nelly P. Stromquist and Karen Monkman, 71–87. Lanham, Md.: Rowman and Littlefield.

———. 2014b. "Searching for Adolescent Girls in Brazil: The Transnational Politics of Poverty in 'The Girl Effect.'" *Feminist Studies* 40 (3):575–601.

———. 2018. *The Gender Effect: Capitalism, Feminism, and the Corporate Politics of Development*. Oakland: University of California Press.

Mohanty, Chandra Talpade. 1988. "Under Western Eyes: Feminist Scholarship and Colonial Discourses." *Feminist Review* 30:61–88.

———. 2003a. *Feminism without Borders: Decolonizing Theory, Practicing Solidarity.* Durham, North Carolina: Duke University Press.

———. 2003b. "'Under Western Eyes' Revisited: Feminist Solidarity through Anticapitalist Struggles." *Signs* 28 (2):499–535.

———. 2013. "Transnational Feminist Crossings: On Neoliberalism and Radical Critique." *Signs* 38 (4):967–91.

Mojola, Sanyu A. 2014. *Love, Money, and HIV: Becoming a Modern African Woman in the Age of AIDS.* Oakland: University of California Press.

Mol, Frans. 1996. *Maasai Language and Culture Dictionary.* Lemek, Kenya: Maasai Centre Lemek.

Molyneux, Maxine. 2008. "The 'Neoliberal Turn' and the New Social Policy in Latin America: How Neoliberal, How New?" *Development and Change* 39 (5):775–97.

Monkman, Karen. 2011. "Framing Gender, Education and Empowerment." *Research in Comparative and International Education* 6 (1):1–13.

Monkman, Karen, and L. Hoffman. 2013. "Girls' Education: The Power of Policy Discourse." *Theory and Research in Education* 11 (1):63–84.

Morris, Monique W. 2016. *Pushout: The Criminalization of Black Girls in Schools.* New York City, New York: New Press.

Moser, Caroline. 1989. "Gender Planning in the Third World: Meeting Practical and Strategic Gender Needs." *World Development* 17 (11):1799–825.

Mukudi, Edith. 2004. "Education for All: A Framework for Addressing the Persisting Illusion for the Kenyan Context." *International Journal of Educational Development* 24 (3):231–40.

Munga, Boaz, and Eldah Onsomu. 2014. "State of Youth Unemployment in Kenya." Washington D.C.: Brookings. www.brookings.edu/blog/africa-in-focus/2014/08/21/state-of-youth-unemployment-in-kenya.

Murphy, Michelle. 2012/2013. "The Girl: Mergers of Feminism and Finance in Neoliberal Times." *Scholar and Feminist Online* 11.1–11.2. http://sfonline.barnard.edu/gender-justice-and-neoliberal-transformations/the-girl-mergers-of-feminism-and-finance-in-neoliberal-times.

Mwangi, Esther. 2006. "The Footprints of History: Path Dependence in the Transformation of Property Rights in Kenya's Maasailand." *Journal of Institutional Economics* 2 (2):157–80.

Mwiria, Kilemi. 1991. "Education for Subordination: African Education in Colonial Kenya." *History of Education* 20 (3):261–73.

Nagel, Tovin. 2001. "Educating Nomadic Herders out of Poverty? A Response to S. Kratli." London: Save the Children Fund.

Narayan, Uma. 1997. *Dislocating Cultures: Identities, Traditions, and Third World Feminism.* New York: Routledge.

Nekatibeb, Teshome, 2002. *Low Participation of Female Students in Primary Educa-*

tion: *A Case Study of Dropouts from the Amhara and Oromia Regional States in Ethiopia*. Paris: UNESCO International Institute for Capacity Building in Africa.

Nkedianye, David, Maren Radeny, Patti Krisjanson, and Mario Herrero. 2009. "Assessing Returns to Land and Changing Livelihood Stategies in Kitengela." In *Staying Maasai?: Livelihoods, Conservation and Development in East African Rangelands*, edited by Katherine Homewood, Patti Kristjanson, and Pippa Chenevix Trench, 115–39. New York: Springer.

Nnaemeka, Obioma, ed. 2005. *Female Circumcision and the Politics of Knowledge: African Women in Imperialist Discourses*. Westport, Conn.: Praeger.

Nzegwu, Nkiru Uwechia. 2006. *Family Matters: Feminist Concepts in African Philosophy of Culture*. Albany: State University of New York Press.

Odem, Mary E. 1995. *Delinquent Daughters: Protecting and Policing Adolescent Female Sexuality in the United States, 1885–1920*. Chapel Hill: University of North Carolina.

Omolo, Jacob. 2012. "Youth Unemployment in Kenya: Analysis of Labour Market and Policy Interventions." FES Kenya Occasional Paper No.1. Nairobi: FES.

Ong, Aihwa. 2006. *Neoliberalism as Exception: Mutations in Citizenship and Sovereignty*. Durham, N.C.: Duke University Press.

Oxfam. 2005. *Beyond the Mainstream: Education for Nomadic and Pastoralist Girls and Boys*. Education and Gender Equality Series, Programme Insights. London: Oxfam.

Oyěwùmí, Oyèrónké. 1997. *The Invention of Women: Making an African Sense of Western Gender Discourses*. Minneapolis: University of Minnesota Press.

———. 2000. "Family Bonds/Conceptual Binds: African Notes on Feminist Epistemologies." *Signs* 25 (4):1093–98.

———. 2003. *Conceptualizing Gender: The Eurocentric Foundations of Feminist Concepts and the Challenge of African Epistemologies*. Conference paper. Dakar, Senegal: CODESRIA. https://www.codesria.org/IMG/pdf/OYEWUMI.pdf.

Parkes, Jenny, and Fatuma Chege. 2010. *Girls' Education and Violence: Reflections on the First Decade of the Twenty-First Century*. Engendering Empowerment: Education and Equality, United Nations Girls' Education Initiative Conference, Dakar, Senegal, May 17–20.

Parkes, Jenny, and Jo Heslop. 2011. *Stop Violence Against Girls in School: A Cross-Country Analysis of Baseline Research from Ghana, Kenya and Mozambique*. Johannesburg, S.A.: Action Aid International.

———. 2013. *Stop Violence against Girls in School: A Cross-Country Analysis of Change in Ghana, Kenya and Mozambique*. Johannesburg, S.A.: Action Aid International.

Parkes, Jenny, Jo Heslop, Samwel Oando, Susan Sabaa, Francisco Januario, and Asmara Figue. 2013. "Conceptualising Gender and Violence in Research: Insights from Studies in Schools and Communities in Kenya, Ghana and Mozambique." *International Journal of Educational Development* 33 (6):546–56.

Pastoralist Child Foundation. 2015. http://pastoralistchildfoundation.org.

Payne, Doris L., and Leonard Ole-Kotikash. 2008. "Maa Language Project." http://pages.uoregon.edu/maasai.

Peck, Jamie, and Adam Tickell. 2002. "Neoliberalizing Space." *Antipode* 34 (3):380–404.

Pigg, Stacy Leigh. 1992. "Inventing Social Categories through Place: Social Representations and Development in Nepal." *Comparative Studies in Society and History* 34 (3):491–513.

———. 1993. "Unintended Consequences: The Ideological Impact of Development in Nepal." *South Asian Bulletin* 13 (1–2):45–58.

Population Reference Bureau. 2008. "2008 World Population Data Sheet." http://www.prb.org/Publications/Datasheets/2008/2008wpds.aspx.

Pratt, Beth Anne. 2003. "Childhood, Space and Children 'Out of Place': Versions of Maasai Childhood in Monduli Juu, Tanzania." PhD diss., Boston University.

Price-Cohen, Cynthia. 1997. "The United Nations Convention on the Landmark Rights of the Child: A Feminist Lnadmark." William & Mary Journal of Women and the Law 3(1), Article 3: 29–78.

Psacharopoulos, George, and Harry Anthony Patrinos. 2002. "Returns to Investment in Education: A Further Update." Policy Research Working Paper 2881. Washington, D.C.: World Bank.

Quan, H. L. T. 2012. *Growth against Democracy: Savage Developmentalism in the Modern World*. Lantham, Md.: Lexington.

Raymond, Adella. 2014. "Girls' Education in Pastoral Communities: An Ethnographic Study of Monduli District, Tanzania." Berkshire, UK: CfBT Education Trust.

Razavi, Shahra. 1998. "Becoming Multilingual: The Challenges of Feminist Policy Advocacy." In Miller and Razavi, *Missionaries and Mandarins*, 20–42.

Razavi, Shahra, and Carol Miller. 1995. *From WID to GAD: Conceptual Shifts in the Women and Development Discourse*. Occasional Paper 1. UNRISD. Geneva: UNDP.

Republic of Kenya. 1964/1965. *Kenya Education Commission Report, Part I and Part II*. Nairobi, Kenya.

———. 2007. *Gender Policy in Education*. Nairobi: Ministry of Education.

Rigby, Peter. 1981. "Pastors and Pastoralists: The Differential Penetration of Christianity among East African Cattle Herders." *Comparative Study in Society and History* 23 (1):96–129.

Ringrose, Jessica. 2007. "Successful Girls? Complicating Postfeminist, Neoliberal Discourses of Educational Achievement and Gender Equality." *Gender and Education* 19 (4):471–89.

Rist, Gilbert. 2002. *History of Development: From Western Origins to Global Faith*. 2nd ed. London: Zed.

Rottenberg, Catherine. 2014. "The Rise of Neoliberal Feminism." *Cultural Studies* 28 (3):418–37.

Rutten, Marcel M. E. M. 1992. "Selling Wealth to Buy Poverty: The Process of the Individualization of Landownership Among the Maasai Pastoralists of Kajiado District, Kenya, 1890–1990." PhD diss., Catholic University.

Sassen, Saskia. 2000. "Women's Burden: Counter-Geographies of Globalization and the Feminization of Survival." *Journal of International Affairs* 53 (2):503–24.

———. 2001. "The Excesses of Globalization and the Feminization of Survival." *Parallax* 7 (1):100–110.

Sena, Sarone. 1986. "Pastoralists and Education: School Participation and Social Change among the Maasai." PhD diss., McGill University.

———. 1994. "Development and Education for Pastoralists: Maasai Responses in East Africa." *CDAS Discussion Papers* 19:13–23.

Sensoy, Özlem, and Elizabeth Marshall. 2010. "Missionary Girl Power: Saving the 'Third World' One Girl at a Time." *Gender and Education* 22 (3):295–311.

Shadle, Brett L. 2006. *"Girl Cases": Marriage and colonialism in Gusiiland, Kenya, 1890–1970*. Portsmouth, N.J.: Heinemann.

Sheffield, James R. 1973. *Education in Kenya: An Historical Study*. New York: Teachers College.

Shell-Duncan, Bettina, Reshma Naik, and Charlotte Feldman-Jacobs. 2016. "A State-of-Art-Synthesis of Female Genital Mutilation/Cutting: What Do We Know Now? October 2016." *Evidence to End FGM/C: Research to Help Women Thrive*. New York: Population Council.

Sheppard, Eric S., and Helga Leitner. 2010. "*Quo vadis* Neoliberalism? The Remaking of Global Capitalist Governance after the Washington Consensus." *Geoforum* 41 (2):185–94.

Sheppard, Eric S., and Richa Nagar. 2010. *A World of Difference: Encountering and Contesting Development*. New York: Guilford.

Sifuna, Daniel N. 2005. "Increasing Access and Participation of Pastoralist Communities in Primary Education in Kenya." International *Review of Education* 51 (5–6):499–516.

Sommer, Marni. 2009. "Where the Education System and Women's Bodies Collide: The Social and Health Impact of Girls' Experience of Menstruation and Schooling in Tanzania." *Journal of Adolescence* 33 (4):521–29.

Sparke, Matthew. 2015. *Introducing Globalization: Ties, Tensions, and Uneven Integration*. Chichester, U.K.: Wiley-Blackwell.

Spear, Thomas. 1993. "Introduction." In Spear and Waller, *Being Maasai*.

Spear, Thomas, and Richard Waller, eds. 1993. *Being Maasai: Ethnicity and Identity in East Africa*. Athens: Ohio University Press.

Spencer, Paul. 1988. *The Maasai of Matapato: A Study of Rituals and Rebellion*. Bloomington: Indiana University Press.

Spivak, Gayatri Chakravorty. 1988. "Can the Subaltern Speak?" In *Marxism and the Interpretation of Culture*, edited by Cary Nelson and Lawrence Grossberg, 271–315. Chicago: University of Illinois Press.

Stambach, Amy. 2000. *Lessons from Mount Kilimanjaro: Schooling, Community, and Gender in East Africa*. New York: Routledge.

———. 2006. "African Education, Culture, and Modernity Unwound." *Comparative Education Review* 50 (2):288–95.

Stanfield, James. 2005. "Kenya's Forgotten Independent School Movement." *Economic Affairs* 25 (4):82.
Strayer, Robert W. 1978. *The Making of Mission Communities in East Africa*. London: Heinemann.
Summers, Lawrence. 1992. "Investing in All People." WPS 95. Office of the Vice President. Washington, D.C.: World Bank.
———. 1993. "The Most Influential Investment." *People and the Planet* 2 (1):10.
Swadener, Elizabeth, Patrick Wachira, Margaret Kabiru, and Ann Njenga. 2008. "Linking Policy Discourse to Everyday Life in Kenya: Impacts of Neoliberal Policies on Early Education and Childrearing." In *Africa's Future, Africa's Challenge: Early Childhood Care and Development in Sub-Saharan Africa*, edited by Marito Garcia, Alan Pence, and Judith L. Evans, 407–22. Washington, D.C.: World Bank.
Swadener, Beth Blue, and Mark Nagasawa. 2015. "Confronting Common Sense Assumptions and Social Exclusion: Transnational Stories and Call to Action." In *Roma Inclusion-International and Greek Experiences: The Present of a Continuum*, edited by Soula Mitakidou, 37–50. Thessaloniki, Greece: City Publishing.
Sutton, J. E. G. 1993. "Becoming Maasailand." In Spear and Waller, *Being Maasai*, 38–60.
Switzer, Heather. 2010. "Disruptive Discourses: Kenyan Maasai Schoolgirls Make Themselves." *Girlhood Studies Journal* 3 (1):137–55.
———. 2013. "(Post)Feminist Development Fables: The Girl Effect and the Production of Sexual Subjects." *Feminist Theory* 14 (3):345–60.
Switzer, Heather, Emily Bent, and Crystal Endsley. 2016. "Precarious Politics and Girl Effects: Exploring the Limits of the Girl Gone Global." *Feminist Formations* 28 (1):33–59.
Taft, Jessica K. 2011. *Rebel Girls: Youth Activism and Social Change across the Americas*. New York: New York University Press.
Talle, Aud. 1988. *Women at a Loss: Changes in Maasai Pastoralism and Their Effects on Gender Relations*. Stockholm: University of Stockholm.
———. 2007. "'Serious Games': Licenses and Prohibitions in Maasai Sexual Life." *Africa* 77 (3):351–70.
Thomas, Lynn M. 1996. "'Ngaitana (I Will Circumcise Myself)': The Gender and Generational Politics of the 1956 Ban on Clitoridectomy in Meru, Kenya." *Gender and History* 8 (3):338–63.
———. 2003. *Politics of the Womb: Women, Reproduction, and the State in Kenya*. Berkeley, Calif.: University of California Press.
———. 2006a. "Gendered Reproduction: Placing Schoolgirl Pregnancies in African History." In *Africa after Gender?* edited by Catherine M. Cole, Takyiwaa Manuh, and Stephan F. Miescher, 48–63. Bloomington: Indiana University Press.
———. 2006b. "Schoolgirl Pregnancies, Letter-Writing, and 'Modern' Persons in Late Colonial East Africa." In *Africa's Hidden Histories: Everyday Literacy and the Making of the Self*, edited by Karin Barber, 187–207. Bloomington: Indiana University Press.

Tikolo, Olayide. 2014. *Digital Campaigning: A New Role for Business in Education.* Policy Brief No. 1. Global Business Campaign for Education. https://issuu.com/olayidetikolo/docs/digital_campaigning_-_a_new_role_fo.

"A Tribute to Jackie Kirk: Activist, Academic and Champion of Girls." Special issue. *Girlhood Studies* 1 (2010):1–191.

UN. 2001. *Beijing Platform for Action with the Beijing +5 Political Declaration and Outcome Document.* New York: Department of Public Information, UN.

UNAIDS. 2012. Fact Sheet: Adolescents, Young People and HIV. http://files.unaids.org/en/media/unaids/contentassets/documents/factsheet/2012/20120417_FS_adolescentsyoungpeoplehiv_en.pdf.

UNDP. 2013. *Rise of the South: Human Progress in a Diverse World.* Human Development Report 2013. New York: UNDP.

UNESCO. 2004. *Educating for a Sustainable Future: Commitments and Partnerships.* Proceedings of the High-Level International Conference on Education for Sustainable Development at the World Summit on Sustainable Development, September 2–3, 2002, Johannesburg. Barcelona: UNESCO.

———. 2006. *Fact Book on Education for All.* Nairobi: UNESCO.

UNICEF. 2004. *Girls, HIV/AIDS, and Education.* New York: UNICEF.

———. 2005. *Female Genital Mutilation/Cutting: A Statistical Exploration.* New York: UNICEF.

———. 2012. *Violence against Children in Kenya: Findings from a 2012 National Survey.* Nairobi: UNICEF.

———. 2013. *Female Genital Mutilation/Cutting: A Statistical Overview and Exploration of the Dynamics of Change.* New York: UNICEF.

Unterhalter, Elaine. 2007. *Gender, Schooling and Global Social Justice.* New York: Routledge.

———. 2012. "Poverty, Education, Gender and the Millennium Development Goals: Reflections on Boundaries and Intersectionality." *Theory and Research in Education* 10 (3):253–74.

Unterhalter, Elaine, Jennifer Anne Karlsson, Veerle Dieltiens, Jane Osongo, Amy North, Herbert Makinda, and Christopher Andrew Yates. 2011. "Gender, Education and Global Poverty Reduction Initiatives." *Report on Comparative Case Studies in Kenya, South Africa and Selected Global Organisations.* London: Institute of Education, University of London.

Unterhalter, Elaine, and Amy North. 2011. "Responding to the Gender and Education Millennium Development Goals in South Africa and Kenya: Reflections on Education Rights, Gender Equality, Capabilities and Global Justice." *Compare* 41 (4):495–511.

Vavrus, Frances. 2002. "Making Distinctions: Privatisation and the (un)Educated Girl on Mount Kilimanjaro, Tanzania." *International Journal of Educational Development* 22 (5):527–47.

———. 2003. *Desire and Decline: Schooling amid Crisis in Tanzania.* New York: Peter Lang.

Vavrus, Frances, and Richey, Lisa Ann. 2003. "Women and Development: Rethinking Policy and Reconceptualizing Practice." *Women's Studies Quarterly* 31 (3-4).
Waller, Richard. 1976. "The Maasai and the British 1895-1905: The Origins of an Alliance." *Journal of African History* 17 (4):529-53.
———. 1988. "Emutai: Crisis and Response in Maasailand 1884-1904." In *The Ecology of Survival: Cases from Northeast African History*, edited by Douglas Johnson and David Anderson, 73-112. London: Crook.
———. 1993. "'Acceptees and Aliens': Kikuyu Settlement in Maasailand." In Spear and Waller, *Being Maasai*, 226-57.
———. 1999. *East African Expressions of Christianity*. Athens: Ohio University Press.
———. 2006. "Rebellious Youth in Colonial Africa." *Journal of Africa History* 47 (1):77-92.
Wangui, Elizabeth Edna. 2008. "Development Interventions, Changing Livelihoods, and the Making of Female Maasai Pastoralists." *Agriculture and Human Values* 25 (3):365-78.
Warner, Ann, Gwenann Hollingworth, Lyric Thompson, Suzanne Petroni, Magnolia Sexton, Josie Song, Jamal Khada, and Kat Jennings. 2013. *I Know, I Want, I Dream: Girls' Insights for Building a Better World*. Washington, D.C.: International Center for Research on Women.
Warrington, Molly, and Susan Kiragu. 2012 "It Makes More Sense to Educate a Boy: Girls 'Against the Odds' in Kajiado, Kenya." *International Journal of Educational Development* 32 (2):301-9.
Weinbaum, Alys Eve, Lynn M. Thomas, Priti Ramamurthy, Uta G. Poiger, Madeleine Yue Dong, and Tani E. Barlow. 2008. *The Modern Girl around the World: Consumption, Modernity, and Globalization*. Durham, N.C.: Duke University Press.
Weiss, Brad, ed. 2004. *Producing African Futures: Ritual and Reproduction in a Neoliberal Age*. Leiden: Brill.
WGG (Working Group on Girls). 2015. *Action for Girls: Newsletter of the Working Group on Girls and Its International Network for Girls* 3 (19): unpaginated.
Williams, Raymond. 1961. *The Long Revolution*. London: Chatto and Windus.
Wilson, Kalpana. 2008. "Reclaiming 'Agency,' Reasserting Resistance." *IDS Bulletin* 39 (6):83-91.
———. 2011. "'Race', Gender and Neoliberalism: Changing Visual Representations in Development." *Third World Quarterly* 32 (2):315-31.
———. 2013. "Agency as 'Smart Economics': Neoliberalism, Gender and Development." In *Gender, Agency, and Coercion*, edited by Sumi Madhok, Anne Phillips and Kalpana Wilson, 84-101. New York: Palgrave Macmillan.
———. 2015. "Towards a Radical Reappropriation: Gender, Development and Neoliberal Feminism." *Development and Change* 46 (4):803-32.
Weinstone, Ann. 2004. *What Girls Need to Grow: Lessons for Social Change Philanthropy*. Impact Report No. 2. San Francisco: Global Fund for Women. https://www.globalfundforwomen.org/wp-content/uploads/2006/11/impact-report-2.pdf.

Wolff, Brent, Ann K. Blanc, and Anastasia J. Gage. 2000. "Who Decides? Women's Status and Negotiations of Sex in Uganda." *Culture, Health and Sexuality* 2 (3):303–22.

Wright, Nazera Sadiq. 2016. *Blackgirlhood in the Nineteenth Century*. Urbana: University of Illinois Press.

Zack-Williams, Alfred B. 2005. "Africa and the Project of Modernity: Some Reflections." In *Negotiating Modernity: Africa's Ambivalent Experience*, edited by Elísio Salvado Macamo. Dakar, Senegal: CODESRIA Books.

Index

adolescence, 19, 39, 114-117, 119, 122, 125, 127, 130, 132-133, 135-136, 140, 143, 148, 152, 155, 157, 162, 168
African Inland Mission (AIM), 33, 41
age-grade system, 22, 38; age-set, 38-40, 43, 45-47, 49, 56, 74, 111, 117
agency, 5-6, 18, 27, 32, 64, 86, 93-94, 115-116, 125, 142, 144, 150, 155
aid, 25, 65, 154-156
authority, 6, 9, 23, 38, 40, 50, 54, 60, 64, 68, 84, 86, 91, 94-96, 99, 101-102, 106-107, 109, 111, 116, 119, 122-123, 126, 141, 152-153

beads, 6, 46-47, 58-59, 62, 82, 86, 146, 166
Beijing Platform for Action (BPfA), 63, 151
bridewealth, 71, 95, 98, 106

capitalism, 9-11, 23, 37, 40, 62, 90, 149, 153, 157, 161-162
cattle, 2, 6-7, 16, 34, 36-40, 43-44, 46, 50-52, 56, 62-63, 69-71, 73, 75-76, 78-79, 81-82, 100, 115, 140-141, 163, 166; cattle raiding, 43
Christianity, 1, 37, 41-42, 137
circumcision, 1, 20-21, 27-28, 38-39, 69, 81, 84, 91, 105, 117-136, 142-146, 166; *emurata*, 21, 38-39, 74, 84, 93, 117-125, 127-128, 132, 134-136, 140, 142, 144, 146, 159, 163; *emuratare oo ntoyie*, 27, 117, 120, 125, 144; female genital cutting (FGC), 119; female genital mutilation (FGM), 124; genital cutting, 5, 119, 152

colonialism, 6, 10, 26, 32, 36-38, 40-46, 48-49, 51, 55, 65-66, 141, 158, 162
Convention on the Rights of the Child (CRC), 108

daughter, 7, 18, 20, 26-27, 38-39, 46, 48, 52, 67-69, 71, 73-74, 84, 90-96, 98-99, 101-104, 106-113, 115-116, 119-120, 125, 131, 134, 136, 138-140, 143, 151, 163, 166
development, 4-5, 7-16, 18, 21, 23-28, 31-34, 37, 43, 46, 48-49, 51, 55-56, 61-68, 71, 77, 85-87, 89-94, 101, 107-110, 112, 114, 116-117, 131, 141, 146-159, 161-163, 166-168; Gender and Development (GAD), 24, 28, 148-149, 152; Girls in Development (GID), 25, 28, 147-148, 157, 167; Millennium Development Goals (MDGs), 152; Women in Development (WID), 28, 148
discipline, 19, 68, 77, 89, 99, 101, 132, 136-137, 151, 161
disturbance, 121, 136-137
dropout rate, 53-54

education, 1, 4-8, 11-19, 21, 23-38, 41-46, 48-57, 59-61, 63-80, 83-93, 95-96, 98, 105, 107-108, 110-112, 119, 123-127, 129, 131, 136, 140, 142, 151-156, 158-159, 161, 163-164, 166-167; primary school, 2, 20, 29, 34, 43-45, 48, 50, 52, 57-58, 63, 70, 76-78, 85, 89, 95, 97-98, 100, 102-103, 105, 123, 131, 135-136, 162, 164; secondary school, 3, 17, 30, 44-45, 52, 88, 90, 100, 109, 111, 146, 162, 164,

166; university, 2, 30, 49, 57, 66, 93, 104, 111, 130, 140, 164-165
Education for All (EFA), 13, 27, 52, 56, 61, 66, 77, 92, 112
education policy, 14, 24, 27, 37, 41, 43, 53, 64-65, 108
empowerment, 4-5, 8-14, 19, 25, 57-58, 61-62, 77, 84-86, 89, 96, 111-112, 114, 116, 143, 145, 147, 150, 153-155, 157, 165-166
enkanyakuai, 27, 114-115, 117, 119, 121, 123, 125-133, 135, 137, 139, 141-144, 159, 163; *inkanyakua*, 125, 127, 129-130, 132, 142, 144
ethnicity, 5, 9, 16-17, 26, 36-38, 40, 44, 46, 48, 52, 56, 61, 147, 149, 159, 162, 168

feminism, 4, 9, 11, 23-25, 40, 62, 148-151, 158, 168; girlpower, 9-11, 15, 89, 91, 112, 148, 153, 157-158, 163; postfeminist, 10-11, 15, 147; transnational, 10, 24
Free Primary Education (FPE), 53, 108

gender, 5, 8-11, 13-14, 16, 19, 21, 24-28, 32, 36, 40, 46, 54, 56, 63-65, 76, 83-84, 87, 93-94, 96, 110, 116, 141, 148-150, 152, 155, 158, 162-163, 166-168
girl-child, 5-6, 22, 27, 62, 68, 83-84, 87, 91-92, 98, 100-102, 108-110, 112, 114-116, 152; girl of the home, 91-93, 105, 107-109, 111-112, 115, 135
The Girl Effect, 11, 61, 90, 153, 155, 158; girl-effects discourse, 16, 19, 32, 61, 67, 76, 90, 114-115; girl-effects logic, 4, 8, 11, 14, 16, 24-25, 27-28, 32, 57, 62, 64, 67, 86-87, 89-91, 101-102, 111, 113, 140, 142, 147-148, 153, 155, 159-160, 164
globalization, 9, 149, 156
Global North, 3, 8-11, 15, 24, 62, 147, 149, 151, 156
Global South, 3, 5, 8, 11, 15, 24, 26-27, 89, 91, 112, 147-149, 151-154, 159

household, 2, 7, 16, 25, 27, 40-41, 43-44, 46, 49, 63, 65-67, 69, 71-73, 79, 82, 89, 91, 100, 103-104, 120, 123, 150, 152
husband, 1, 19, 39, 46, 68-74, 76, 79, 82, 84-87, 90, 96, 105-108, 112, 114, 117-119, 123, 128, 130-131, 146, 159

imperialism, 10, 32, 40, 43. *See also* colonialism
independence, 19, 28, 45, 48-49, 54, 58, 64, 68-69, 76, 83-84, 114-115, 130-131, 157

individualism, 11, 91
International Monetary Fund (IMF), 152
intersectional, 10, 24, 147, 162

Kajiado District, 2, 52
Keekonyokie Central Location (KCL), 2, 17, 19, 34, 62, 119, 131,
Kikuyu, 43-44, 51
kinship, 47, 111, 149, 163
Kiswahili, 3, 20, 26, 48, 58, 77, 79, 88

labor, 14-16, 19, 31, 43-45, 56, 63-64, 66-67, 71, 73-74, 77, 79, 85, 90, 93, 101, 115, 142, 150, 152-153, 158, 162-164; girls' labor, 74; "hard work," 19, 77-78, 82-83, 86, 88; pastoral labor, 43, 56, 63; wage economy, 42, 69, 141
lifestyle diversification, 66
literacy, 17, 42, 57, 77, 158, 162
Loodariak, 2, 17, 20, 33-34, 54, 71, 73-74, 85, 88, 118, 129, 134, 145, 167

Maa, 3, 26, 42, 59, 86, 95, 104, 132, 160, 166
Maasai, 1-8, 11-14, 16-19, 21-63, 65-67, 69-70, 72, 74-80, 82-89, 91-96, 98-103, 107-108, 110-112, 116-121, 123-126, 131, 133, 141-144, 146-147, 158-164, 166-168
Maasailand, 14, 18, 31, 37-38, 41-46, 48-49, 52, 60, 67, 166
marginalization, 10, 26, 56, 61, 147, 156-157, 168
marriage, 5, 7, 9, 19, 24, 39, 60, 68, 73, 77-78, 83-84, 86-87, 89-91, 93-94, 96-98, 100-101, 105-112, 114-115, 118, 120-123, 126-128, 131-133, 137, 139, 143, 146, 152, 157-158; arranged, 5, 86, 90-91, 94, 97, 106-109, 112, 118, 120-122, 127, 131, 139; early, 19, 84, 87; forced, 5, 158; polygyny, 158
modern, 6, 9, 12, 14, 16, 18-19, 37, 40, 44, 54-55, 62, 76, 80, 112, 141, 147, 154, 158-59, 161-162, 166-167
motherhood, 9, 19, 40, 60, 78, 83, 87, 89-91, 118, 127, 157

neoliberalism, 8-11, 15, 65-67, 77, 89, 101, 147-148, 150-152, 161-162, 167
NGO, 2-4, 6, 62-63, 68, 71, 92, 102, 154
Ngong Division, 2

obligation, 15, 19, 71-74, 77, 85-86, 89-90, 100-102, 104, 106-108, 111, 150-151, 157-158, 163, 165

218 • Index

parents, 1, 7, 39, 44-45, 48-53, 56, 59-61, 64, 66-67, 70, 73-75, 78-80, 84, 86-87, 90-91, 99, 104-108, 111, 115, 118-127, 130-134, 136-137, 139-140, 143, 161, 166; father, 6-7, 23, 26, 29, 38-39, 43, 46, 49-52, 59, 68-69, 72-74, 78, 84-86, 90, 93-99, 101-102, 104-112, 115-116, 118, 122-123, 126, 130, 133-134, 137-139, 144; mother, 6-8, 13, 16-17, 25-27, 29-31, 35, 38-39, 46-47, 49-52, 54, 57, 59-63, 65-75, 77-83, 89-90, 94, 96-102, 104, 106-108, 111-113, 117-118, 120, 122, 126-127, 129-135, 139-140, 143, 146, 151, 158-161

pastoralism, 36, 41, 43-44, 52, 56, 65-66, 69, 72-74, 82, 141, 144

patriarchy, 6-7, 12-13, 16, 41, 69, 74, 84-86, 90-96, 99, 101-102, 106-109, 112, 115-116

postcolonial, 23, 26, 32, 38, 40, 49, 51, 55-56, 65

poverty, 1, 3-5, 7-8, 11, 13-16, 25-27, 30, 54, 62-69, 73, 77, 84, 89, 91, 95, 98, 100, 104, 107, 112, 114-15, 138, 147, 150-57, 159, 161-62, 165

pregnancy, 1, 15, 19, 78, 90, 105, 119, 124, 127, 133-138, 140, 158

race, 3, 8-9, 11, 15-16, 40, 148-149, 153, 155, 157, 168

respect, 20-23, 39, 51, 59-60, 71, 76-77, 87, 91-92, 94, 99-102, 108, 111, 116-117, 121-123, 125, 127, 132, 137, 141, 160, 166. *See also* discipline; *enkanyit*

responsibility, 11, 15, 19-20, 25, 40, 64, 68, 71-73, 77, 85-87, 89, 91, 93-94, 101, 107, 110, 112, 125, 133, 139-140, 150-153, 157, 164-166; responsibilization, 151-153, 157-158, 163-165

schoolgirl, 1, 3-8, 11-14, 16, 18-33, 35-36, 38, 47-49, 51-52, 54, 56-62, 65, 67-68, 70, 72-94, 96-102, 104, 106-113, 115-117, 119-127, 129-144, 146-147, 158-159, 162-168; girl of the school, 91, 95, 109

school uniform, 59-60, 80

sexism, 148

sexuality, 9, 14, 32, 40, 116-117, 129, 131-132, 149; play, 39, 81, 112, 116-117, 121, 134; sexual activity, 78, 120

Swahili, 30, 42, 80, 95, 97, 141

teacher, 1-3, 6, 8, 13, 16, 25-27, 30-31, 34-35, 42-44, 47, 49-50, 52-54, 56-57, 59, 61-62, 65, 67-68, 70, 74-77, 79-81, 83, 86, 90, 92, 94, 96-97, 100, 102-103, 105-106, 109-110, 115-116, 120-121, 124, 129, 131, 133, 135, 138-140, 142-143, 158-159, 161, 163, 166

violence, 2, 6, 31, 139, 147, 157, 164-165

warrior, 38-39, 41, 43, 46-47, 51, 59-60, 117; *ilmurran*, 43, 46, 50, 59, 96; moran, 47, 50-51, 69, 76, 161; *olmurranni*, 47

wife, 6, 21, 26, 38-41, 46, 49, 51, 60, 69-71, 73-74, 78, 83, 89-90, 94, 99, 104, 107-108, 110, 112, 117-118, 120, 123, 126-127, 133, 141, 143, 146, 151, 153, 160-161

womanhood, 19, 71, 93-94, 126, 135, 143, 159

World Bank, 8, 49, 64, 66, 151-152, 154-155

Heather D. Switzer is an associate professor of Women and Gender Studies in the School for Social Transformation at Arizona State University.

The University of Illinois Press
is a founding member of the
Association of American University Presses.

University of Illinois Press
1325 South Oak Street
Champaign, IL 61820-6903
www.press.uillinois.edu